RAISING HELL
THE REBEL IN THE MOVIES

RAISING HELL
THE REBEL IN THE MOVIES

TERENCE PETTIGREW

COLUMBUS BOOKS

PICTURE ACKNOWLEDGEMENTS

Kobal Collection: 6, 9, 14, 18, 27, 34, 40, 50, 56, 58, 61, 72, 74, 79, 89, 92, 94, 107, 110, 123, 128, 131, 132, 136, 139, 144, 147, 149, 151, 164, 168, 171, 173, 175, 182, 186

Napthine-Walsh Collections: 142

National Film Archive: 11, 37, 45, 53, 62, 70, 76, 81, 104, 115, 119, 159, 178

Topham Picture Library: 99

Pictures reproduced by courtesy of Allied Artists Inc., Columbia Pictures Industries, Inc., MCA/Universal Pictures, Metro-Goldwyn-Mayer, Inc., Paramount Pictures Corporation, RKO General Pictures, Twentieth Century-Fox Film Corporation, United Artists Corporation, Universal City Studios, Inc., and Warner Bros. Inc.

Title page photo shows James Dean as Jet Rink in *Giant* (1955) (Topham Picture Library, courtesy of Warner Bros. Inc.)

First published in Great Britain in 1986 by
Columbus Books
Devonshire House, 29 Elmfield Road, Bromley, Kent BR1 1LT

Designed by Roger Walker

British Library Cataloguing in Publication Data
Pettigrew, Terence
Raising hell: the rebel in the movies.
1. Characters and characteristics in moving-pictures.
I. Title
791.43'09'09   PN1995.9.C36

Phototypeset by Falcon Graphic Art Ltd
Wallington, Surrey
Printed and bound by
R.J. Acford, Chichester, Sussex

ISBN 0 86287 235 9

CONTENTS

Successful gangster Tom Powers (James Cagney, left) tastes the high life with ritzy
blonde Gwen Allen (Jean Harlow) in *The Public Enemy* (1930).

CHAPTER ONE

THERE'S A RAINBOW 'ROUND MY ANKLES

The stock market crash of 1929 and the Depression of the 'thirties in many ways saved the American movie industry from going under. It is doubtful whether the novelty of sound by itself could have averted the threat of extinction which the industry faced in 1927. As the 'twenties ebbed away, the film industry had become noticeably starved of cash and ideas. Attendances had dwindled, and in a mood of growing desperation moviehouse managers staged burlesque shows between screenings to try to encourage audiences to return.

With the Depression, people needed to be entertained again. Cinema attendances shot back up and variety acts found themselves on the end of the lengthening dole queues. With its merchandise in hot demand again, and no one to curb its wilder excesses, Hollywood cashed in with brassier musicals, more frivolous comedies and more violent action films than ever before. Audiences wanting to see life in the raw were not disappointed – that would come later with the arrival of Will Hays and his infamous Production Code.

Commentators refer to the 'thirties as the 'golden age of Hollywood', but in reality the decade divides into two segments – the period before the Production Code came into effect in 1933, and its aftermath.

The pre-1933 Hollywood movies attempted to seduce audiences with breathtaking action, realism and generous use of dramatic sound effects. Their preoccupation with sociological issues was, as yet, not properly defined. The fact that a high proportion of the movies of that period which remain memorable had urban-social overtones stems more from commercial expediency than a desire to ventilate moral issues. Crime melodramas gave film-makers a wonderful opportunity to use all sorts of violent sound-effects – screeching tyres, machine guns, smashing glass – in settings which were recognizably a part of everyday life.

Thus they fed the audience's craving for both excitement and honest revelation, a heady mixture to combat the aches and pains brought on by the Depression.

It would be inaccurate to blame the stock market crash entirely for the misery which followed it. Certainly, the abrupt transformation from the euphoric, easy-credit days beforehand to the subsequent severe credit restrictions played a large part in creating the conditions which led to the slump. However, a number of root causes lay in commercial mismanagement, over-trading and blind faith in the value of 'paper' money, none of which during the heady, expansionist days of the 'twenties seemed to conceal any danger.

By the end of the decade, however, industrial workers' wages had failed to increase at the same pace as product output which left the home market cluttered with all manner of high-price consumer goods which increasingly fewer ordinary working people could afford. Neither was it feasible that these products could find a ready export market to Europe or Canada, in view of the high tariff barriers that stood in their way.

Unavoidably, the concentration of unsold cars, gadgets and domestic appliances had reached danger proportions by the late 'twenties, forcing their manufacturers to dispose of existing stock-piles at considerably reduced prices. This at least generated cash-flow, but at the expense of severe financial losses. As a result, and in accordance with lower levels of demand, production rates were reduced. Both developments dramatically reduced job opportunities. Adding to the chaos were the thousands of businesses being strangled by lack of working capital or credit.

Economic collapse and the effect it had on society created a style of cinema far removed from the frothy inanities of the 'twenties. In the real world, life savings were dwindling, hunger was rife, mortgages were foreclosed, evictions had become commonplace. Shanty towns constructed of scrap metal, cardboard boxes and knocked-up canvas tents grew up around industrial communities. People were lured there by the hope of employment, sometimes to have their pathetic dwellings raided and destroyed because the local townspeople feared for their own jobs. However, more often than not they were allowed to remain, occasionally enjoying handouts of soup and bread donated by some of the more prosperous citizens.

By any reckoning, it was a desperate, uncomfortable existence for millions of slump victims, exacerbated by the fact that nobody, not even the top figures in the Administration, could predict an end to it all. As the army of unemployed grew, and conditions worsened, there came signs that not only the financial structure but, indeed, the very social fabric of the nation was coming unglued. The suicide rate in 1932 overtook all previous totals by an appalling margin. Casual street crime, quite apart from the organized thuggery which had wasted no time in cruelly exploiting the nation's economic malaise, also rose dramatically.

The rebel character in films of the early 'thirties – boldly and aggressively intent on self-preservation – was a creation sparked off by a response to the hard times, a model for survival in a world going rapidly to the dogs.

In the gangster movie, Hollywood gave 'rugged individualism' its head, and came up with an anti-Depression figure which symbolized better than any other kind the resilience and nerve needed to pull the nation through. Gangster movies, more than any other genre, crystallized the flavour of the 'thirties, with its portent for chaos and social disaster. Hollywood gangsters inhabit and dominate a world where social

Tom Powers (James Cagney, left) and Matt Doyle (Edward Woods, centre) get some advice on the rackets from Putty Nose (Murray Kinnell) in *The Public Enemy* (1930)

and economic norms have broken down. It is a world which has been slammed into reverse, denying the honest protagonist a visible way out of the mess.

The gangster figure was an energetic, resourceful go-getter, hungry for success, taking what he wanted from a society too timid or dim-witted to obstruct him. Gangster-rebels were tough, single-minded, self-assertive and unstoppable (except by a bullet or the electric chair). Lack of formal education was no obstacle in their climb to power – their rise depended on an ability to pick their friends carefully and to outfox or outshoot the opposition. It was hardly surprising, therefore, that a generation soured by the absence of a viable future should see in the gangster and his methods a blueprint for getting out of the rut.

But if Hollywood-style gangsterdom had the appearance of being merely another form of private enterprise engaged in by people sick of pious bromides and worthless promises, it did at least point a finger at where most of the worthless promises came home to roost – namely the neglected, overcrowded immigrant areas of big cities where the lack of legitimate opportunities and the lure of quick rewards combined to turn young men to crime who, given a reasonable alternative, might have chosen a more honest future.

James Cagney leapt to stardom by embodying more convincingly than other Hollywood actors at the time the working-class response to the political and economic turmoil of the period: disillusion, quickly superseded by a drive to succeed in which courage, stamina and unwillingness to compromise all played their part.

9

Cagney's appeal had echoes of Charlie Chaplin's, whose audience saw in the little fellow's ups-and-downs a reflection of their own predicament. Replacing the artful innocence of Chaplin's comedies, however, were a new toughness and cynicism befitting the Depression years. Both were, essentially, champions of the 'little man', whose fight to overcome rough, unpromising origins both had experienced at first hand.

The Public Enemy (1930), Cagney's first gangster performance of note, and still rated by many as the pick of the crop, interweaves contemporary social comment with tragedy. It traces the progress of two radically different sons of a working-class, Chicago-Irish policeman father and a gentle, over-indulgent mother. Tommy (James Cagney) is the smart-ass, dissatisfied at home, attracted to easy money, for which he is quite prepared to commit petty thefts, run errands for established mobsters, take part in armed robbery and murder. Matt (Donald Cook) is his diligent brother, a hard-working streetcar conductor who wants to get ahead the honest way, and attends night school to further that ambition.

The contrast between the brothers is extreme and leads to enmity between them. Tommy despises his brother's conformity and ridicules his decision to enlist for World War I, seeing little value in putting his life on the line for no profit! And, sure enough, it is the profit motif which hooks Tommy (Cagney) and his boyhood chum (Eddie Woods) on to their doomed trajectory, associating with prominent gangsters, robbing government warehouses and muscling in on rival gangs' territories.

By the time Matt returns from Europe, a fêted but wounded local hero, Tommy's alienation from his family, and the honest values which it represents, is almost complete. Confronted with a keg of illicit liquor which Tommy has fetched home for the homecoming celebrations, Matt hurls it to the ground in a rage. Tommy's indignant reply is, 'You ain't so good yourself – you didn't get those medals for holding hands with the Germans!'

Prohibition gives Tommy the chance of easy money. Disgusted by the situation at home, he vents his spite on his girlfriend (Mae Clarke) shortly afterwards, in the infamous grapefruit-in-the-kisser incident. The build-up to it is short and snappy and typically Cagney. Sourly appraising the breakfast which his girlfriend has lovingly prepared, he growls, 'Nuts to that stuff! Ain't ya got a drink in the house?' (A mild rebuke about drinking before breakfast has provoked the memorable outburst.)

'I wish you were a wishin' well so that I could tie a bucket to you and sink you!' snorts Tommy, using her nose as a juicer. After a brief flirtation with a worldly dame (Jean Harlow) who proves too hot to handle, a machine-gun burst kills Tommy's boyhood pal. Mayhem ensues, with reprisals hurtling on to the backs of earlier reprisals, leaving Tommy uncharacteristically subdued and hospitalized from gunshot wounds while the killers of his buddy are left either dead or in disarray.

But the question of whether or not he is redeemable remains unanswered, for the remnants of a rival gang abduct Tommy from his hospital bed and, in another of the film's many powerful images, prop his rigid corpse against the family's front door. When his brother, with whom he was briefly reconciled before being murdered, answers their knock, the grotesque, bloodstained parcel topples into the hallway.

The familiarity of the ending may now rob it of real surprise, but in its day, viewed for the first time, Tommy's off-camera murder and the callousness of the deed startled audiences out of their wits. So, too, did the grapefruit attack on Mae Clarke, who had to go through a similar ordeal in *Lady Killer* (1933) when, in a scene clearly inspired by the grapefruit incident, Cagney drags her round the room by her hair before kicking her into the hallway.

The Public Enemy really was Cagney at his best, whether giving or taking the

'Shoot first, argue afterwards.' Rico Bandello (Edward G. Robinson) survives another attempt on his life in *Little Caesar* (1930).

rough stuff. The similarity of backgrounds shared by character and star, plus director William Wellman's attention to detail, lends authenticity, even down to Cagney's now-famous square stance and loosely-balled fists at his sides, mannerisms copied from a real-life gangster he remembered vividly from his childhood.

The contrasts between the drudgery and cheerlessness of the family apartment and the illicit excitement of the speakeasy and the gambling den are effectively drawn. One is allowed to see, and understand, how someone like the Cagney character, ambitious, gutsy, thrill-hungry, would be attracted to the easy money and the excitement of racketeering.

Another great rebel gangster figure of 1930 was Edward G. Robinson's Rico Bandello in *Little Caesar* (1930). 'One of the first legitimate anti-heroes in the American cinema', Robinson beat Cagney to his New York opening of *The Public Enemy* by only four months. Production of both films overlapped at Warner Brothers, as a hedged bet against the failure of either one of them. These canny insurance measures proved quite unnecessary. Robinson was not a tough guy in the Cagney mould, though an equivalent streak of ruthlessness and audacity permeated his personality like the lettering down the inside of a stick of rock.

Cagney's villainy was all the more excusable because he really looked and sounded like a kid from the wrong side of the tracks, inadequately schooled, socially rejected, with crime his only way forward. Though it was frequently suggested that deprivation similar to Cagney's lay at the roots of Robinson's gangster figures, it was harder to believe – Robinson simply did not look like an adult version of a hungry street urchin.

Robinson, however, made contemporary handsomeness look tame and ordinary by asserting from the very beginning an intense animal superiority – and that was the key to his success. He looked nastier, talked faster, played rougher than anyone else. His armoury of fast movements, gestures and mannerisms – the jabbing of a pudgy finger in his opponent's face, the sign-writing in the air with a huge cigar, the deadly effect of words and bullets being discharged at the same rapid rate – an eloquent essay in the art of bringing people down to size.

In *Little Caesar*, the movie that established him, Robinson's 'Rico' is a small-time hold-up artist with ideas of grandeur. He seeks status as much as profit. 'Money's all right, but it ain't everything!' he says. 'Be somebody, have a bunch of guys who will do anything you tell 'em, have your own way, or nothin'!' Joe Massaro (Douglas Fairbanks Jr), his accomplice from the early days, dreams of stardom as a dancer. As they begin their ruthless climb to power, Rico warns Massaro, 'Shoot first, argue afterwards – if you don't, the other fellow gets you . . . This game ain't for guys that's soft!'

His fierce ambition is matched by a trigger-happy instinct that worries Massaro, who nevertheless recognizes that without it they are both probably doomed. The power of his gun, says Rico, is 'all I got between me and . . . the whole world', and in a corner he is more than willing to use it.

Disposing of everyone likely to prove troublesome, Rico becomes undisputed boss of the North Side, second only to Mr Big, although his grasp on the mechanics of running a modern crime empire is at times alarmingly naïve. Also, there is a cuckoo in the nest; his former pal Massaro refuses to abandon a thriving dancing career to help him exert control. Massaro is in love with Olga Strassof (Glenda Farrell), another dancer. His rejection of Rico's offer provokes a mad fit of jealousy and an irrevocable split. Desperate for protection for himself and Olga, Massaro, who was a witness to the murder of the Crime Commissioner, decides to turn State's evidence.

This proves to be the turning point of Rico's fortunes. The gang is dispersed, and Rico goes on the run, hiding in a flophouse, indistinguishable from the other down-and-outs. His sworn enemy on the police force decides to flush Rico into the open by attacking his vanity, which he accomplishes by means of a planted newspaper story saying that Rico is hiding like a rat in a hole.

Enraged, the megalomaniac Rico emerges from hiding for one final confrontation with the police. He is outmanoeuvred and gunned down in a state of sorry bewilderment. 'Mother of Mercy, is this the end of Rico?' he croaks at the end, as if repulsed by his newly-discovered mortality.

Rico's philosophy – 'shoot first, argue afterwards' – was, of course, nothing new. It had been the staple of action films since the silent days. He is prepared to go all the way, to back his words with fierce aggression, to invite showdowns and to risk his life in order to achieve the glittering prizes, which for a time he manages to enjoy. The drab environment of his early days is replaced by a lavish apartment, hand-cut clothes and flashy jewellery. Any pretence at restraint is tossed overboard. He swaggers round the room, jabbing his finger in people's faces, spitting out instructions and ultimatums like a repeater rifle about to overheat.

Rico was the last word in film rebeldom in 1930: the brash kid from nowhere who breaks all the rules, insatiable for power and success, deaf to appeals from others to change direction or slow down. He is at odds with his environment, determined to better himself, remorseless in his efforts, snobbish in his tastes even before his rise to power, convinced of his own invincibility.

This determination translated on to the screen as something admirable. The Great American dream is, in part, a reflection of the common belief that ordinary people can fulfil their ambitions if they have sufficient drive and talent, and Rico's progress is merely another example of this. As with Tommy in *The Public Enemy*, Americans saw in the character's battles with the criminal establishment and with the law a reflection of their own struggles to improve their lot against heavy odds. The people Rico terrorizes on either side of the law are no better than himself and deserve no more than he does to succeed. His most dangerous enemy is not the force of law and order – here depicted as weak and vacillating – but the flaws in his own personality which prevent him killing the old friend whose testimony will ultimately destroy him. This sense of loyalty, the only visible counterpoint to his murderous nature,

Gangboss Tony Camonte (Paul Muni) finds 'Goodbye' a difficult word to say in *Scarface: Shame of a Nation* (1932).

helped audiences to come to terms with his blind ambition – he could murder enemies and strangers without hesitation, but friendships mattered.

Tony Camonte (Paul Muni) in *Scarface* (1932) was chronologically the third but arguably the best of the three memorable gang-boss figures of the early Depression cinema. Like Tommy in *Public Enemy* and Rico in *Little Caesar*, Camonte was from impoverished Catholic immigrant origins, propelled forwards and upwards by the same maniacal lust for power and social acceptance.

Camonte begins his climb as a resourceful minder for a bootleg firm which he takes over as a prelude to eventual supremacy over the combined Chicago rackets. Despite his tactical strengths and ruthlessness, an incestuous interest in his sister Cesca (Ann Dvorak) proves, in the end, to be his Achilles' heel.

Returning from a trip to Miami, Camonte finds that his sister has secretly married his top lieutenant, Guido (George Raft). His terrible jealousy eventually traps and destroys all three – Guido murdered by Camonte, Cesca accidentally mown down by police rifle-fire minutes before Camonte, desperately trying to evade capture, meets an ignominious, bullet-ridden end.

All the familiar ingredients are there: the street-wise delinquent's hunger for success and acceptance; the best friend who turns out to be a cuckoo in the nest; the fluffy gangster's moll; trigger-happy cops; sheister lawyers; and flashy nightspots.

Based loosely on the life and times of Al Capone, with occasional nods towards the Borgias, where murder and incest frequently came to dinner, *Scarface* boasted a string of real-life incidents in its narrative. The St Valentine's Day Massacre, a major outrage even for those lawless times, is featured, as is the telephone-booth killing of a rival – the real-life victim was Big Jim Colosimo. A hospital assassination is modelled on an event in the life of Legs Diamond. The machine-gunning of Capone's headquarters is also represented.

No effort was made to distinguish the Camonte character from that of Capone. In fact, the opposite occurred, with particular emphasis being placed on Camonte's liking for Italian opera, his penchant for flashy possessions and his livid facial scar, all faithfully reflecting his real-life model.

The gun battles reverberate as Camonte effects his perilous climb, progressively shedding his thick immigrant accent, improving his wardrobe and acquiring on the way the obligatory status symbols such as a flashy car and a resilient blonde girlfriend. With all rivals removed, Camonte is vulnerable only from the inside. Slower than his sister Cesca to abandon the strict, traditional Italian codes of family conduct, he is driven insane by her defection to the stone-faced Guido, but by killing him he merely choreographs his own bitter and violent end.

As with many later Howard Hawks films, the action has the flavour of an elaborately staged contest between competent protagonists, each of whom is capable of drawing out the best of the other. The internecine struggles of power-crazed crime czars are as removed from everyday living as an Arabian Nights fantasy, yet the power of the images, the surrealist quality of the spooky silhouettes filling the screen which change without warning into armed emissaries of death, contain a chilling realism which is not easily explained.

Encouraged by the success of a number of Broadway productions which showed what happened after criminals went into custody, Hollywood turned its cameras on the prison yard and the cell block. Here was not only a microcosm of society functioning within a recognizable rulebook, but a perfect allegory for the misfortunes of the period – basically decent men driven to desperation by a corrupt system operated by bullies and reactionaries. The sadistic prison guard, and every cell block had one, was a symbol of the Depression, wringing all the humiliation and misery he could from his victims throughout their incarceration.

In the same way that the early 'thirties gangsters were in a sense folk heroes who challenged the established social order, the convict in films like *The Big House* (1930) won admiration for his refusal to conform. It was not that the early prison-yard movies, any more than the gangster cycles of the same period, were consciously mounting any kind of crusade; prison was simply a good setting for a gritty yarn about survival under stress. However, a number of prison riots had made the news in the long, hot summer of 1929, notably at Dannemora and Auburn. Though penal reform was not a burning issue (indeed, with the degree of fear and lawlessness around, many citizens felt that captured criminals deserved rough treatment), prisons and the prison-yard setting, guards and captives alike – and often they *were* alike, distinguishable from each other only by the uniforms they wore – became fair game for film-makers. Thus, with *The Big House* in 1930, began a tradition that would continue to embrace such noteworthy movies as *Angels with Dirty Faces* (1938), *Invisible Stripes* (1939), *Each Dawn I Die* (1940), *Brute Force* (1947), *The Big House USA* (1955), *Birdman of Alcatraz* (1962), *Cool Hand Luke* (1967) and *Brubaker* (1978).

Prison, in *The Big House*, proves to be a stalwart test of the human spirit. The awful food, claustrophobic conditions and degrading routines either drove men crazy or helped them on the road to self-discovery and ultimate redemption. Kent Marlowe (Robert Montgomery) is an affable good guy who is jailed for an accidental killing, but he lacks what it takes to survive behind bars. He suffers badly at the hands of his fellow inmates and eventually goes under, whereas John Morgan (Chester Morris), a gutsy forger, shrugs off everything which the system can throw at him and emerges at the end as a man who has earned, through good judgement and resilience, the right to happiness. Butch Schmidt (Wallace Beery), who is serving a life sentence for murder, leads a doomed escape bid and is killed.

The Big House is noteworthy for setting a style which countless prison yard movies would emulate – the fly-on-the-wall glimpses of a violent, oppressive, insular society where men are bullied and depersonalized by their guards and by each other. Frances Marion's intelligent, probing script creates cell-block characters who are all too plausible: the weak guy whose nerve collapses; the tough inmate who keeps his humanity under wraps and the brutish no-hoper who is nearing the end of the line. Among the prison staff is the authoritarian chief warden, who is gruff but fair, and a brutish guard, figures who are familiar to cinemagoers now but who in 1930 were innovative and utterly plausible.

The film's main strength lies in its documentary-style approach, coupled with sensitive camera work. The camera noses along narrow, ill-lit corridors, peers into cramped cells, follows the path of a concealed knife as it passes from hand to hand under a mess-hall table and overviews a cell-block mutiny as it blazes into action. The scenes where Kent Marlowe is admitted to prison have a special power because of the matter-of-fact way in which the procedure is carried out. The physical examination, followed by photography, uniform issue and routine introductory lecture realized through clinical movements and empty words, provides a chilling foretaste of what is in store.

A more moving and conscious indictment of the American penal system occurred in *I Am a Fugitive from a Chain Gang* (1932), a controversial, politically sensitive film which put at risk, for a time, the Southern markets for Warner Brother's entire output because of the uncompromising way in which it depicted the treatment of criminals in Georgia. The controversy was welcomed by prison reformers through-out the country, since it heightened the film's impact – if the people responsible for having men chained together like pack animals and worked half to death by bullying overseers were shouting 'foul', then it was surely no bad thing.

More than any movie of the period, *Chain Gang* justified Warners' eloquent claim to be the company which 'combined good picture-making with good citizenship'.

In *Chain Gang*, the central character, James Allen (Paul Muni), is a war hero whose determination to succeed as a skilled professional engineer, instead of settling for a mundane clerk's job in a shoe factory, is stonewalled because there is no work. Slowly it dawns on him that he is not going to get anywhere – all decent jobs are filled, and his Belgian *Croix de Guerre* is a worthless decoration in a land of diminished opportunities.

Unemployed and destitute, he teams up with a shifty-looking vagrant to intimi-date a hamburger stallholder into giving them food. But Allen's partner suddenly pulls a gun and forces the stallholder to hand over the day's takings, a meagre five dollars. They are quickly apprehended, the other tramp killed by the police, and Allen with no one to substantiate his plea of innocence is sentenced by a hostile judge to hard labour, which means a chain gang. The awfulness of the sentence is conveyed in a series of disturbing images. Dank, verminous huts provide the living quarters. Floggings and indiscriminate victimizations abound. Escape or some other end to the agonizing daily grind dominates the convicts' thoughts.

Helped by a Negro fellow-prisoner, Allen manages to escape and put the past behind him. Five years later, he has a good job and a bright future, but the idea of squaring matters with the law still nags at him. Assured by the authorities that by voluntarily surrendering himself to the Georgia courts which originally sentenced him he will merely receive a token ninety days in jail, he decides to purge the past and give himself up. To his horror he finds that the promises were meaningless, and he is tossed back into the chain gang for an indefinite period.

Once again he succeeds in escaping but he is unable to rebuild any kind of future and is forced into permanent hiding. In his own bitter words, he has 'no friends, no rest, no peace . . . keep moving, that's all that's left!' The film's last, harrowing glimpse of him is as a pathetic, unshaven fugitive who keeps himself alive by stealing.

Apart from the downbeat ending, the story follows with reasonable fidelity the true-life experiences of chain-gang escapee Robert Elliott Burns, who lived success-fully on the run for seven years after his estranged wife's betrayal. The film's power lies in its authenticity (Burns was hired as technical adviser on the production), the semi-documentary treatment by director Mervyn Le Roy and the general excellence of the leading performers.

The film's desire to overstate Allen's innocence at times undermines the force of its sociological observation. The audience gets sidetracked into condemning the cruelty and degradation meted out to an innocent man when the real issue, the true outrage, is that it was ever meted out to anyone. The innocence or guilt of the victim has no bearing on whether or not the barbaric treatment of prisoners should be condemned. It should be and is wholeheartedly in this remarkable, crusading film.

Nobody loves you when you're down and out. Roy Earle (Humphrey Bogart) is
floored before taking a bigger fall in *High Sierra* (1940).

CHAPTER TWO

THE ROARING 'THIRTIES

*H*ollywood crime films of the early 'thirties, with their stark, uncompromising view of slum life, stunted opportunities, speakeasies and the politics of violence and intimidation, gave cinema audiences a taste of social comment more vivid and thought-provoking than that of which newspapers were capable. They also provided much-needed escapism – escape from the awful realities of poverty and hopelessness. Will Hays had sought to establish that films depicted violence as an unfortunate by-product of the gangster's climb to power, not something that he revelled in or resorted to unnecessarily. But despite the studios' strict compliance to edicts which they considered reasonable, accusations of glorifying the unspeakable, of pandering to lurid tastes and of undermining the nation's morals, continued.

As the Depression progressed, the watchdogs grew more uneasy at the number of movies which, despite their exposé tag, seemed hell-bent on exalting a way of life which was utterly unacceptable in a civilized society.

The Quigley-Lord Production Code of 1930, created to oppose moral debasement in talking pictures, had had only limited effectiveness. Anxious to keep audiences happy by giving them what they wanted, producers tried, to circumvent the regulations (and generally suceeded) by incorporating steamy language, near-nudity, extra-marital philandering and violence.

For a time the recipe worked and cinemas did fill up again. However, with more and more studios paying only lip-service to the self-censorship demanded by the Production Code, it was clear that they were embarking on a collision course with religious pressure groups who saw the nation's morality as more important than the studios' balance sheets.

In 1933, supported by other institutions, the Hays Office tightened its control on what was acceptable on the screen. Among its supporters were the Catholic Bishops of North America, whose plans included a boycott of crime movies to bring the industry to its senses.

The Catholic clergy represented a single ideology backed up by an organizational structure without equal in the Western world – a formidable enough opponent even without the Vatican support which it claimed to have. When its committee on the motion picture industry, calling itself somewhat provocatively the League of Decency, distributed pledge forms to support a boycott of movies which the Catholic Church declared indecent, the response was certainly enthusiastic, not merely from Catholic and lay organizations but from Protestants and Jews, too. Within weeks of the forms being circulated, 11,000,000 people had pledged to boycott improper films. Events quickly conspired to force the Motion Picture Association of America to accept the conditions of a re-strengthened code without reservation: the choice was either to accept the recommendations for self-discipline made by a sympathetic friend of the industry, or to submit to a possibly tougher code imposed on it from the outside.

What the revised Code did was to remove the arbitrary right of the studios to have the final say on what did nor did not represent good taste. From 1933 onwards, motion pictures which lacked the approval of Hays' Los Angeles-based Production Code Authority were deprived of distribution. It was as simple and as devastating in its effects as that. In order not merely to comply but to be seen publicly to be willing to obey the Code to the letter, the studios which had previously championed most strenuously the social-reforming powers of modern movie-making deliberately excluded controversial themes from their storylines.

By 1934, gangster films had seemingly run their course, and with the revamped Production Code keeping its eagle eye on the genre, nothing very startling happened in crime movies that year. After the fast and ferocious patterns carved on the screen during the previous couple of years, the breathing space proved timely.

It was not that crime movies had lost their crowd appeal – far from it, audiences still cherished the crackle of the sub-machine gun, the automobile chases, the posturing of big-time crooks and the classy dames they kept in tow. But with the tightening of censorship, explicitly violent scenes and individuals profiting from lawlessness were ruled inadmissible, and since gangster movies without either were like sandwiches without the filling, alternative themes less reliant on savage action and the dollar motif were dusted off the shelves and put in front of the cameras in increasing numbers.

'Safe' family pictures such as the Andy Hardy series starring Mickey Rooney, westerns and musicals – most enduringly the Gold Diggers series by Busby Berkeley – began to roll off the production line in ever-increasing numbers. Even horror films such as *Frankenstein* (1930) and *Dracula* (1931) were acceptable, since their obvious unreality cleared them of any suspicion that they could corrupt impressionable minds. However, if the idea had been to divert the public's attention from the lawbreakers, the real-life hoodlums themselves were not about to retire gracefully. Crime continued to made headlines, often accompanied by lurid close-ups of bullet-riddled victims.

For a while, the law's apparent powerlessness had the effect of turning public enemies such as John Dillinger and Machine Gun Kelly into folk-heroes. The early 'thirties crime movies often showed the law out-manoeuvred at every turn or in some smart gangboss's pocket – which in many cases was no exaggeration of the truth.

The Lindbergh Kidnap case in 1932, described at the time as 'the crime of the century', had nothing to do with hoodlum empires, and perhaps because of this its impact on the American consciousness was significant. Government resources were deployed to strengthen the federal agencies and improve their track record in major crime-busting. Known as the Lindbergh Law, and passed in 1933 (one of the first bills to be enacted by the newly elected Roosevelt Administration), it brought within the list of federal crimes a number which previously had been the sole responsibility of local police forces, such as ransom demands and crossing over a state boundary in kidnapping offences. The Bill was scarcely out of its wraps when a further amendment to it extended the Bureau of Investigation's jurisdiction to include armed robbery, taking stolen goods across state lines, and resisting arrest by a federal agent.

The Bureau, under its glamorous new name, the FBI, gave law enforcement its brightest chance for several decades to bring the big-time criminals to heel.

Unrestricted by local red tape, and staffed by volunteers who were recruited cautiously and who took a pride in the job, the FBI agent became the New Deal hero, a symbol of a much wider American crusade to throw off the bad old days and get the nation functioning along the right lines once again.

Their successes were spectacular. FBI agents trapped and shot both Pretty Boy Floyd and Baby Face Nelson in two separate incidents in 1934. John Dillinger met a hail of FBI bullets as he strolled with two women from the Biograph movie theatre in Chicago having just seen Clark Gable and William Powell in *Manhattan Melodrama*, a crime movie in which the hoodlum Gable dies in the electric chair.

Ma Barker and one of her delinquent sons were surrounded and shot by the FBI in January 1935. Not surprisingly, the Bureau's new-found momentum and the clean-cut image of its agents was noticed by Hollywood. Here, surely, was another way of giving audiences the exciting gangster shoot-outs they adored, but by shifting the emphasis on to the gang-buster and by presenting the story from his viewpoint, they were also satisfying the demands of the Production Code.

Warner Brothers certainly thought so, and it was Jack Warner who finally persuaded FBI chief Herbert Hoover to consent to the Bureau being shown in a fictionalized though factually constructed story which highlighted the training, codes of behaviour and effective deployment against a ruthless gang of bootleggers. Hoover's anti-Hollywood feelings were well-known. He was miffed at the way it had glorified crime in the days when the Bureau was having only limited success, and had turned down any request for information from his files, until Warner, who knew him personally, managed to change his mind.

Among the package of goodies which Warner was able to put before the wary Hoover was James Cagney as the film's FBI officer – a sensible choice, in view of the star's huge popularity and his charismatic tough guy rating. But it was also a cheeky idea since Cagney's gun-happy killer image represented an affront to everything for which Hoover and his organization stood.

G-Men (1935) shows how Brick Davis (James Cagney), a New York slum urchin and former delinquent, makes a success of his life thanks to two lucky breaks. The first occurs in the shape of a genial top gangland mobster, Mac (William Harrigan), who takes Davis off the streets and propels him through law school, an investment of $20,000 which Mac airily dismisses as 'chicken feed when you like a guy'. Davis qualifies, and starting humbly in a spartan office on the East Side, passes his time rehearsing eloquent court-room pleas, or flinging knives at insects crawling across his door.

Declining the 'sheistering and ambulance chasing' route to success, Davis has plenty of spare time, but this ends when a law college pal, Buchanan (Regis Toomey), introduces him to the FBI. It is not until Buchanan is killed with a bullet intended to silence the hoodlum he was questioning that Davis gives serious thought to the idea of joining the Bureau. When he does eventually join up his reasons are personal, the overriding reason being to use the well-oiled investigation machinery within the Bureau to nail his chum's murderers.

Davis is Cagney at his archetypal and energetic best. In retrospect, it is unthinkable that anyone else could have played the role. At the Washington Training School for FBI recruits, his breezy repartee goes down badly with the no-nonsense training instructor McCord (Robert Armstrong). When Davis scores magnificently on the pistol range and a puzzled McCord asks where he learnt to shoot, Davis replies witheringly, 'I used to be marbles champion of the Bronx!'

The bad feeling between them causes Davis to be passed over when after fingerprint evidence has linked one of Mac's cronies (Barton Maclane) with the Buchanan murder, an agent is to be sent to New York to make the arrest. Later, when McCord discovers that it was a top mobster who funded his pupil's legal training and that the two still meet in secret, Davis comes within a hair's-breadth of being thrown off the force for 'falsifying details of his personal history on his entrance papers'.

Davis's gratitude at not being instantly dismissed does not curb his wry humour. When McCord points to a wall map explaining that the remnants of the gang are confined to 'that circle somewhere' Davis's wry comment is: 'Only six States – we've practically got 'em cornered!' But corner them they do in Cagney's customary biff-bang fashion, with plenty of gunplay and sardonic lines to round off a consistently action-packed film.

G-Men marked the start of the climb-back to prominence of the gangster movie in a slightly different guise. It also marked the start of the second most interesting phase of Cagney's development. All the mannerisms familiar from his gangster films are here: the cocky, pugnacious stance, the sharp, machine-gun bursts of dialogue and the athletic movements. Cooped up in a cheerless office, he is like a fish in a net and his feisty reaction to a gangster's proposition that he becomes their front man shows both his mettle and his inner craving for action. The first real test of his character comes in the gritty exchanges with McCord, who fails to knock Davis off his stride until his mobster patron is discovered; even then, only fear of getting his marching orders brings a momentary sobering of his attitude.

In 1936, escaped convict Duke Mantee (Humphrey Bogart) blasted his way into the cinema's consciousness in *The Petrified Forest*. Mantee is no glamorized, all-purpose wiseguy. He is, instead, a perfect illustration of how gangsters were meant to fare under the re-strengthened Hays Code — a haggard, unattractive fugitive, uninterested in the goings-on around him other than to save his own skin, sullenly taking his revenge on that section of society which he believes has wronged him. On the run after killing several prison guards, Mantee and two fellow convicts take refuge in a remote filling station which has an adjoining café. The owner's wistful and romantically-inclined daughter Gabrielle (Bette Davis) has already expressed a considerable interest in a footloose, impoverished poet-traveller named Squier (Leslie Howard), whose shy yet intense manner initially unsettles but later reassures her that life beyond the confines of her humdrum waitress job at her father's café can have some purpose.

Mantee's abrupt arrival disturbs the tranquillity, but he makes it clear that he wants no trouble, merely a hiding-place until a girlfriend shows up with a fresh getaway car. Her failure to arrive makes the increasingly jittery Mantee and his henchmen even more desperate.

When Squier provokes Mantee into shooting him, having at first bequeathed the proceeds of his life insurance policy to Gabrielle to give her a start in life far away from the repressive atmosphere of the café, the cornered killer solemnly obliges, apparently envious of Squier's courage and resigned to meeting a similar fate. This he does, off-camera, when G-men trap him shortly afterwards.

Though Mantee is a supporting role, and his appearance in the movie is delayed until the relationship between Squier and Gabrielle is established, his famished-wolf look and cruel heritage dominate the film in a manner similar to that in which he personally dictates the course of events inside the dining room. Mantee is walking — rather, shuffling — proof of what prolonged prison terms can do to a man. Aloof and unrepentant, he waits for death to close in like a rescuing angel, acknowledging his powerlessness to affect the eventual outcome.

From an entirely different standpoint Squier, too, contemplates the futility of his own existence, and sees in society's mad rush to urbanize and mechanize the great outdoors a depressing parallel with the curtailment of his own freedom. Soon there will be nowhere for a true poet to find his soul: it will all be swallowed up by concrete blocks and bulldozers. This, however, in no way devalues the noble sacrifice which he makes at the end in order to secure Gabrielle's future.

Both the nomadic, penniless poet-aesthetic and the surly gangster are victims of the changing times. Each is doomed by his inability to adapt. Squier drifts and talks aimlessly about a dream-world which the Depression has destroyed — if, indeed, it ever existed. Mantee peers through furtive eyes and a crushed spirit, reflecting without bitterness, at one point, on a life which has yielded precious little joy — 'I've spent most of my time since I grew up in jail. . . and it looks like I'll spend the rest of my life dead!'

The law enforcer as gangland infiltrator was another way of circumventing the Hays Code. In *Bullets or Ballots* (1936), Nick Fenner (Humphrey Bogart) runs a criminal empire that is host to an undercover cop, Johnny Blake (Edward G. Robinson), whose mission is to uncover the men who control the syndicate. Blake's masquerade is eventually seen through by Fenner, who is killed in the shoot-out, and Blake, too, is mortally wounded, but he survives long enough to lead government agents to the brains of the mob, several smooth bankers whose political, financial and social elitism has so far guaranteed them immunity from prosecution. Again, there is the good guy ostensibly turned bad – a believable switch in the case of Edward G. Robinson – glad-handing it with his opposite numbers as he ferrets out the damning evidence. As in *Little Caesar*, Robinson overcomes his lack of inches with a crackling, word-spattering performance which completely dominates Bogart in the lesser role of a compulsive triggerman.

The suggestion that the real power behind the rackets hides within plush Wall Street offices, escaping retribution because the same people control the mechanisms of justice which allow their underlings to function outside it, is briskly and convincingly made. A recurring feature of many socially conscious crime movies is the implicit connection between the mobs and shady figures in higher authority as, for example, in *Force of Evil* (1948) and *On the Waterfront* (1953). The real-life inspiration springs from the well-documented relationship between the Capone gang and Chicago's civic leaders in the 'twenties, and from other subsequent though less spectacular examples of hoodlums operating under the unseen protection of the authorities.

Though a minor film in other respects, *Bullets or Ballots* was the first to propose forcefully that respected legitimate concerns were not always as clean as they appeared to be. This was also one of the first films actually to engage the character of an undercover agent who was indistinguishable in attitude and temperament from the people whom he had infiltrated.

Bogart participated in several documentary-style social-observation movies during the late 'thirties, more often than not in a supporting role since these were made before his breakthrough film, *High Sierra* (1941). All bore the hallmark of a Warner Brothers crusade, though one was made while he was on loan to Goldwyn. Many of these films focused as keenly on the unfavourable social conditions which bred crime as on the criminals themselves.

These films fall into approximately three categories. In the first category is the criminal whose opposition to the law can be traced directly to his slum origins, his early hardships and the absence of any legitimate outlet for his burgeoning talents. In other words, his behaviour expresses the magnitude of his frustration, a way of repaying the condemnation and hostility shown to him, and in many cases to his honest, hard-working parents, by a dispassionate and inflexible social system. In the second category, the criminal rises from identical beginnings but, unlike the other one, has acquired a relish for robbery and murder and is irredeemable. Duke Mantee in *The Petrified Forest* came broadly within this category as did quite a few other late 'thirties Bogart characterizations. The third category, though, in a sense it is just a broadening of the same focus, looked at the effects of institutionalized reform on young offenders, how the warping effect of bad living conditions on young minds continues in these so-called reform schools where cruelty and repression conspire with past frustrations to harden the offender against ever going straight.

Dead End (1937) combined elements of all three categories. A successful criminal, Baby Face Martin (Bogart) returns on a visit to the New York waterfront of his childhood, to straighten out matters with his mother and re-establish a relationship of sorts with former childhood sweetheart Francey (Claire Trevor). Down on the East Side nothing much has changed: in the grime and squalor, a gang of noisy slum kids (the Dead End Kids, as they came to be known) run riot, intimidating the doorman of a ritzy apartment block just across the divide, harassing grown-ups and spoiling for trouble.

Martin's visit is plagued by disappointment. In a classic scene, his mother spurns his attempts at a reconciliation, and Francey destroys another illusion by confessing that she is now a prostitute. Determined that his trip should not be a total disaster, Martin enlists the street gang's assistance to kidnap a wealthy kid from the neighbouring well-to-do apartment block, but even this fails when the plan is overheard by former boyhood rival Dave (Joel McCrea), an unemployed architect. Spurred to take the law into his own hands, Dave survives a murder attempt to silence him, and finally kills Martin after a violent fight.

In the original stage play, Dave had been a cripple who merely tips off the police about Martin, but Hollywood insisted on a physical trial-of-strength between two near-equal combatants. Either way, the two were natural opposites, representing the worst and best type of individual which slum life can produce. It is a nervy, claustrophobic film, a classic of its kind, which even in its quieter moments seems to be crying out with pain and class tension. The Dead End Kids were an incredible discovery, the only group of youngsters to make a full-blown career out of street-wise yobbery. They never played anything else, nor did they ever have to, because Warner Brothers had plenty of socio-conscious vehicles into which they dropped as comfortably as peas into a shell.

Angels with Dirty Faces (1938) was probably their best film, and good though they were, the fine performances of James Cagney and Pat O'Brien, as hoodlum and priest respectively, overshadowed them completely. It is set in the familiar *Public Enemy* locations and milieu, with Cagney as a slum kid, Rocky, aided and abetted by his childhood chum Jerry (Pat O'Brien) beginning his descent into crime initially through bravado, stealing pens. Rocky is caught and sent to reform school, thereafter serving various prison sentences en route to becoming a hardened criminal. Jerry escapes on that first occasion, and later redeems himself by becoming a priest in their old neighbourhood, a figurehead of respectability and reason amid the teeming squalor and lawlessness.

The oppressive slums are imaginatively recreated in the opening montages by Michael Curtiz, one of the great film stylists of the 'thirties. Rocky's breezy invincibility makes him a hero to the local toughs which, in turn, weakens Father Jerry's corrective influence. But Rocky has his own problems. He is double-crossed by his lawyer-partner Frazier (Humphrey Bogart), which gets him a prison rap during which time Frazier sets himself up in the nightclub business with Rocky's money.

When Father Jerry publicly condemns the criminal behaviour, Frazier takes it rather personally and decides it is time the priest joined his Maker in the sky, but Rocky overhears the murder being planned and seizes the initiative. He forces Frazier, at gunpoint, to empty his safe and then kills him, but in making his escape is obliged to shoot a cop who intervenes. A tense shoot-out follows in the deserted warehouse where Rocky is trapped by police fire, with Father Jerry, a voluntary intermediary, being taken hostage by the increasingly desperate Rocky.

Caught and awaiting execution, he is visited one last time by the priest, who begs him to destroy the hero-worship which the local kids feel for him by renouncing his tough-guy image. At first, Rocky brusquely dismisses the appeal – 'Crawl on my belly? Nothin' doin'!' – but in front of the pressmen and judiciaries witnessing his final moments, he suddenly starts to whine and plead for his life, sobbing abjectly and struggling with his escorts.

Headlines such as 'Rocky Dies Yellow' and 'Killer Cowardly At The End' are followed by graphic reports of how Rocky lost his nerve at the last minute. The effect on his impressionable devotees, whose denouncement of Rocky is more strident than even the newspaper reports, is catastrophic.

Angels with Dirty Faces, by the crime movie writer Roland Brown (who also wrote *Quick Millions* for Spencer Tracy, *Hell's Highway* and *Blood Money*), is an ideal vehicle for the tough, hard-bitten Cagney rebel, seen here riding on top of the messy, vice-ridden environment like a cork on oily waters. Though part of it, he is also detached and self-contained, and he cares for nobody's plight but his own, unlike the priest whose commonsense caring attitude – the familiar Pat O'Brien character, in or out of a dog collar – shows him to be a man of wider horizons.

The contrast in their adult lives is captured in two key scenes, in the teeming, run-down streets and inside the church, the former being Rocky's natural habitat, the latter Father Jerry's. The drab surroundings, the inescapable mediocrity of a cheap rooming-house, tatty street corners, anonymous crowds, the decayed basement hide-out revered in Rocky's memory, say far more about the emptiness and turmoil of his life than his snappy repartee. Similarly, Father Jerry's church, an oasis of calm and decency, equates strongly with the characteristics of the priest himself.

Compassionate priests were dab hands at pulling up juvenile offenders in pre-war Hollywood movies, none more solidly than in *Boys' Town* (1939), in which real-life

Handouts for the boys: Rocky Sullivan (James Cagney) gladhands the Dead End Kids in *Angels with Dirty Faces* (1938).

do-gooder Father Flanagan (Spencer Tracy in Oscar-winning form) achieves amazing results by giving problem city kids a taste of the countryside. Instead of official encouragement and support, Flanagan gets into difficulties with nervous financial backers and unhelpful superiors, and to make matters worse a new boy, Whitey Marsh (Mickey Rooney), turns out to be an unprincipled little tearaway.

The film's success rests centrally on the quality of Tracy's performance, though his selection for the part was not really surprising – he had played a Catholic priest before, in *San Francisco* (1935), and as a young college student in Milwaukee had once contemplated becoming one. What he brought to the role was his familiar amiable roughneck charm and a refreshing absence of overt piety. Here was a priest who knew what it was like to lunch with the devil, and would do it again if it suited his purpose. This makes the eventual straightening out of Whitey Marsh more plausible, for it is Flanagan's strength and sanguinity as a human being, not as a holy roller, which finally wears Whitey down.

In *The Roaring Twenties* (1938), the Cagney rebel is again a catalyst between good and evil. The priest figure is replaced by honest lawyer Lloyd Hart (Jeffrey Lynn), but apart from that it is the familiar Cagney gangster scenario. Humphrey

Bogart appears, again, as an unsavoury villain. There is also a flawed attempt to make Cagney a victim of love.

Eddie Bartlett (James Cagney), George Hally (Humphrey Bogart) and Lloyd Hart meet up in the World War I trenches shortly before the German surrender, and an unquestioning sort of friendship develops in their shared dug-outs. After the war, Eddie returns home full of optimism about earning an honest dollar, but jobs are scarce and opportunities all but non-existent. Disillusioned but uncomplaining, he teams up with a pre-war buddy, Danny (Frank McHugh), in a one-cab taxi business which Eddie makes profitable by running errands for local mobsters.

His business flair and audacity keep him out of trouble, while simultaneously putting him on the bottom rungs of the ladder to crime. The transition from rebuffed war veteran to successful bootlegger is achieved in a series of vivid brushstrokes – cinematically as well as in the story – which include the off-shore hijack of a liquor hoard on which George, his pal from the trenches, is riding shot-gun.

They join forces, mutual suspicion for a short time taking second place to their collective greed. ('I'm going to have to keep an eye on you.' – 'You could stand a little watching yourself!') George has more opportunity to watch his partner. Eddie's love-life has collapsed because the lady in question, night-club singer Jean Sherman (Priscilla Lane), has fallen for Lloyd, the third member of the foxhole friendship, a qualified lawyer whom Eddie has hired to watch over his business affairs.

After Eddie's violent reaction to the news of their affair, Lloyd breaks with the gangsters, marries Jean and becomes a public prosecutor, the instigator of a vigorous campaign to combat crime in the city. Lloyd's burgeoning career and happy marriage contrasts starkly with Eddie's slide into obscurity after Jean's desertion. Effortlessly deposed by George, and drinking heavily, he reverts once more to cab driving, having been left one solitary cab by George as a final knee-in-the-groin gesture when he dissolved their partnership.

Feeling threatened by what Lloyd knows about his past, George decides to kill him. Jean, who knows how rotten George can be, digs Eddie out of a morbid, drunken daze and begs him to reassure George that Lloyd has no intention of letting the Crime Commission know anything about their past connections.

Eddie obligingly confronts George in his nightclub stronghold, where his scruffy appearance provokes considerable amusement. But George is too powerful and malevolent to concede anything. He decides the time is right to dispose of Eddie, too. But Eddie turns the tables on him, sidesteps the hitmen, and annihilates a very surprised George. On Hays Code insistence, to atone for past indiscretions, Eddie, too, dies in a hail of bullets from George's bodyguards, surviving long enough to reach some nearby church steps and be comforted by the sounds of a choir-practice.

The Roaring Twenties was Cagney's farewell, for a period of ten years, to the gangster film, and even without the choral send-off, he departed on a high note from the genre he had dominated for nearly a decade. It was a film of considerable merit, and justly deserves its near-cult status.

As in *Angels with Dirty Faces*, Cagney finds himself pinned between good and evil. Familiar reasons are offered for his downfall – the downward pull of a system which has no room for his burgeoning talents. He becomes a criminal without wanting to be one, as much the victim of his fate as its architect. Even more strongly than in previous films he is the well-intentioned rebel who is pushed off-course by a series of unfortunate circumstances.

Without a Pat O'Brien figure to deflect our interest, the characters played by Cagney and Bogart provide eloquent contrasts. Eddie is loyal to his friends whereas George callously murders his when they have served their purpose. Eddie yearns for respectability – as evidenced by his love for the virtuous Jean, his hiring of the straight-laced lawyer and his disintegration after Jean's defection. George, on the other hand, has not a single respectable thought in his head. In a sense, each is a cypher for survival in the modern urban jungle. Eddie is reluctant to surrender traditional courtesies yet he competently, if sparingly, applies his talents for violence until Jean's cry for help lights the fuse. George, the winner at any price, is accomplished in the art of treachery and unstinting in his uses of them.

Critics love to compare Bogart and Cagney in this film, the only time they played near-equals. This is unfair in my view, since Cagney was at the peak of his powers and obviously in his element in a role that demanded a multi-layer performance – brash and ebullient during his ascendancy of the criminal ladder, dispirited and emotionally wrung-out after his world collapses. Bogart, however, was merely biding his time with another killer-stereotype until he got the chance to infill his characters with his own brand of colour.

A fairer comparison would be between Cagney in *The Roaring Twenties* and Bogart in *High Sierra*, for in the latter film Bogart's role allowed introspection to be interleaved with the toughness. Given room to manoeuvre he was an actor who unfailingly delivered the goods, and one who, unlike Cagney, discernibly kept on improving with age.

Bogart's Roy Earle in *High Sierra* (1940) is a loser and he knows it. Prematurely greyed by his long years in prison, Earle needs to be reassured after his latest pardon that 'grass is still green and trees are still growin' '. His release has been arranged by a powerful but ailing gangland baron, Big Mac (Donald MacBride), who needs him to take charge of a jewel robbery at a holiday resort in the California mountains.

Before the hold-up, Earle gets involved with two attractive women – Velma (Joan Leslie), a partially-crippled farmgirl, and Marie (Ida Lupino), a dance-hall hostess whose boyfriend is one of the two fledgling hoods recruited by Big Mac, and who are already installed at the hideaway when Earle arrives.

Despite his tough appearance, Earle is a pushover for both girls, each of whom proves troublesome in her own way. He falls in love with the ungrateful Velma and is rejected in favour of a small-town city slicker, despite having funded the medical treatment which transforms her ugly-duckling world into one where she can 'dance all night if I want to!'

Marie is troublesome because she is a born loser, attracted to no-hopers like the stray dog which hangs around the hideout – 'I was never hooked on any guy that wasn't wrong'. The raid is successful, but its aftermath is a disaster. Earle's two assistants take the wrong turning and their car spins off the highway bursting in flames. 'Small-timers, they lost their heads,' is Earle's acid comment as he accelerates past the wreckage of their vehicle.

The postponement of his departure due to a delay in the pay-off caused by Big Mac's death – of natural causes – enables the police to pick up his scent, and having despatched Marie separately to Los Angeles, Earle takes his chances with the pursuing hordes of police cars and outriders scorching rubber a few yards behind him. They finally corner him on a ledge, and a marksman's bullet brings him crashing down – or crashing out, to use his own colourful prison-yard vernacular, meaning total and irreversible release from captivity.

The anachronistic quality of Earle's life is referred to visually and textually throughout the film. At the beginning, his sombre, dark-suited figure contrasts with the merriment of children playing football in the park outside the jail. Even the ball, when it lands accidentally at his feet, is white against the drab, black shoes.

Later on, as he studies the hotel set-up, his gloomy presence contrasts starkly with that of the holidaymakers strolling around and chatting happily. Other people's enjoyments mean nothing to him and, deservedly, his presence goes unnoticed. He moves among them like some ghostly confirmation of John Dillinger's quoted description of 'guys like [Earle] and him rushing towards death'.

Earle is a rueful, Rip Van Winkle figure awakening from his prison stint to find that the world has moved on without him. Only the amiable hayseed whom he befriends ('Me and Roy are old-timers') and Big Mac, whose death-bed lament is for 'all the Al guys' that have passed on, remain on his wavelength.

The callow young villains represent the 'soda-jerk and jitterbug' generation, the 'twerps' whom Big Mac so despises who are waiting to take over and make a mess of things, as their counterparts have done in government, business and banking. Earle stares at a grubby, unfamiliar world where traditional values are disappearing fast.

The picturesque mountains have been desecrated in order to create a gigantic amusement arcade for the rich. Even honesty is in short supply and yields little reward – the honest farmer is forced off his land by debts, the sincere marriage proposal is rebuffed. 'Sometimes I feel like I don't know what it's all about any more,' he tells Big Mac.

Squeezed by moral corruption on one side and the forces of retribution on the other, Earle's escape route leads naturally and spectacularly to the wide open sierras, his last refuge from trigger-happy cops, and his last chance to wipe clean the last thousand years of civilization. 'I've done all the time I'm ever going to do,' he remarks shortly before the end, indicating clearly that when death comes, as inevitably it must, with three more killings on his slate, the marksman will merely be accomplishing what Earle urgently wants him to do.

One of the most influential figures in the 'thirties (and 'forties) sociological cinema was John Garfield. More than any actor of his generation he epitomized the outsider in society, the underdog struggling for recognition and acceptance against overwhelming odds. Garfield offered passion, anger and an all-pervading sadness in poetic symmetry, housed in the body of an aggressive athlete. He was the classic outcast, partly through self-alienation, partly because the system had no slot which contained him comfortably. Garfield himself would have been the last person to claim that he spoke for anyone, but clearly a strong affinity existed between the bitter, street-scarred character he played (and indeed *was*) and the born losers of the Depression era.

All the great rebel actors have made their impact in a hugely personal way. Many shared origins which were strongly anti-establishment – Cagney, Raft, Garfield and Steve McQueen all had frequent run-ins with the law during their adolescent years – so that when they came to play rebels later in life their portrayals contained an intrinsic honesty that went far beyond acting skills. When Garfield complained, 'The fates are against me', in his first Hollywood film, *Four Daughters* (1937), his eyes conveyed those sentiments more eloquently than the dialogue. With McQueen he shared an almost uncanny ability to register depth of thought and conflicting inner tensions without the slightest visible flicker of emotion.

The quality that Garfield offered which was original even in movies which expressed fundamental social concerns during the late 'thirties and afterwards, was his ability – and complete willingness – to play characters who were incapable of helping themselves.

Cagney, Raft and Bogart either solved their problems or died in spasms of life-sapping violence – their films offered simplistic solutions which nobody questioned because the characters themselves, apart from Cagney's later *tours de force*, such as *White Heat* (1948), were refreshingly free of consciences or complexes. Which Cagney character of the 'thirties ever paused for a moment to reflect on the consequences of his actions? Which Bogart figure of that period ever expressed remorse? The supposition that a grim environment breeds toughness at the expense of all sensitivity was one to which Hollywood adhered all too rigidly, in order no doubt to cash in on their numerous tough-guy stars, but in the light of what we have since learned about human behaviour patterns in response to conditioning, not always convincingly.

John Garfield represented the other side, the human side, of that equation, as an underprivileged immigrant poor boy who *knew* he was getting a raw deal from society but who had enough gumption to realize that he was helpless to reverse the situation. The Garfield film character was in essence a creation of this mixture of impotence and rage against middle-class conventions and snobbery which the actor, as a crinkly-haired Jewish kid making his way in the world, had encountered all too often at first hand.

An objective assessment of Garfield's work on its own is near impossible, for the

31

on-screen character he became remains inseparable from his own life and beliefs. To attempt to understand the Garfield movie rebel without relating it to the actor's development as a young man running wild in the streets of New York is equally futile. If Garfield symbolizes anything, it is the penniless underdog beset by hardship and injustice, and if his characterizations embody the kind of stubborn pride and hurt indifference which people in adversity who are denied an escape possess, and I believe these are the qualities which he most powerfully conveys, then those performances draw their strength from real-life experience.

Born on New York's notorious East Side in 1913, the son of an immigrant Jewish garment-presser, Garfield's first tragic experience occurred when his mother Hannah died, in 1920. Robbed of her affection, and thereafter cared for by a busy father who spent most weekends serving as a cantor at the local synagogue, Garfield, in his own words, 'got to know the streets'. When his father remarried three years later, Garfield referred to his new stepmother as 'the woman my old man lives with'. Not surprisingly, the company he kept comprised other disaffected youths and delinquents, and before long, at the authorities' insistence, he was enrolled in a special school for problem children supervised by an understanding psychologist, Dr Angelo Patri.

Selective in his praise of others, Garfield later said of Patri, 'I owe him everything for reaching into the garbage pail and pulling me out'. It was the kind of self-effacing candour which later endeared him to free-thinkers and would make him a target for those capable of applying devious methods to bring a good man down.

Behind the mask of toughness, there was always with Garfield an appealing naïvety, a stray dog's trust of strangers that would prove problematic, and a desire to earn respect. Though fame and wealth eventually distanced him from his humble beginnings, he never showed the slightest inclination to play down the rough side, although anyone questioning his abilities because of that background invariably received a sharp retort. Near the start of his film career, one director who had been lined up to work with him remarked that because of Garfield's lack of film experience he would be taking a chance, to which Garfield snapped, 'I've never heard of you either, so we're both taking the same chance!' In the company of acknowledged intellectuals such as the top brass of the Group Theatre, or writers such as Arthur Miller, Abraham Polonsky or Clifford Odets (who wrote *Awake and Sing* in which Garfield appeared in 1935, *Golden Boy* – for Garfield – in 1937, and *The Big Knife*, in which he starred on the New York stage in 1949), Garfield carried his lack of formal education like a hump on his back.

While he would readily admit his discomfiture in private to people he held in high esteem, he would tolerate no putdowns from anyone he considered to be merely his own intellectual equal.

Garfield's entrance into films created as great an impact as his entrance into the quiet, small-town family with whom he boards in *Four Daughters* (1938). Mickey Borden (John Garfield), a some-time composer and life-long pessimist, encounters his first taste of genuine love from Ann Lemp (Priscilla Lane), but it is not enough to heal the bruises of a lifetime. A fugitive from the big city, Borden does not understand small-town communities, and is contemptuous of middle-class convention and weary of the pretentious time-wasting which passes for life in small American towns.

He makes no attempt to conform, nor does he attempt to offend purely for effect. He is, by his own definition, a realist, by which he means that nothing – not even life itself – ought to be thought of as sacred. The story contains overtones of the romantic interludes of *The Roaring Twenties*, in which Priscilla Lane and Jeffrey Lynn were the fey young lovers and James Cagney the odd man out left to nurse his sorrows. In *Daughters Courageous*, Lane and Lynn (the latter playing Felix Deitz) are again the lovers, engaged to be married when Garfield, as Borden, arrives at the house. Though Borden succeeds in snatching her from Felix, it proves to be a hollow achievement, for her experiences with Borden merely confirm in her own mind the enormity of her error, an impulsive act committed as a result of her mistaken belief that Felix preferred one of her sisters.

Though Ann gamely tries to make something of her marriage to Borden, it is a hopeless mis-match, the realization of which drives Borden to suicide, or rather, to put himself out of the picture – literally – so as not to impede further her chances of happiness with Felix.

The film started out as a relatively innocuous and gentle account of the temporary disruption of a solid middle-class family life by a shabby iconoclast, but in the making got transformed, by Garfield's wholly unexpected incisiveness as the intruder, into a thoughtful evaluation of middle-class American values. Nobody was quite prepared for the plausible ease with which Garfield slotted into this, his very first film role. Hindsight tells us, of course, that Garfield could have played Borden, or something very similar, without being given a script, but in 1938, before the facts of his early life were known outside the fringe theatre audiences around New York, there was nothing to detract attention from his performance, which was hailed as 'brilliant' and 'inspirational'.

Though the nearest comparison to the impact made by Garfield in *Four Daughters* was that made by James Dean, eighteen years later, in *East of Eden* (1954), Garfield can more easily be twinned with Steve McQueen as a romantic rebel. In his biography, *McQueen*, William F. Nolan describes his subject as 'a man whose often awkward and frustrated attempts to find the love denied him as a child reflected the depth of his need for human intimacy'. This summary can be applied equally well to Garfield, whose need to be accepted by the intellectuals was another facet of that striving for human intimacy. Given his background, his political naïvety and the left-wing leaning of so many of the intellectuals whose respect he wanted, it was not surprising that he endorsed a number of causes that offended Hollywood's right-wing establishment and for which he paid, as so many of his screen characters did, a terrible price.

33

Sergeant Bill Dane (Robert Taylor, left) and Corporal Barney Todd (Lloyd Nolan) in
Bataan (1943).

CHAPTER THREE

CONQUERING HEROES

*7*he hopeful sentiment that World War I had been 'the war to end all wars' was unfortunately an unfulfilled prophecy that lasted for little more than two decades. Long before the outbreak of hostilities in 1939, it could be foreseen (though not apparently by the British government) that the tensions and injustices raging across Europe would lead to some awful reckoning.

The inter-war years witnessed both Fascist and Communist uprisings within Europe. To offset the Communist gains powerful partisan groups of right-wing fanatics and disaffected World War I veterans in Germany and Italy vowed to destroy the Red Menace and to solve the increasing economic and political strife in their countries by suppressing and persecuting alien minorities, predominantly the Jews. Mussolini's Fascist successes in Italy in the early 'twenties prefaced and, indeed, fuelled a similar rise in Germany of Hitler's Nazism a decade later, aided and abetted by the social disorientation precipitated by the world depression. Jews and other resident non-Aryans were stigmatized as being directly responsible for the nation's difficulties and by September 1935, when Hitler legislated against German Jews, the Holocaust had begun in earnest.

The Spanish Civil War drew Germany and Italy to the support of the right-wing insurgents while for a time the Soviets aided the Spanish Republic. However, disenchanted with the poor organization and constant in-fighting between leading Republicans, Stalin withdrew his support in 1938. This, along with the cessation of support from the International Brigades, left the Republicans in a desperately vulnerable position.

Anxious to avoid a threatened bloodbath as the Fascists pressed home their advantage against Spain's ill-defended cities, the British and French premiers, Neville Chamberlain and Edouard Daladier, bowed to Hitler's counterbalancing demands to annex Austria and also Sudetanland, the German-speaking border areas of Czechoslovakia, to the Third Reich. The sell-out, for such it was, occurred at Munich in September 1938, from which Chamberlain returned to Britain declaring that 'peace in our time' had been secured. It was probably the worst example of misplaced optimism in modern history. Chamberlain had been hoaxed into believing

35

that Hitler had fulfilled his global ambitions. Hitler next took over Czechoslovakia, in March 1939: his threat to flatten Prague unless the Czech government acceded to his demands had been enough to persuade President Hacha to comply.

With Czechoslovakia under the swastika, the British and French governments saw how totally they had been duped. Their response was an Anglo-French-Polish treaty which guaranteed assistance to Poland should Hitler invade. (Poland was the next logical target if Hitler's vow to control the entire land mass between the Atlantic Ocean and the Urals was to be fulfilled.) At dawn on Friday, 1 September 1939, Germany launched a huge offensive against Poland, precipitating Britain and France into their long-awaited counter-move.

Hollywood was neither prompt nor eager to acknowledge the slide into full-scale war in Europe. It was a subject which the film-makers had found to be both politically and commercially expedient to ignore. With its unrivalled domination of the Western European market for films, rejection by any particular country of its films would have been costly. By the late 1930s, the new rulers in Germany had shown their willingness to censor and ban movies with Jewish involvement on either side of the camera, or movies in which the regime's view offended or contaminated public morality.

The films of Johnny Weissmuller, for example, were unacceptable because of his German-Jewish blood. Fred Astaire, who was really Fred Austerlitz, the son of an Austrian-Jewish immigrant, was similarly banned, as was Peter Lorre. Among the more ridiculous bans was Mae West, considered too vulgar for the masses, though what, if anything, the average German cinemagoer would have made of those juicy American double-entendres is anybody's guess.

Hollywood's response was to look the other way, as, indeed, did Congress. To be fair, America had large-scale domestic problems to contend with, and however disquieting the events in Europe seemed to those Americans who bothered to read about them, the economic difficulties nearer home were far more urgent. Hollywood economists were in no doubt that the storms brewing in Europe were best left out of screenplays for the time being.

In addition, direct or implied criticism of any nation that was not officially an enemy of America would have encountered censorship difficulties. This was why Walter Wanger's film *The Blockade* (1937), starring Henry Fonda and Madeleine Carroll and set during the Spanish Civil War, declined to indict, or even identify, either side of the conflict. Great care was taken to avoid mentioning incidents or locations which might lead anyone to suspect they were watching something about the Spanish Civil War. What cinemagoers saw, in fact, was a completely anonymous civil war being waged for no apparent reason in a deliberately fictitious and scarcely credible country. But at least no foreign government could take offence and that meant no restrictions on the exporting of Hollywood films.

The first and most welcome sign that Hollywood was about to shift its stance and stop shifting its feet came with *Confessions of a Nazi Spy* (1939), made by Warner

Brothers. The company's antipathy to Hitler dated back to 1936, the year its German-Jewish salesman in Berlin had been interrogated and then bludgeoned to death in a Berlin alleyway by Nazi murderers.

Personal antagonisms aside, it was appropriate that a studio which had launched and led the wave of social realism films during the 'thirties should again be first off the blocks to attack political injustice. Of all the major studios which later joined in the propaganda war, Warner Brothers' output remains the most consistently honest and journalistic. It knew better than most how to turn an eye-catching headline into a good film, and this wealth of experience in documentary-style story-telling gave it an enviable edge over studios which had up till then majored on romantic fiction, glossy musicals and fantasy.

Following the declaration of war in September 1939, America passed 27 months in confusion, self-examination and indecision as to what it should do. Lifelong isolationists had a field day, but historical ties with Britain, the common language bond and a long-standing love of all things British pricked at the American conscience. Nevertheless, there was widespread relief when American military help

Spycatcher Edward Renard (Edward G. Robinson) quizzes a suspect in *Confessions of a Nazi Spy* (1939).

was neither requested nor expected. American losses during the final phases of World War I had been horrific and nobody had any reason to believe that the fatalities would be fewer this time round.

Though still officially at peace, by August 1941 America was repairing British warships. American warships were escorting British merchant shipping convoys across the Atlantic as far as Iceland, where they could rendezvous with the British Navy, thereby saving Britain from having to deploy dozens of warships urgently needed elsewhere to keep the busy Atlantic trade routes open. The Germans regarded this effrontery as an act of war and from September 1941 onwards American navy personnel came increasingly under fire from German submarines and U-boats. Neither side was keen to declare war formally, however, and this bizarre situation, in which German ships wantonly fired on any American vessel which took their fancy, remained unresolved until after the Japanese attack on Pearl Harbour in December 1941. Until this time Germany also continued to enjoy diplomatic representation in the USA.

Since its silent era, Hollywood had been a melting-pot for European movie talent, driven to California as much by the absence of a comparable industry in Europe as by the lure of Hollywood. Film bosses and directors of European origin could scarcely be expected to reconcile what was happening in Europe with the official isolationist policies of the American government. But neither could they get away with making films with a political or ideological stance that opposed the official view. For the 27 months between the declaration of war in Germany and America's active involvement, Hollywood sat on the fence. Films made which were sternly anti-Fascist in tone were wholly unreal, the message being tactfully diluted by the packaging.

European expatriates, not surprisingly, had a field day whipping up emotions and displayed the greatest commitment towards exposing Hitler's tyranny. Chaplin's *The Great Dictator* (1940) had already been in production before the outbreak of war, and was halted only during the first week after war was declared. Characteristically, the more warnings which the politically nervous Hays Office and Chaplin's own studio gave him, the more he was encouraged to press on regardless. Chaplin's hiss-boo send-up of the Germans – Adolph Hitler becoming Adenoid Hynkel complete with hysterical oratory – was very effective though the sporadic force-feeding of sentimentality, as in the 6-minute final address to camera, works less well.

Hitchcock's *Foreign Correspondent*, an anti-Nazi movie commenced in 1938, the year he made *The Lady Vanishes* (1938), which expressed similar sentiments, was scripted originally by John Howard Lawson, but was reworked numerous times by various writers, including eventually the director himself.

Joel McCrea plays the foreign correspondent who uncovers the truth behind a Fascist conspiracy led by an apparently innocent leader of a peace organization (Herbert Marshall). Hitchcock fills the film with memorable setpieces – for example, the assassination of a Dutch diplomat by a killer masquerading as a press photographer who conceals the gun in his camera. But despite the thriller elements, its central appeal is the power of its political statement, one in which Hitchcock's patriotic feelings are given full expression, mainly through the correspondent's impassioned broadcasts across the Atlantic from a badly-blitzed London, urging America to be vigilant and to ring itself 'with steel' (sentiments echoed closely by broadcaster Ed Murrow in his famous reports).

Fritz Lang's *Manhunt* (1941) shows a gallant big-game hunter, Thorndike (Walter Pidgeon), stalking Hitler as he would an African lion, being discovered by patrolling SS guards just as he has the Führer in his sights. The SS torture him in an attempt to wring a confession from him that his mission was to kill Hitler on the orders of the British government. When their tactics fail, they shoot him and toss him off a cliff, leaving him for dead. Thorndike, however, survives his ordeal and manages to return to England concealed in the hold of a freighter.

The realization that he may still be alive starts a huge search for him, and he is eventually tracked down by a tenacious enemy agent (George Sanders) to an underground hideout in the New Forest. Entombed and finally forced to confess his misdeeds, Thorndike, however, has the final word, when he returns the fountain pen used like a makeshift bow-and-arrow which the agent had passed down to him for signing his confession up through the spy-hole with such force that it embeds itself in the SS man's skull.

Whilst *Manhunt*, like *Foreign Correspondent*, encompassed its director's hatred and distrust of Germany under the Nazis, other expatriate European directors, too,

Thorndike (Walter Pidgeon) evades his Nazi assassin in *Manhunt* (1939).

employed subtle devices to get their message across. Michael Curtiz's *The Sea Hawk* (1940), contained a wealth of anti-Fascist sentiments delivered with swashbuckling swagger by Errol Flynn. Philip of Spain (Montagu Love) is a Hitler figure, albeit in Elizabethan guise, who muses malevolently over his world map about outright domination, describing England as a 'puny, rock-bound island' secretly giving aid to his enemies and impatient for it to be crushed.

For much of the picture, Queen Elizabeth (Flora Robson) dismisses Flynn's warnings about the futility of delaying her attack on Spain and of her insistence on diplomacy, clinging resolutely, if somewhat forlornly, to the notion of appeasement. In the end, she is forced to denounce Spain's double-speak, and gives her blessing to preparations for war, declaring her change-of-heart to have been because 'the earth belongs not to any man but to all men, and that freedom is the deed and title to the soil on which we exist'.

In *The Mortal Storm* (1941), the incarceration of a kindly Jewish academic, Professor Roth (Frank Morgan), in a concentration camp provokes bitter recriminations within his immediate family. Fritz Marberg (Robert Young), the ardent young man in love with his daughter, and his stepson side with the Nazi cause, while his natural family, including his daughter Freya (Margaret Sullivan) opposes the regime. Freya is romantically drawn to Martin Breitner (James Stewart), whose views echo the liberalism of Professor Roth, his former university tutor.

The professor's death in captivity is the final straw for Freya following her own detention and interrogation by the Gestapo. Desperate to make a fresh start in life

Martin Reitner (James Stewart) and Freya (Margaret Sullivan) witness a sinister show of hands in *The Mortal Storm* (1941).

across the German border Freya and Martin head for the Alps, but she is cut down by German bullets at the frontier and dies within the sight of freedom. Ironically, the detachment of border guards responsible for her death is commanded by Fritz Marlberg, her one-time fiancé.

The eruptions of passion and the polarization of the beleaguered family following the professor's arrest and his callous treatment in SS hands are believable enough, as the hot-headed stepsons put fatherland before father, while mother and daughter turn increasingly for support to the professor's genial star pupil. The sufferings of the concentration-camp victims are equally vivid, and again benefit from the film's general atmosphere of restraint – Gestapo agents are brutal but matter-of-factly so, taking no obvious pleasure from their actions.

Less successful was the casting of Robert Young and James Stewart as the young male protagonists, which gave the conflict a divertingly wholesome American feel, both actors having made their names as hometown good eggs. The illusion of reality was not helped by the casting of Frank Morgan, the previous year's Wizard of Oz, as the Jewish professor. These irritations, however, do not outweigh the merits of a film which not only exposes the bigotry and injustice behind Nazism but also portrays the humanitarianism and compassion which are its logical counterpoints.

Alexander Korda, Hungarian by origin but British by adoption, used historical fact to add weight to the British argument. 'There are always men who, for the sake of their insane ambition, want to destroy what others build,' says one character in *Lady Hamilton* (1941), an obvious reference to contemporary politics. Nelson (Laurence Olivier) is highly sceptical of the peace of Amiens and warns the Admiralty of the consequences of taking the agreement at face value: 'You can't make peace with a dictator!' Again, the sentiment has its parallel in the Munich peace pact and Neville Chamberlain's misguided faith. At one point Nelson is taking a battering from Napoleon until help in the form of supplies and extra armaments arrives, whereupon he exultantly declares to his absent adversary, 'Look out. . .we shall lick you now'. The Americanism used in this so-called warning leaves little doubt as to whom Korda was addressing.

Other than verbal support and encouragement, help of the kind intimated by Korda did not materialize until a week after the invasion of Pearl Harbour by the Japanese on 7 December 1941, by which time the war had assumed a wider and more deadly perspective.

Despite the substantial deterioration in diplomatic and commercial relations between America and Japan, and even taking into account Japan's expansionism in the Pacific, the idea that this could lead to a full-scale war crossed the minds of few observers. Japan had a wealth of plunder available under its very nose from the British, French and Dutch possessions in the Far East. Also, while the USSR's attention was diverted, to repulse the German invasion, its mineral-rich eastern flanks were theoretically up for grabs.

Japan had no logical reason to view America either as a candidate for conquest or as a threat to its own imperialism. Logic was, alas, sadly missing from the plan which launched that fateful assault on Pearl Harbour. It was the result of a combination of political arrogance, military naïvety and tactical incompetence by the military clique under General Tojo.

The losses suffered by the Americans at Pearl Harbour were initially less severe than their embarrassment at having been caught napping. Some 2,400 personnel died, and half that number again were injured in the attack. Half the base's air-strike power was wiped out, humiliatingly, on the ground and five battleships were destroyed. But considering the 292,000 American servicemen killed in the war that followed, and the £85,000 million – $340,000 in 1945 – spent by the Americans in the war effort Pearl Harbour was, as it were, a drop in the ocean.

For the Japanese, however, it was a terrible omen. They failed to track and destroy the three US Pacific fleet carriers absent from Pearl Harbour on the morning of the raid. They failed to knock out the base's substantial fuel reserves, or communications installations – whether it was through incompetence or delusions of their own invincibility hardly matters. What does matter is that the Japanese initiative was gained and lost in a single day, and that the raid, while failing miserably in what should have been a clear-cut tactical objective, succeeded only in unifying and galvanizing the strength and the will of a previously divided nation against them.

From the outbreak of 'its own' war, America suffered a series of embarrassing and costly defeats. The legacy of Pearl Harbour seemed unshakable, and until late 1942 the USA and her Allies were subjected to one military battering after another. The American army was routed on Guam, Wake Island and the Bataan peninsula, while Britain lost its grip on the strategically vital Singapore. The battle for Midway Atoll in June 1942 swung the pendulum decisively the Americans' way. In the months which followed, US marines and infantrymen leap-frogged from one Pacific island to another, and some of their names, for example, Guadalcanal, Iwo Jima, Okinawa, have become immortalized in Hollywood movies.

The mortality rate on both sides was enormous. Over half the US assault troops who stormed Iwo Jima died in the attempt. The Japanese casualties were appalling, too. Also at Iwo Jima, twenty thousand Japanese were killed, with less than one per cent of them taken prisoner – surrender was simply not in their vocabulary. The Americans quickly learnt to be wary of their white flags, which all too often were used to lure GIs within range of grenades concealed under their tunics.

More than 100,000 Japanese troops took up positions to defend Okinawa, but the Americans captured it in spite of everything which the Japanese could throw at them, including the infamous kamikaze suicide squadrons. The Japanese made excellent propaganda out of the so-called fanatical dedication of these fearless volunteers, but conveniently forgot to add that the pilots' canopies were sealed on the outside of the aircraft. Volunteers they might have been, but there was certainly no scope for second thoughts.

The island war gave American movie producers something else to think about besides Europe. It also signalled an end to the propaganda restraint which had been imposed upon its European focus. No longer were their sentiments about democracy and the overthrow of repression the sterile musings of an onlooker.

Bataan (1943) has Sergeant Bill Dane (Robert Taylor) in charge of a platoon which is assigned to destroy a bridge, and thus to obstruct the enemy's advance while General MacArthur rethinks his strategy. The Americans are hopelessly outnumbered and eventually overwhelmed, including, last of all, Dane, who in anticipation of his fate has tidily prepared his own resting-place and constructed his own memorial cross.

Here was a piece of recent history re-enacted with a commendable respect for the facts, though some of the dramatic interludes, such as Dane reciting aloud a fellow-soldier's final letter home – 'it don't matter where a man dies as long as he dies for freedom' – are obvious crowd-pleasers.

In *Flying Tigers* (1943) John Wayne commands a platoon of fighter pilots engaged in dogfights with the Japanese. John Carroll is the cavalier newcomer who challenges Wayne's rule-book command. The same plot, with Robert Ryan as the insubordinate second-in-command, resurfaced as *The Flying Leathernecks* (1952). Its aerial sequences, with cockpit windows shattering under machine-gun bursts and evil Oriental faces vomiting blood as their planes spiral out of control, remain memorable enough, but unfortunately the human dramas counterpointing the action are nothing to get into a spin over.

As the title suggests, *Guadalcanal Diary* (1943) focuses on what was, without doubt, one of the bloodiest showdowns in the entire war, the crucial engagement at Guadalcanal between August 1942 and the following February. Again, the tale of ordinary guys *versus* the verminous yellow hordes helped recruitment figures. The ordinariness of the fighting marines is emphasized by an absence of any big-name star to head the heroics. Instead, a stalwart troupe of character actors, among them Preston Foster, William Bendix, Lloyd Nolan and Richard Conte, go through their daily routines of killing, cracking jokes, writing home, bragging about their families, praying and dying. Because they are indistinguishable from real troops, the realism is heightened. At one point, Bendix, pinned under heavy enemy fire, declares, 'I ain't no hero. I'm just a guy. I'm here because someone sent me and I just want to get it over with. . .', a sentiment shared by almost everyone in uniform.

Broadly speaking, though, the island war had little to offer cinematically, and only a handful of films commemorating the brutal campaign is worth remembering. All were made after the war: for example, *Sands of Iwo Jima* was made in 1950 and *Halls of Montezuma* in 1951. In contrast with the Germans and their puppet officials, who could assume characters unpleasant but at least recognizable, the Japanese had no point of contact with a Western audience whatever, and were invariably shown as demented, short-sighted little sadists. Fidelity to the propaganda image of a despicable enemy unfortunately made monotonous, repetitive cinema even when major stars were brought in to polish them off in morale-lifting numbers.

By comparison the war in Europe continued to offer an exciting mixture of incidents, nationalities and characterizations for film-makers to choose from. The overriding problem, as always, lay in the inaccuracy of the reconstruction. Well-intentioned though much of it was, the atmosphere conveyed was generally phoney, but as the war progressed after the terrible reverses of the early years, a firmer grasp of what was happening permeated back to Hollywood and movies began to tap richer veins and strive for greater realism.

Mrs Miniver (1942) belongs in the former starry-eyed category. Sincerity oozes from everywhere, as from an aerosol with a slow puncture, and its depiction of Britain under siege is unintentionally comic at times. Set during the Dunkirk retreat, it shows how one staunchly patriotic middle-class family do their level best for king and country. Father (Walter Pidgeon) rounds up his chums, a group of small boat owners, and sportingly they all head off into the choppy English Channel to rescue the beleaguered Brits. All classes are swept up in this scramble to be heroes, including one volunteer who turns up at the quayside in top hat and evening dress, having felt the call of duty midway through his Savoy dinner.

Mother (Greer Garson) captures a German pilot who has crash-landed on to the shrubbery, disarming him in more ways than one with a cosy lecture on duty and boys loving their Mums. Servants with names like Ada and Gladys float in and out with endless trays of food like comedy supports in a zany 'thirties musical.

The huge popularity of *Mrs Miniver* stems from the very fantasies which devalue its social observation. Despite the production-line tragedies which occur, such as the death of daughter-in-law Carol in an air raid, it retains the flavour of a pious charade. The irony largely overlooked at the time it first appeared was the depiction of the Minivers' social inferiors as being quaintly moronic, yet these are the people who constituted the vast majority of the brave expedition forces trapped on Dunkirk beaches.

The ordinary British tommy got a better deal in *This Above All* (1942), although with Tyrone Power as the working-class Briggs some concession to fantasy was made. Briggs, a Dunkirk hero, deserts his unit because he objects to the way his working-class brothers are being sacrificed in battle to defend a despicable class system. Redemption, however, is at hand for him in the guise of an upper-class WAAF (Joan Fontaine), whose blistering tirade against the futility of the German oppression ('We'll never give in. . . We won't be beaten. We won't. We just *won't!*') dislodges the rocks from his head.

On his way to surrender himself to the authorities, he is critically injured rescuing the victims of an air raid. R.C. Sherriff's screenplay sustained the patriotism making Briggs' desertion seem like an isolated act of folly rather than the result of deep-seated animosity to which the character succumbs in Eric Knight's original novel. Despite the pairing of Hollywood's handsomest duo, Tyrone Power and Joan Fontaine, the movie strikes some honest chords and its rub-down of the British class system is more intelligently stated than in *Mrs Miniver*, which had implied that one of the real tests of British resolve under siege was its ability to feed itself on the servants' night off.

Satirizing the Nazis as being nothing worse than a bunch of unpalatable goons had its problems: doing it sophisticatedly drew accusations of helping enemy propaganda whilst doing it hamfistedly attracted hostility for debasing the efforts of those busily opposing it. Ernest Lubitsch's comedy *To Be Or Not To Be* (1942) starred Jack Benny and Carole Lombard as an engagingly witty married couple, members of a Polish Theatre company in occupied Warsaw, who out-manoeuvre the Nazi authorities and cause the death of an undercover Nazi agent before swanning off to freedom. It is another of those films which has inherited a belated gloss due to the indelicacy of its theme at the time of its making – in this case, the supposition that it was acceptable to make jokes about the tragic fate of Poland and the fortitude of Polish resistance fighters. Aside from the frantic wisecracking of Benny and Lombard, even the heavies were given so-called laugh lines such as Sig Ruman's jolly explanation of his nickname 'Concentration Camp' Erhardt – 'I do the concentrating, they do the camping!'

Once upon a Honeymoon (1942) similarly attempts to tiptoe between comedy

Mrs Miniver (Greer Garson) copes with an intruder in *Mrs Miniver* (1942).

45

and thrills with pauses for romance along the way and with Cary Grant and Ginger Rogers as the love interest one could expect more deftness of touch than is seen here. Grant plays Pat, an American radio correspondent whose reporting of a society wedding between a local baron and Katie (Ginger Rogers), a ritzy showgirl, leads to the unmasking by Pat of the baron's pro-Fascist activities.

This, rather naturally, swings the bride's affections Pat's way, and the pair manage to escape the wrathful reprisals of the baron and his ugly friends. Director Leo McCarey's attempt to extract humour along with phoney confessions in a grim concentration-camp setting hits well below the belt. That, alas, is one of the dangers of trying to be funny at the expense of barbarians.

Hangmen Also Die (1943) had worse casting problems than *Once upon a Honeymoon*, with perennial tough-guy Brian Donleavy inexplicably hired to play the Czech patriot who bumps off the notorious Nazi gauleiter Heydrich. Making his escape after the successful assassination Svoboda (Donleavy) is helped by a young girl, Marsha (Anna Sten), with whose family he finds temporary sanctuary at the insistence of Marsha's stoically anti-Fascist historian father, Professor Novotny (Walter Brennan). The German officials exert pressure on the townspeople to reveal Heydrich's killer by taking hostages and ritualistically murdering them in reprisal, the independent-minded Novotny being among the first to be rounded up.

The second half of the film focuses on the efforts of the resistance to prevent Svoboda's arrest, and to incriminate a podgy quisling, Czaka (Gene Raymond), who not only forfeits his life at the hands of his paymasters but also ends the slaughter of the hostages. Svoboda escapes detection, but Czaka's ritualistic gangster-style execution – at the end of a car ride – by a Gestapo murder squad is too late to save the professor, who is shot alongside other patriots to a rousing chorus of 'No surrender', the hostages' anthem composed during captivity by one of the prisoners.

An intriguing postscript shows a coded German report admitting that Czaka did not murder Heydrich, but having failed to intimidate the Czechs into surrendering the real assassin, they had no alternative but publicly to swallow the sacrificial offering in order to save face.

A more philosophical projection of Nazi tyranny occurs in *The Seventh Cross* (1944) which differs from other stories by making the victims Germans themselves. Set in 1936, thereby revelling in a kind of smug hindsight, it follows the fate of seven concentration-camp escapees, among them Ray Collins, who narrates the story from beyond the grave as he is the first to be re-captured. When the Nazis discover their escape, they erect seven crosses in the prison yard, one for each runaway's execution after recapture, as a grim warning to other prisoners.

Heisler (Spencer Tracy) heads for Mainz where he has friends, among them a Jewish physician who fixes his badly infected hand, and a married couple who shelter him from patrolling SS squads under equally threatening circumstances. With all the other six escapees either executed or killed during capture, Heisler becomes a *cause célèbre*. The authorities' failure to bring him to heel acutely embarrasses them.

As they increase their efforts, and reward money, others enable Heisler to bid a thankful farewell to Germany.

Director Fred Zinnemann's delicate touch is constantly in evidence and he refrains from any vulgar depiction of Nazi torture, creating instead a subtle, optimistic tone. Ray Collins describes what happens as the story of 'a few little people who proved there is something in the human soul which sets men above the animals, and beyond them'. Crucifix motifs abound throughout the film – telegraph poles in silhouette against the night sky, telephone wires on buildings and so on – offering subliminal messages of hope for the escapers. Occasionally, their despair is glimpsed, and each time it registers vividly on the memory: the fleeing circus acrobat trapped on a roof who dives spectacularly into the crowd; the escaper who surrenders, vowing that 'it's better to be dead and rotting and not have to see man's inhumanity to man'.

Heisler's optimism is its keynote. Here is a man with every reason to curse humanity and to give up, yet alone and wounded he struggles on, refusing to acknowledge that 'this degraded Germany' is irretrievably ruined. Nobility under duress or the gradual discovery of it is a recurring feature in the central characters in Zinnemann's films – for example, *The Men* (1950), *From Here to Eternity* (1953), *A Man for All Seasons* (1966) – and in Heisler Zinnemann created an eloquent symbol of rugged defiance.

By 1944, the propaganda format was clearly established, and unlikely to change however long the fighting lasted. Army platoons were intentionally made up to represent a microcosm of American society with Jews, such as Sam Levene in *Action in the North Atlantic* (1943); Italians, such as Richard Conte in *A Walk in the Sun* (1945); and Irish, among the rank and file. Cameras supporting the case for democracy infiltrated the clandestine resistance groups in occupied territories including France, Poland and Czechoslovakia. France was cinematically Hollywood's first choice for illustrating how a noble, cultured race should behave under barbarian occupation, and there was no shortage of French officials putting the boot into Fascism from behind a masquerade of tame acquiescence.

Claude Rains' endearingly corrupt police chief in *Casablanca* (1942) was a classic example of this. In the same film, Bogart plays an American, but during the war he played a French resistance fighter (*Passage to Marseille* [1944]), convincing audiences with raw passion alone, and with no concessions towards a French accent, that he was every bit as French as a Gauloise.

The Purple Heart (1944) features Dana Andrews (a busy if somewhat stilted wartime actor), Richard Conte and Farley Granger as three of the eight US flyers shot down after a bombing raid on Tokyo whom the Japanese put on trial for their lives – in defiance of established conventions of war which accord captured servicemen the status and attendant privileges of being prisoners of war. Their captors justify this action by claiming that civilian targets were the Americans' real objective. Interrogation, blackmail, a crude attempt at bribery – recognition of their POW status in return for confessing where the raid took off from – and finally torture fail to loosen the crews' tongues. At a short trial, staged before Axis and other interested observers, they are found guilty and sent to their deaths.

The Purple Heart decoration, created during the American Revolution by General George Washington, is the top honour that can be bestowed on any American soldier during active service. A film with such a title is clearly not going to let the Yanks in the hold slink away ignominiously, so the verdict and sentence at the end is a foregone conclusion. So, too, is the shrill invective used against the Japanese, whose behaviour throughout the film suggests a total absence of the honour and inscrutability with which they like to be regarded.

Interestingly, the release of *The Purple Heart* was postponed from 1943 to the following year because of the State Department's reluctance to divulge, for fear of repercussions at home, that American prisoners in Japanese hands were, in many cases, not protected by the Geneva Convention. This regrettable state of affairs was officially acknowledged by the American government in 1944, and the film was accordingly released, provoking, as had been expected and as its producer Darryl Zanuck had expressly hoped, a considerable furore.

Another of the better films to appear towards the end of the war was *Thirty Seconds Over Tokyo* (1944), which viewed the same incident from another angle: the actual planning and carrying through of the raid. Afterwards, one of the B25 bombers is brought down over China, but instead of capture by Japanese sympathizers the airmen are fussed over and nursed by friendly villagers. The pilot loses his leg – a grimly realistic amputation without the use of anaesthetics – but a happy ending sees the pilot reunited with his tearful, pregnant wife.

Realism based on personal eye-witness accounts of the Italian campaign is what keeps *The Story of GI Joe* (1945) as fresh today as when it was made. War correspondent Ernie Pyle was on hand to authenticate the film version of his syndicated war reports, for which he gained his profession's approximation of the Purple Heart, namely the Pulitzer Prize. The film retains consistently Pyle's perception of the fighting as it follows the indomitable Infantry Company C from its bivouacked stake-out in North Africa to the bruising, drawn-out battle to liberate the monastery at Monte Cassino.

Director William Wellman's fly-on-the-gun-turret technique allows the audience to be one of the group, to eavesdrop on conversations which have the sharp ring of truth. Burgess Meredith plays the plucky newsman who instinctively dishes the dirt with the rest of the guys, but who retains his professional objectivity despite being knee-deep in carnage and suffering.

The progress through Sicily and Italy saps the company's physical and mental reserves. San Vittorio is reduced to a pile of rubble as the advancing US Fifth Army snatches it back, eating up enemy mortars and sniper fire.

The bloody siege of Monte Cassino provides the film's explosive climax, where among the fatalities is the rueful, independent-minded CO (Robert Mitchum), who is returned to his men draped unceremoniously over a mule.

Aptly summarizing Hollywood's view of the war as it entered its closing stages was *A Walk in the Sun* (1945), which combined action with good, snappy dialogue. It was nevertheless a distant cry from the fiery rhetoric and flag-waving excesses of the early years. The entire action of the film shows the experiences of a group of US infantrymen from the time they hit the beach at Salerno until they capture a fortified farmhouse which is important to the Allies for strategic purposes.

Disasters befall them quickly. The officer-in-charge is badly shot up and his replacement is quickly laid out with a nervous breakdown. After a series of violent encounters, including being strafed from overhead by enemy fighter planes, they come upon a farmhouse packed to the rafters with German troops and weapons. Orders are relayed through – the position must be secured. After a brave but obviously doomed frontal assault fails when the oncoming Americans are pinned on their bellies by fierce enemy fire, they regroup and try again, but through the back door. This time the Germans are overwhelmed, at terrible cost to the Americans.

Again, there is the familiar cross-hatching of US ethnic nationalities – Poles, Italians and the like – making up the tight little group whose experience the audience shares and whose conversations it overhears. The dialogue has a crisp theatricality, the humour is tersely ironic. The gruelling slog of war and its effects on the soldiers are matter-of-factly shown.

Made at a time when victory was in the bag but focusing on an earlier period when the outcome was less certain, the dialogue mixes unreserved patriotism ('I wish I had every Nazi in the palm of my hand – I'd crush them to a pulp!') with honest-to-God circumspection ('I just want to live long enough to be a civilian').

The air of futility and helplessness shared by the soldiers is conveyed with impressive subtlety. Only the platoon hot-head talks about 'crushing' the enemy. One sergeant composes letters home in his head which he has no time to write. Another bemoans the woeful condition of Italian soil ('too many soldiers have been walking on it'), while other soldiers jaw about popular bandleaders, Hollywood movie starlets and the beauties of nature. Perhaps the most telling comment about war and the state of mind which it imposes on fighting men is made near the end of the film, as the remnants of the platoon prepare to storm the fortified farmhouse. Sizing up the opposition with prophetic accuracy, one of the soldiers mutters, 'Looks like we'll be getting a new platoon pretty soon!'

The film was made before Hiroshima, yet it contains moments of acute condemnation of what is happening to the US platoon ('There's a lot of good men going down in this war!'), to the enemy, to the Italians (gullible at the outset and finally devastated as a nation 'left holding the bag') and to the landscape itself, left barren and desolated. *A Walk in the Sun* is conspicuously short of heroics; the victims either die or have to be abandoned, the survivors move on to another skirmish where more of the same happens. After six years of willing compliance to the propaganda needs of the nation, Hollywood was discovering its conscience, and showing the first signs of a mood of protest which would not reach its apotheosis until two decades later.

Sergeant Joe Gunn (Humphrey Bogart) and his beloved tank, the Lulubelle, in *Sahara* (1944).

CHAPTER FOUR

BOGEY AT WAR

*H*umphrey Bogart had a distinguished war, despite being denied active participation in it on grounds of age when America entered the fight. At forty-one and a seasoned hard liquor-drinker, his ability to pass the physical for active service would have been in doubt even had he been allowed to take it. Having spent a year in the earlier war on Atlantic convoy duty as a young navy volunteer, militarily speaking he had already acquitted himself adequately in the service of his nation. He remained, nevertheless, keen to do whatever his age and stature in society allowed, and declared his readiness right at the beginning to tackle propaganda roles and undertake personal appearance tours to wherever the authorities willed. They, in turn, were not slow to recognize the powerful propaganda tool which Bogart's established screen persona represented.

In film after film he had proved himself a tough and resourceful adversary. He was a no-bullshit, no-surrender type of fighter, a little short on social graces perhaps, but unlikely to turn tail at the first setback, or pussyfoot around when dangers had to be faced.

The prematurely gnarled face and rasping voice which audiences had loved to hate became suddenly comforting and reassuring when deployed on the side of democracy. 'These guys [Nazi agents] make you and I look like Little Bo-Peep,' he tells Barton Maclane, his erstwhile rival in *All Through the Night* (1941) and it is a characteristically down-to-earth appraisal. Hitler's gangsters had made the worst Mafia excesses seem tame by comparison.

Warner Brothers was the first studio to condemn Fascism on screen, with *Confessions of a Nazi Spy* (1939). Though vigorously anti-Nazi as an organization, the studio nevertheless had to restrict itself to muted criticism of the conduct of a foreign nation with whom the American government was not at war.

All Through the Night (1941) got round the problem by setting up a Nazi spy ring in the heart of New York City, which allowed a stream of forceful tirades against the evils of Nazism to balloon from the mouths of Humphrey Bogart and Barton Maclane, two weathered gangster players from whom one would never seriously consider buying a used car. It was a clever way of circumventing accusations of unwarranted political bias – after all, who could believe anything which the likes of Bogart or Maclane might say? But the fact was they said it, and people believed it, and Warner's was able to get a sombre message across by spoofing it up for the censors.

Bogart plays 'Gloves' Donahue, a New York gangboss sufficiently miffed by the curtailment of supplies of his favourite cheesecake, following the murder of his local Jewish baker, to start investigating the circumstances of his death. The only clue he has is that a mysterious-looking blonde was seen leaving the bakery around the time of the murder. He discovers she is employed as a singer in a nightclub owned by a rival underworld figurehead, Marty Callaghan (Barton Maclane).

The girl is an unwilling accomplice in a plan by a Nazi group to devastate the New York dockland – her father is in Dachau and unless she co-operates fully his life will be forfeit. Once Donahue learns the truth, he enlists his old rival's help to smash the subversives.

The film is a curious mix of gangland spoof and sober warning about enemy infiltration. Donahue's successful attempt to pass himself off as one of the saboteurs, during a meeting in which the destruction of the New York waterfront is being planned, is played strictly for laughs. Posing as an explosives expert, he and accomplice Frank McHugh bewilder the other would-be saboteurs with pseudo-technical gobbledegook – 'the scradoran is on the paratube right next to the moctus-proctus.' Despite his illegal activities, Donahue is appalled when Nazi chief Ebbing (Conrad Veidt) suggests that neither of them respects democracy: 'I pay my taxes and wait for traffic lights!' he retorts angrily.

The attack on Pearl Harbour, around the time of the film's release, and a real-life attempt to destroy ships in New York harbour made it difficult for Americans to appreciate the central joke. They were, however, ready to absorb the implicit warning that when, if ever, the threat materialized, it would be from infiltrators more competent than Ebbing's comic army. The notion of gangsters closing ranks against a common foe was plausible enough, and given extra bite by the casting of Bogart and Maclane, hard-faced adversaries from way back, as the rival gangbosses reluctantly swallowing their mutual enmity to serve the national interest.

Selling military secrets to the highest bidder was the theme of *Across the Pacific* (1942), with US Army officer Rick Leland (Humphrey Bogart) the ex-soldier of fortune ready to part with defence information likely to be of interest to the Japanese. To make himself more readily accessible to enemy agents, Leland books his passage aboard a Japanese freightship heading for Yokohama via the Panama canal, where among his fellow-passengers are a Canadian socialite (Mary Astor) and an oriental expert, Dr Lorenz (Sydney Greenstreet).

Leland's knowledge of military defence installations around the Panama region appears useful to Lorenz, who is really a traitor planning to bomb the canal and disrupt vital US arms shipments. However, Leland is not what he appears – his well-publicized dishonourable discharge from the army ('the brass hats tied me up with pink ribbon and threw me to the wolves') and subsequent pseudo-treasonable activities are an intelligence ploy to unmask the spies. Leland's intervention saves the canal and brings Lorenz and his pals to book. As the outsmarted doctor dejectedly contemplates suicide at the end, Leland draws his attention to a squadron of US fighter planes passing overhead. 'If any of your friends in Tokyo wanna commit hara-kiri,' he observes dryly, 'those are the boys to help them out!'

As well as being the romantic movie to outshine and outlast them all, *Casablanca* (1942) is a clever political allegory. Every nation with a say in contemporary politics and some who might have preferred to remain silent had its spokesman in the film. It is an enduring tribute to its makers that not one line of the dialogue has grown whiskers, nor has the atmosphere become diluted by any subsequent reshaping of the global map. *Casablanca* is practically everybody's favourite film and no better testament to wartime film-making at its most cryptic and morale-boosting survives.

Wartime Casablanca was a dumping ground for refugees of diverse political persuasions, awaiting escape to Lisbon and the Free World. Without proper documentation, however, they remain trapped like relics under glass, victims of German oppression and brutality.

Police Captain Renaud (Claude Rains, second left) diverts the militia while patriot leaders Lazlo (Paul Henreid, centre) and his wife Ilsa (Ingrid Bergman, extreme right) make their escape in *Casablanca* (1942). Rick Blane (Humphrey Bogart, second right) watches approvingly.

Two bitter enemies converge on Casablanca at roughly the same time. Major Strasser (Conrad Veidt) arrives to take personal charge of the arrest of a saboteur, Ugarte (Peter Lorre), whose capture is being staged with a fine theatrical flourish by the French chief of police, Captain Renaud (Claude Rains). Renaud has arranged for his men to seize Ugarte at Rick's Café Américain, a colourful nightclub owned by Rick Blane (Bogart), an unaligned cynic who endures constant reminding by Renaud that he is a 'sentimentalist at heart'.

Strasser's main enemy is Lazlo (Paul Henreid), a tenacious Resistance leader who has been promised the travel visas stolen by Ugarte to enable him and his wife Ilsa (Ingrid Bergman) to escape to the Free World and continue his propaganda war against Nazism. Desperate to silence Lazlo in another German concentration camp but content for the time being to trap him in Casablanca, where his every move can be watched, Strasser needs to get hold of the two visas to ensure that Lazlo's nuisance value is successfully curtailed.

Unbeknown to Strasser or his puppet-like police chief, Ugarte brings the documents to Rick and hands them over for safe keeping only moments before his arrest, knowing that Rick will give him a square deal. Ugarte is also anxious to convince Rick, who can put other lucrative black-market deals his way, that he is no longer a despicable 'cut-price' crook.

Rick's all-round diffidence extends to politics. When Ugarte is trapped in the café, Rick dispassionately abandons him to his fate: 'I stick my neck out for nobody!' With women he is equally remote and evasive, though his regard for Renaud and for Sam, a Negro pianist-companion who has been with him for several years, is genuine enough. Renaud, in turn, admires Rick for qualities he is unable to share, such as indifference to beautiful women ('Watch out – one day they may be scarce!') and a liking for doomed causes which Renaud's probings into Rick's background have revealed.

Strasser senses that Rick's much-flaunted neutrality is a lie, but his questions are wittily deflected during their first encounter. With the arrival of Lazlo and Ilsa comes the wholly unexpected revelation that Rick and Ilsa were lovers in Paris just before the city fell to the Germans. Having promised to accompany him to the safety of Marseille, Ilsa had deserted him without any explanation. With the inquisitive Renaud and Lazlo looking on, Rick treats her like a stranger, and later, in the deserted bar, he remains grudgingly unconvinced by her explanation as to why she had no choice but to let him leave Paris alone.

Her pursuit of alternative visas leads her via a cagey black-marketeer, Ferrari (Sydney Greenstreet), back once more to Rick, but he stubbornly refuses to help. Eventually, however, confronted by her tearful admission that it is he, Rick, whom she truly loves, he agrees to furnish Lazlo with a single exit visa, on condition that she remains behind.

The climax is neat and memorable. Rick tips off Renaud to be ready to arrest Lazlo as he takes possession of the stolen visa – a treasonable offence, and grounds for locking him away for good. It looks as though he might seriously have Lazlo's downfall in mind, but when Renaud arrives, Rick forces him to escort all three of them to the airport where a plane for Lisbon stands ready to take off.

Strasser's last-minute intervention at the departure point proves futile, for Rick kills him before he can summon help. Instead of handing over a single visa, Rick produces two of them and urges Ilsa to leave with her husband ('It's where you belong.') Tearfully she does, leaving Rick and the bemused Renaud to sort out the mess on the ground. A short breather in the safety of neighbouring Brazzaville seems about right for the pair of them, given the Germans' murderous reaction when they discover how brilliantly they have been outfoxed.

The allegorical make-up of *Casablanca* is about as subtle as one of Strasser's prison-cell interrogations. Rick is pre-Pearl Harbour America, weary, self-contained, and politically neutral. A lecherous Russian barman inherits his boss's liking for tuxedos and beds his discarded bar-girls. Strasser is Nazi Germany: insufferable, arrogant, contemptuous of everyone – including the eager-to-please Italian and Spanish toadies who accompany him everywhere.

Lazlo represents the oppressed non-Aryans, admirably disobedient and proud in defeat, drawing strength from outside, converting the neutrals, *vis-à-vis* the enchanting Ilsa and, through her, the solitary Rick. Ugarte, the despised North African murdered by the Germans during interrogation, provides an accurate projection of his nation's stature in world opinion, a barren sandstrip about to be steamrollered by convoys of panzers.

Rick's café characterizes the war zone, with words substituting for tanks and bullets. At one point, Lazlo conducts a chorus of the Marseillaise loud enough to drown out the German national anthem, an insult which results in the café being declared off-limits. Renaud's unashamed self-interest makes him more pliable and appealing than a bendy toy; compulsively chameleon-like, he is determined to sup with the eventual victors, whichever side that proves to be, and it is due in no small way to Claude Rains' gallant yet roguish charm that Captain Renaud is *Casablanca*'s second most watchable character.

Action in the North Atlantic (1943) provides an eloquent tribute to the US merchant marine service. Rossi (Bogart) is second in command to Jarvis (Raymond Massey). The two men are essentially opposites; Jarvis is quiet, cultured, long-married and a big-brother figure to Rossi, who between voyages lives it up in nightclubs – until, that is, he meets Pearl (Julie Bishop), an attractive singer. Out at sea their ship is holed and set afire by an enemy U-boat, which then proceeds to ram the survivors in blatant disregard of the ethics of naval warfare.

When Jarvis calls at Rossi's apartment to bring him up to date on their latest mission (their new ship is to be part of a major task force heading for the Russian port of Murmansk) and discovers Pearl there, he suspects that once again Rossi has been sweet-talked out of his wages, He soon learns to his considerable embarrassment that the two are already married ('You know a lot about boats, Steve, but you

Rossi (Humphrey Bogart) confers with his captain, Jarvis (Raymond Massey), in *Action in the North Atlantic* (1943).

don't know anything about people,' Rossi tells him). When Pearl tries to talk Rossi into staying at home, his response is equally forthright ('We can't sit around holding hands with all *that* going on!').

Out in the Atlantic, dogged by atrocious weather conditions, Jarvis spots a U-boat trailing them, the same U-boat in fact which destroyed his earlier command. To divert the enemy submarine away from the main body of the task force, Jarvis decides to change course, and what follows is a tense game of cat and mouse between the two vessels. When the Germans summon aerial assistance and wave upon wave of Lüftwaffe striker planes bombard the American ship, seriously wounding Jarvis, it begins to look like a re-run of their earlier encounter. Having taken charge, Rossi initiates a plan that will make it appear to the enemy that the ship is in its death throes: he orders the engines to be silenced and fires to be lit on deck. Believing their work finished, the German planes retire, and the U-boat surfaces to take a close-up gloating look. Just as it nears the bows of his ship, Rossi orders full steam ahead. The American ship charges forward, crushing and sinking the enemy. By keeping the throttle open, Rossi and the delighted Jarvis manage to catch up with their colleagues as they steam towards Murmansk harbour safe-guarded by a welcoming squadron of Russian fighter planes.

Commendably put together (the *New Statesman* called the film 'the American equivalent of our war documentary. . .tough and exciting with no concessions to the flim-flam'), *Action in the North Atlantic* never loses sight of its propaganda mission, which is achieved through realism and understatement. The fears and phobias of ordinary seamen are expressed as openly as the calm reservations of their officers. At a burial-at-sea service Bogart tells the survivors, 'A lot more people are going to die before this is over; it's up to the ones that come through to make sure they didn't die for nothing!' Rarely, if ever, has a studio tank looked so real.

Sahara (1944) is the story of a multi-national coterie of stragglers stranded in the desert as the allied armies retreat towards El Alamein following their defeat at Tobruk. The showpiece of the drama is the Lulubelle, a US army tank commanded by Sergeant Joe Gunn (Bogart) who, rather than abandon her to the advancing panzers (Joe is sentimental about tanks), heads her off into the desert in pursuit of the retreating Eighth Army. Soon the Lulubelle has attracted a motley collection of misfits and runaways, including an Italian prisoner-of-war, all of whom Gunn endeavours to bind into a small, viable fighting unit. However, opposing political creeds, clashing temperaments and a pervading sense of doom combine to frustrate his efforts.

With the advancing Germans gaining ground day by day while they struggle on through sandstorms and other misfortunes, the motley platoon stumble into Bir Acroma, a derelict caravan station where there is a limited quantity of fresh water. Their numbers are augmented shortly afterwards by a German pilot, brought down while attacking them, and a scout for a motorized German battalion who reveals that enemy troops in large numbers are just over the ridge and desperately in need of water.

The advancing battalion is part of the enemy's build-up towards a final decisive assault on the Allies. Gunn cajoles the diffident group into delaying the Germans for as long as possible at the waterhole, which means a shoot-out and possible annihilation. The Germans, however, are unaware that the waterhole is dried up. Realizing that it is only the promise of water which is detaining them, Gunn decides to fool them into thinking there is plenty of water to be had, which he agrees to share with them on condition they surrender. To achieve this, he imitates the delights of taking a shower (in imaginary water), feigning merriment, gurgling noises and splashing around in arid air.

The inevitable pitched battle occurs, but despite heavy odds Gunn's ragbag platoon keeps the Germans at bay. With only one other survivor – the symbolic Britisher – Gunn prepares for what he imagines will be their last stand, but instead of seizing the advantage, the thirsty Germans decide to throw in the towel (a very dry towel in this case) in order to qualify for the water. Ironically, one of their mortars manages to score a direct hit on the waterhole and open up a fresh supply, so they are not disappointed. Later, Gunn learns that the British have held El Alamein, so the stand-off at Bir Acroma has paid dividends.

Making the best of a bad connection. Matrac (Humphrey Bogart) is forced on the run because of his anti-Fascist views in *Passage to Marseille* (1943).

In *Passage to Marseille* (1943), Captain Freycinet (Claude Rains), liaison officer of a striker airbase in rural England, is host to an influential journalist (John Loder) who is convinced that he recognizes Matrac (Bogart), a Bomber Command gunner at the start of a major sortie on Berlin ('I've never seen a stronger face or a stranger one'). Freycinet discloses Matrac's strange story, but for security reasons the journalist is obliged to keep the details to himself. At the start of the war, Freycinet and some other French Army officers including Captain Duval (Sydney Greenstreet) return from the Orient to Marseille via the Panama Canal in a freighter carrying six thousand tons of nickel ore for the Allies. Duval, a Nazi sympathizer, is bitterly and outspokenly resentful of his country's alliance with Britain ('The British will fight to the very last drop of French blood') and believes that France would be better to throw in its lot with Hitler, an attitude which Freycinet and others, including the ship's captain, sternly oppose.

Safely through Panama, they run across a small boat adrift in the ocean with five semi-conscious men aboard. Their leader Matrac (Bogart) explains that they have been without food for twenty days and without water for five, and later confides to Freycinet, whom he trusts, that they are escaped convicts from Devil's Island. The others are keen to return to France to join the war, but Matrac, a one-time crusading journalist whose outspoken anti-Fascist editorials have landed him on Devil's Island on a phoney murder charge, is sour and disillusioned and wants only to rejoin his wife Paula (Michele Morgan).

After receiving the news that France has surrendered, the captain plots a course for England, but Duval seizes control and changes course, only to lose the initiative

58

to Matrac and the other convicts. However, because they managed to radio their location first, they attract a German air attack. Matrac's hatred for the Germans explodes after tracer bullets have killed the cabin boy, and he kills the shot-down enemy air crew floundering helplessly in the water.

Arriving in Britain, Matrac promptly joins Bomber Command, and his surviving compatriots also enlist. On the night of the reporter's visit, as the narrative is brought up to date, Matrac's plane fails to return: he has been shot down in a duel with three Messerschmidts. At his funeral service, Freycinet reads aloud Matrac's final letter to his son, which was never delivered, urging the boy in later life to treasure and safeguard the freedoms earned through the vigilance and sacrifice of others.

In *To Have and Have Not* (1944), Harry Morgan (Bogart) hires out his cabin cruiser as a fishing boat along the coastline of Martinique. He lives at the Marquee Hotel, whose nervous owner Gerard (Marcel Dalio), alias Frenchy, a staunch supporter of de Gaulle, implores Morgan to allow his boat to be hired to a group of French patriots who are about to converge on the hotel, but Morgan firmly declines ('I can't afford to get mixed up in your local politics').

In the hallway he gets a come-on from Marie (Lauren Bacall), a footloose nightclub singer on her way home to the States from Trinidad, out-of-pocket and stranded against her will in Martinique. Later their paths cross again when Marie palms the wallet of an American fishing enthusiast, Morgan's latest client, and Morgan lectures her ('You ought to pick on somebody to steal from that doesn't owe me money').

After a raid by police to snatch the terrorists Morgan and Marie are arrested and interrogated by Captain Renard (Dan Seymour). Asked her business in Martinique, Marie explains that she came to buy a new hat, a remark which gets her a slapped face from one of Renard's assistants. Morgan immediately squares up to the bully: 'Go ahead, slap *me*,' he invites him.

With his money confiscated pending further investigation of his affairs, Morgan remembers the Free French cash offer is still open and about-turns on his vow to Frenchy ('I need the money now. Last night I didn't'). His task is to smuggle two escaped patriots into Martinique from a nearby island, the opening move in a daring plot to spring a top resistance fighter from Devil's Island.

Morgan attempts to ditch his alcoholic old partner Eddie (Walter Brennan) because of the dangers, but Eddie hoists himself back on board before the boat departs. Discovering that his passengers are a married couple, Morgan lectures the husband ('I don't understand what kind of war you guys are fighting, dragging your wives around... Don't you get enough of them at home?'). A Vichy patrol boat opens fire on them and Brussac (Walter Molnar), the husband, is seriously wounded. He is smuggled into the hotel and concealed in the cellar, where the full extent of his injuries becomes evident. In the bar above, the wily Renard buys Eddie drinks to loosen his tongue, unaware that drinking has the opposite effect. When Morgan intervenes, Renard offers the return of his money, passport and additional $500 blood money, but without success. Realizing that by now the police are on to him, Morgan decides to vanish, news which genuinely grieves Frenchy, who had hoped to convert him gradually to the cause of de Gaulle and also Brussac, who openly admires his resilience ('I wish I could borrow your nature for a while, Captain. . . The word failure does not even exist for you').

The formal arrest of Eddie and his obvious discomfort in police custody brings Morgan, finally, off the fence. Renard is battered into authorizing harbour passes for the Brussacs and into phoning through instructions for Eddie's release. He is then coldly abandoned by Morgan to a traitor's fate at the hands of the freedom fighters.

Morgan finally throws in his lot with the Brussacs, offering his boat in whatever capacity it can be used to help free the resistance hero from Devil's Island; his reasons, in Morgan's own words to a delighted Frenchy, are simply 'because I like you and I don't like them'.

Taken as a slice of contemporary propaganda, *To Have and Have Not* works exceptionally well because the elements making it up are nicely judged — too nicely judged, perhaps — and the plot moves purposefully towards the final dénouement from the moment that Renard confiscates Morgan's cash and documents.

In considering the loose political overtones — much looser than in *Casablanca* — Morgan's prickly lack of patriotism for nine-tenths of the film is less acceptable than Rick's, coming three years later and with the worst of the fighting and dying already over. What was so admirable about a supposed tough guy 'minding his own business' in a safe tropical backwater?

Morgan's head-in-the-sand egocentricity, dismissing the hostilities as a matter of 'local politics', refusing to acknowledge — because acknowledgement would tie his hand to one side or the other — that this is a global fight ('You save France, I'll save my boat,' he tells Brussac, which neatly sums up his priorities), is hard to take.

Because of the timing, his live-and-let-others-die attitude appears on the surface indefensible. 'I don't care who runs France,' he declares, but has he not seen what the people currently running France are capable of? It is not until the final reel that we are let in on what director Howard Hawks and the others are up to. By making Morgan fiercely neutral, oblivious to patriotic sentiment and appeals to his better nature, the anti-Fascist statement contained is a personal one not a political one, thus making the parallel between Fascism and the surrender of individual liberty all the more vivid.

Integrity prompts the action against the evil abuse of power in both *Casablanca* and *To Have and Have Not*, but in the later film the outrage is a personal one, and Eddie is merely the tool to get at Morgan. In *Casablanca*, Rick is not personally involved, his action is voluntary, out of affection for Ilsa and a sneaking regard for what Lazlo represents. In *Casablanca*, he could have done almost anything without compromising his personal integrity, whereas in *To Have and Have Not*, because the seizure of Eddie is an act of calculated aggression against himself, the violent

Learning to whistle. Skipper Harry Morgan (Humphrey Bogart) and his tutor, nightclub singer Marie (Lauren Bacall), in *To Have and Have Not* (1944).

response (unlike the moral outrage which provokes it) is a spontaneous personal declaration of war.

By the end of the war, it had become strongly apparent that it was the war itself, not the New Deal, which had ended the Great Depression. The need for America to maintain its armed and economic strengths had entered the nation's consciousness, engendering optimism and single-mindedness on a scale not seen since the 'twenties.

Promoting capitalism, the source from which abundance flowed, became a major preoccupation of government during those early post-war years. With the emergence of the Cold War so suddenly after the fighting ended, extreme right-wing propagandists, among them a number of unscrupulous opportunists intent on hiving off power for themselves, stridently proclaimed the existence in America's midst of an enemy far more sinister and challenging than anything which it had faced before – an enemy sworn to usurp power without a vote being taken or a shot fired. The Communist scare, and its repercussions, were about to plunge American politics and Hollywood into their darkest years.

Homecoming serviceman Fred Derry (Dana Andrews) returns to a troubled marriage in *The Best Years of Our Lives* (1946).

CHAPTER FIVE

RED SCARES IN THE SUNSET

*T*he death of Franklin D. Roosevelt in April 1945, four months before the declaration of victory over Japan, was the bad news before the good. Roosevelt was a father figure, solid and dependable. The awesome military and economic might of America required a steady hand at the controls and Roosevelt had provided that.

Just as America was unrivalled in its position of influence over the world in 1945, so Hollywood, too, had unchallenged supremacy at the box office. After the war the cinema industries of France and Germany were devastated; only Britain put up any kind of competition. During the 'forties the British output crept higher in quality but failed for a variety of reasons to achieve success internationally.

Ruling the roost as it did, it is not surprising that the influence exerted by the American post-war film industry was far-reaching behaviourally, sociologically and culturally. From American films of the time, many generations got their first lessons on how to behave with the opposite sex, on the value of honest effort and moral behaviour, on how the law and the police worked and on the evils of racism. Hardly a problem faced by the modern world escaped Hollywood's scrutiny and scarcely a film dealing with a problem refrained from offering a solution. Usually the solutions offered suffered from over-compromise in deference to the box office, but the fact that the problems were even considered was no bad thing at all.

The Best Years of Our Lives (1946) was one of the best examples, showing the rehabilitation problems of America's fighting men – to be exact, three fighting men who collectively represented not only the three divisions of the services – army, navy and air force – but also the heart and spirit of the returning heroes themselves.

Fred (Dana Andrews) returns to a broken marriage and a wife no longer interested in home-making. The film depicts her as a slut and contains, by implication, a rather graphic condemnation of wives who could not, or would not, wait. Al (Frederic March), a former banker, encounters problems at home, too, but it is the resumption of his career and the difficulty he has applying the old, narrow-minded code of play-safe banking after his horizons have been widened by his combat experiences which plague him most. Homer (Harold Russell) is a war-wounded sailor who remains cheerful despite the loss of both arms at the elbow. They have been replaced with clumsy metal callipers, which he operates with rueful resignation.

All three are too obviously sympathetic figures. The working-class soda-jerk Fred earns our sympathy because he deserves more happiness than his feckless wife can provide. Al, too, shares the bewilderment of homecoming veterans as the emphasis changes from killing Japs to making money. Homer's disabilities and his tough struggle to regain normality, borne in a matter-of-fact way are all too evident.

The film is a sober assembly job, the timing and sociological aspirations of which belie its outward honesty. In fact, by interweaving the lives of the three protagonists so cleverly, by rewarding the good and castigating the not-so-good, the censorial moral tone devalues what might otherwise have been a powerful documentary-style assessment of immediate post-war adjustment.

Coping with, though in some cases succumbing to, the pressures of re-establishing a post-war lifestyle provided the basis of many films of the late 'forties and early 'fifties. More recently the Vietnam War was followed by a similar batch of protest movies showing the effects on soldiers of the sustained brutality of warfare. By then, of course, strong protest was acceptable. After World War II, the climate was not right for criticizing the system which had created the conditions, and to have done so would have led to a severe clamp-down on any studio offering such a viewpoint.

Despite the success America had had on the battlefield, and a largely solvent nation which celebrated victory with the returning troops, memories of the Depression remained vivid. Many people believed that the economic viability of their country was a freak solution created by the War, and that once it was all over the country would plunge again back to the bad old days of race riots, labour unrest, left-wing inspired violence and a retaliatory crackdown on civil liberties.

Behind many of the films made shortly after the War, therefore, there was a moralistic overtone aimed at showing the virtues of a strong America. Films showing the fighting man's ability to overcome physical and mental injuries were one of Hollywood's ways of reassuring the nation that its resolve remained unbroken. Doctors and psychiatrists replaced crusading cops and lawyers with social consciences as the movie do-good heroes. Preoccupations with health and mental stability became cyphers, cinematically, for what was a more profound preoccupation: that of sustaining and defending the economic health and political well-being of the nation.

Perhaps the prototype 'readjustment' movie of the 'forties was *Pride of the Marines* (1946), in which war hero Al Schmidt (John Garfield), blinded at Guadalcanal, takes refuge behind a wall of resentment. He spurns all attempts to help or sympathize with him and is rude to hospital staff, tossing his Braille alphabet aside and refusing to feed himself. When the permanence of his condition is explained to him, he regresses even further, recalling the actual receipt of the injuries and imagining his girlfriend's rejection of him in a series of tormented dreams.

Out in the hospital ward he remains aloof and bruised, refusing the well-intentioned reassurances of fellow-patients, avoiding human contact wherever possible. The generally optimistic tone of the other patients' conversations are an anathema to Schmidt, who wastes no opportunity to drive home his callous indifference to events going on around him. When one patient declares, 'We can make things work in peace as we did in war, don't you see, Al?' the brusque and honest retort is, 'No, I don't see!'

As in other films in this category (notably, *The Men*, with Marlon Brando similarly embittered by, in his case, a sniper bullet which paralyses him from the waist down), the chip on the shoulder is eventually whittled down by the fidelity of a loved one and a caring society as depicted by the authorities in charge of rehabilitation. Refusal at first even to meet the girlfriend gives way, at her insistence and with the benign connivance of the authorities, to a grudging attempt at reconciliation. Once the hero believes he is wanted for what remains of himself rather than any moral obligations on the girl's part to do the right thing, his behaviour mellows and he undergoes a resurgence of optimism and gradually conquers his underlying neurosis.

The consistent view throughout these movies is that society is decent and understanding and that the individual who holds out against this caring society is wrong. Happiness will continue to elude him until he acknowledges that he is the one at fault. He must be the one to come inside and close the door. This benign view of society contrasts vividly with its image in films of the 'thirties when the rebel character was usually seen as the victim of society's indifference.

In films of the 'forties, the rebels were the maladjusted ones, attempting either through moral waywardness or because of some personality defect to undermine the system. As such, it served society's grand purpose to make them appear as individual pockets of distress rather than, as had been the case during the 'thirties, depicting them as proof of a widescale malaise.

These rebels also purported to show the futility of finite resistance, and that eventual integration with the view of the majority is the only solution to one's problems. The message was clear – get the strength of society behind you and all will be well. In movies during the 'forties all the great rebels worth their salt in the end had to sort themselves out and return to the main pack. From Garfield in *Pride of the Marines* through to Brando in *The Men* and *On the Waterfront* and to James Dean in *Rebel without a Cause*, all made their protests, sulked and threw tantrums, but eventually came in out of the cold because there was nowhere else for them to go.

Films of the late 'forties and early 'fifties agonized about social control. Its imprint was felt on all the popular genres, and its purpose was to warn and unify the nation against attack from whatever source it was likely to come. Although 'McCarthyism' is now enshrined in the language as a rabid attempt by right-wing troublemakers to rid America of Communists, such fears had been around before Senator Joseph McCarthy appeared centre stage in 1950.

The House of Un-American Activities Committee (HUAC) had been looking for

Communists and other subversive influences since the late 'thirties, but at that time left-wing attitudes encompassed no particular threat. On the contrary, it could be argued that a left-of-centre counterbalance provided a healthy reminder for the government not to take the sorry plight of the nation too leisurely.

War had made Russia a blood brother whether America liked it or not, and for its duration, dissaffection with the Soviets' doctrinaire politics was superseded by the need for a second powerful ally in the East. With the return of peace, however, came the inevitable resumption of the old suspicions, exacerbated by Russia's prompt rejection of the terms of the Yalta agreement in 1945, and the abandonment of all pretence at being neighbourly.

Inflammatory talk about Communist plots found a willing audience among ordinary Americans experiencing the pressures of post-war re-adjustment and they were only too willing to believe the worst about their former ally. The conviction of Alger Hiss, who had been one of Roosevelt's advisers at the Yalta Conference, for passing secrets to the Soviets, in January 1950, caused a tremendous uproar, and with it came the demand for greater vigilance in the selection of individuals who ran for public office.

In between Hiss's two trials – the first one ended inconclusively – the Communists overran China, the Red Army threw out all notions of democracy in Eastern Europe and Russia detonated its first atomic bomb, aided in a wholly unexpected way by the donation of blueprints and other top secret US information by the Rosenbergs, who went on trial for their crimes in 1950, only weeks after the Hiss conviction.

Gradually the idea that American political and cultural life had been infiltrated by Communist sympathizers and wreckers began to take hold. The inevitable backlash occurred, whipped up with almost evangelical fervour by McCarthy and his supporters. There was already enough dirty linen in the bag before the Rosenbergs' trial and execution for McCarthy to launch his assault, which he did in Wheeling, West Virginia, in January 1950. There he waved a piece of paper in the air declaring that it contained a list of 205 names of 'members of the Communist Party who are still working and shaping policy in the State Department'.

No such list existed, of course, and he was never able to produce factual evidence that would convict anyone in a proper court of law. But such was the hysteria which resulted from the accusations, and the newspapers' reaction, that in no time at all he had climbed to a virtually unassailable position where even the slightest challenge to his wild claims ran the risk of being interpreted as disloyalty.

Newspapers had been a valuable ally in his quick climb to power, and he thought that television would make him an even greater star, by reassuring Americans that he was a tireless champion of democracy, and that their welfare was in safe hands. Television coverage of the 1954 hearings on Communism in the US Army had precisely the opposite effect. In March that year Ed Murrow's documentary series *See It Now* showed clips of McCarthy in action. That was enough to convince millions of viewers they had been railroaded by a bully and a sheister. His downfall came, in the end, not because he hated Communists but because he saw them everywhere, and because he lacked the sense to realize that he had gone too far.

What he had done, and skilfully accomplished, was to tap into a vein that ran deep in the American psyche after the end of the War. The discovery of a Russian spy ring in Canada in 1947 had alerted the US Government to the possibilities of a similar situation occurring there. President Truman required all federal agencies to submit lists of their employees to the FBI for screening, and 'loyalty boards' were established to interview suspects. Hollywood was thought to be a likely hotbed of subversion with its liberal and left-wing writers and a crop of recent movies whose warts-and-all glimpses of contemporary American life might seem, to anyone looking for evidence of un-American sentiment, to be showing the nation in poor light.

Exploratory enquiries into the extent of the influence of Communism on the film colony commenced in 1947. In that autumn the hearings switched to Washington, amid a welter of publicity, unavoidable since so many of the witnesses were household names. A group of writers and directors who declined to give evidence and instead took the Fifth Amendment, and who were later known as the Hollywood Ten, received prison terms, and it was many years before the climate changed sufficiently in their favour for any of them to work again under their own names.

There were many blacklists, the most notorious of which was a publication called Red Channels, a so-called 'directory of subversives'. Anyone whose name appeared within it became too hot to handle and their careers were virtually over. People found themselves on the scrapheap without ever having being told that the only reason they could not be employed was their inclusion in a list of names compiled from rumour and innuendo.

These shenanigans inevitably affected the studios' choice of themes and treatment of stories. The Hays Office, now renamed the Johnson Office following the succession in 1945 of Eric Johnson as President of the Motion Picture Association of America, subserviently attempted to impose upon Hollywood the desire of the New York administration offices of the major studios to outlaw stories which, however indirectly, could be accused of having a socialist bias.

Ironically, this new era of censorship in the interests of so-called democracy was disturbingly totalitarian in its applicaiton. Stories which contained any implied criticism of how the country was being run were strictly taboo. Heroes could no longer raise hell in defiance of the system, and opposition to it was denied. Not surprisingly, a number of leading writers and directors, some of indeterminate politics, who found it unattractive to work under these strictures, packed up and departed. Many more stuck it out, making films which, on the surface, adhered to the new regulations, but which, at a deeper level, reflected their acute alarm and despair. Many of these remain as 'film noir' classics.

Hollywood's answer to outsiders, or rebels, was simple. They had to be given every opportunity to see the error of their ways, by gentle persuasion and by a coherent example. If it succeeded and the rebel decided to conform, then society, being in its own view all-benevolent, welcomed him back, possibly after a reasonable period of atonement. If all efforts failed, he could be, and usually was, killed off.

In westerns and gangster films, the final-reel shoot-out served handsomely to eliminate the no-road-back rebel. Political allegories were rife in films of the 'forties, from the more obvious *Key Largo* (1948) to the innocent-looking *Drumbeat* (1954), with Alan Ladd. In the latter, Ladd plays an Indian agent charged with the task of capturing a renegade Apache chief, Captain Jack (Charles Bronson, in an early role), who murders whites and triumphantly wears their clothes. Jack is an alien force as much an enemy to his own tribe as to the palefaces whose job it is to round him up.

In the end he is caught and hanged and the canyons can practically be heard sighing with relief. Settling up with Jack posed no problem for the scriptwriters because he was a savage who had murdered indiscriminately, and his death was richly deserved. In the same way, the use of military power to destroy sci-fi invaders caused nobody any pangs of conscience. Both were unreasoning and unreachable creatures, so good riddance to them.

The same logic could hardly be applied to contemporary social misfits some of whom were polite, white and middle-class. They were too much like the rest of us to vaporize with carrot-guns. More reasonable ways had to be found for dealing with them, physical force being the least acceptable because it amounted to an admission that the cerebral argument had been lost. It was also a *prime facie* denial of the very freedom of thought and action which the establishment were at such pains to show they endorsed.

Those who functioned outside society and refused every olive branch offered had to be restrained from affecting, or infecting, the rest of us. But they could not be seen to be crushed by the State because that degree of power, in any hands, would be unacceptable and dangerously divisive, making it necessary later on to find a cure for the cure.

One straightforward answer, used in many films, was to appoint a leader of the dissidents, isolate him from the rest either physically or intellectually, and then convert him to society's view. He could even fall in love with an attractive girl, thereby declaring his willingness to conform right down the line. Audiences would see his conversion as a voluntary endorsement of the values they stood for and equilibrium would be preserved. If, on the other hand, our hero rejected the ideological arguments or its attendant inducements, he was already isolated sufficiently from the pack to be disposed off without too much fuss, whereupon a second-in-command, promoted from the pack to defuse the situation, could be seen as more amenable to the offer on the table and effect the awaited compromise.

Another tried and tested method of disposing of enemies of the established social order was to enslave them sexually. Society got its desired result while judiciously – and this was important – keeping its hands clean. Predatory women feature boldly in post-War movies, adding the 'deadly sin' perspective with which the loner's downfall can conveniently and plausibly be associated.

Sexual licence was frowned on during the repressive 'forties and 'fifties as much as the other side of the coin – healthy, happy family life – was applauded. Characters indulging in sexual activity outside marriage were morally reprehensible whatever other views they had, and if they were social dissidents, too, then the rest of us could feel very comfortable about making them pay dearly.

What was conveniently fudged on these occasions was whether the individual was paying for his dissident views or for his moral dissolution. In other words it was not clear whether society was punishing him for being an outsider, or whether his destruction, when it came, was prompted by the self-destructive urges of which we had already been given glimpses. The sexually-enslaved were losers, momma's boys who had merely transferred their dependence to younger women, and the women themselves were cold and dispassionate despite the surface allure whose offer of happiness can never be anything more than a cruel hoax.

Before Eisenhower became President in 1952, consensus was a dirty word, and the harsh shadows thrown across the screen during the 'film noir' period depict a world where the rebel cannot breathe or hide. Everyone in social drama before 1952 is either good or bad, a survivor or doomed. Bogart's Philip Marlowe in *The Big Sleep* (1946) is a survivor because he won't compromise or take the easy way out of the case when Vivien (Lauren Bacall) attempts to buy him off. 'We made a deal and you're going to stick to it, right or wrong,' he tells her, and walks out the door almost straight into a beating-up, which is the going rate for integrity in a San Francisco back alley.

By contrast James Cagney's Cody Jarrett in *White Heat* (1948) is doomed. He is a demented, mother-fixated killer with about as much social conscience as a hole in the ground. The menace he represents parallels the sickness that threatens society. It can be neither reasoned with nor excused. Cody's isolation is stressed throughout the film. The only people he encounters outside his closed little circle of relatives, crooks and cellmates are those whom he either robs or kills, or sometimes both. Enemies of society in 'forties films who are beyond redeeming function in a vacuum and have to be exterminated for the good of the majority.

The Soviets' success with the atomic bomb in 1950 intensified America's jitters. Here was the one power above all the others which they wanted to stay ahead of in the A-bomb race. More than any other incident Russia's setting off of its A-bomb switched the mood of the nation, quite literally, on to 'Red alert'. Before that, and even through the torturous HUAC hearings, people wondered what might happen *if* Russia launched an offensive. After 1950, people thought about it in terms of *when*.

The only physical possibility was an air attack, so people began, unconsciously at first, to scan the skies, thus giving their worst nightmares a semblance of respectability. It was a scenario just begging to be rewritten by Hollywood and, sure enough, the creative juices of tinsel town were waiting to absorb the idea.

Since no hostilities existed between East and West – other than in Korea, a land mass sufficiently remote and conventionally contested to be thought of in less than Armageddon terms – films depicting a Russian invasion were not allowable. However, storylines which showed America, that is, civilization, under attack from various extra-terrestrial beings, giant ants and lagoon creatures – all handy cyphers for Communism – were snapped up eagerly.

Right and left ideologies found vivid expression in the science-fiction films of the 'fifties. Right and centrist viewpoints depicted the aliens as enemies of the people, either monsters or zombies running amok causing wholesale death and destruction, or creeping in, masquerading as 'us', in order to take us over surreptitiously. The former had its logical counterpart in Soviet military expansionism throughout the Far East, whilst the latter graphically hinted at the shocking penetration of American political and cultural life by socialist ideas.

By contrast, the left saw the aliens as unthreatening, more in the form of docile interplanetary travellers who had taken a wrong turning between galaxies and had fallen foul of the Earthlings' tendency to beat up anything they cannot understand. The right saw the outsider as the aggressor, whereas the left identified strongly with the difficulties which the intruder encountered. Hostile authoritarianism, the

Cody Jarrett (James Cagney) takes a fretful nap, watched by his mother (Margaret Wycherley) in *White Heat* (1948).

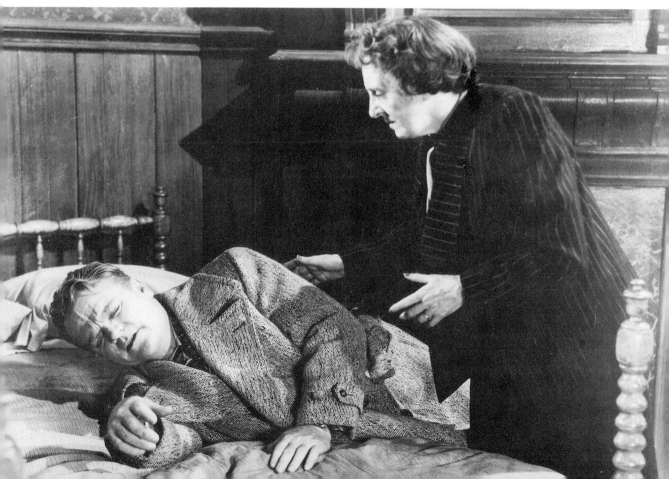

burn-'em, flog-'em, mortar-happy reactionaries, and so on, these were all an extension of what they already had to contend with.

'Fifties sci-fi films were all about power – the power of technology, the power nature had to fight back and even the power of Faith. (Indeed, biblical themes made a dramatic comeback during the 'fifties, with such blockbusters as *Samson and Delilah* [1950], *David and Bathsheba* [1951] *The Robe* [1953] and *Salome* [1954] coming off the production line.) However, it was the power in man's hands to blow its enemies sky-high, and to resist the forces buzzing around the universe, which concern us here.

The Day the Earth Stood Still (1951) was a fair example of leftish philosophizing dressed up in a quasi-religious setting. Klaatu (Michael Rennie), a gentlemanly, word-perfect visitor from outer space, arrives in Washington in a gleaming spaceship on an errand of mercy. He wants 'peace and goodwill' to be established, and to meet with the world's leaders to bring about an end to world tension. One of the first things to happen to Klaatu is that he is wounded by a bullet from a nervous National Guardsman who thinks he means trouble. In retaliation, Klaatu's metallic robot Gort barbecues some of the weapons of destruction ringing their spaceship, just to show who is boss. Klaatu is hospitalized but his powers of recovery are colossal and in no time he is up and around, out on the streets, trying to rent lodgings, mixing with ordinary people to take soundings about their attitudes to universal love.

Calling himself Mr Carpenter, he passes off easily as one of us – if anything, he is too genteel and courteous to be one of us – and makes friends with a small boy who takes him to see the Lincoln Memorial and reads the famous Gettysburg address. 'That's the kind of man I'd like to talk to!' Klaatu murmurs approvingly. Alas, only lesser mortals are available to debate the threat to universal stability and security being posed by Earth's atomic bomb, which he suspects is about to be borne aloft in the first Earth spaceship.

A respected scientist, Professor Barnhardt (Sam Jaffe) gets the message after Klaatu has stopped the Earth's rotation as a demonstration of his power, and soon Barnhardt is busy organizing an East-West congress to discuss the problem. Some dismiss Klaatu's oratory as the ravings of a lunatic while others applaud it. But Klaatu's message is clear: unless we can learn to live in peace with each other, and with other planets, a coalition of interplanetary forces will convert us all into cinders.

As well as being a cypher for a benign and immeasurably tolerant alien force Klaatu has an unmistakable touch of divinity about him. He is shot twice and each time heals himself. He calls himself Carpenter, an obvious allusion to Christ's earthly trade. Finally, in case some of us have not spotted the clues, his departure by spacecraft, having preached at length about living piously and decently, has a New Testament Ascension feel about it. Straying little from the Church's teachings, Klaatu's recommendations are voiced with the calm authority of 'Someone Who

Knows'. Not surprisingly, when the role of St Peter in *The Robe* needed to be filled shortly afterwards, the actor who played Klaatu, Michael Rennie, got the job.

War of the Worlds (1951) sets the Martian invasion at 1950 – a cinema is showing *Samson and Delilah* in the small Californian town where the first spaceship lands. All aspects of American authority, that is, government, the military, scientists and churchmen, mount a combined but unsuccessful attempt to repel the outsiders after they have converted three yokels assigned the task of watching them into a pile of ashes. 'It's an enemy sneak attack,' shouts one onlooker, in an obvious reference to Russia, and to underline the aggressive attitude of the Martians, the three victims are barbecued as they advance towards the spaceship shouting, 'We are friends!'

Soon the heathen nature of the invaders is confirmed when they zap a local pastor for coming towards them with a crucifix and prayer. The local military commander adopts a pro-McCarthy view, 'If they start anything, we can blast them right off the earth!', but the bombs and powerful explosives which rain down on them cause our visitors no worries at all.

Hostility towards the aliens increases as it becomes obvious their intention is to 'murder everything that moves'. An eminent scientist (Gene Barry) is more circums-

Space invader Gort is zapped by the US military in *The Day the Earth Stood Still* (1951).

pect about them, however, suggesting 'they could be as curious about us as we are about them'. This view is not borne out by the way they later demolish the farmhouse in which he is hiding.

Hundreds more spaceships land all over the world, at which point gloom and panic take over. 'We're beaten,' howls a scientist, predicting a total wipeout of humanity within six days. As the news spreads, despondency gives way to panic and mindless violence as mobs run riot, stealing cars and looting shops, even dragging off the scientific instruments which are man's only hope of survival.

In a nearby church, a despairing priest appeals for 'divine intervention', and no sooner is the request lodged than a miracle occurs. A Martian spaceship crashes into the street nearby, its occupant poleaxed by a 'flu germ from which it has no immunity. The rest of us can all breathe again, because of 'the littlest thing which God, in His wisdom, had put upon this Earth'.

A less conciliatory view of space invaders is taken in *The Thing* (1951), in which the creature found embedded in Arctic ice – at first, rather ominously, taken to be a Russian warplane – represents real menace, and anyone associating with it in any way is depicted as either crazy or subversive. It is quite revealing that the scientist who aligns himself most strongly with the Thing, in opposition to the official US Army line on things, sports a goatee beard and a Russian fur hat.

A more alarming cypher for Communism emerges in *Them* (1954), which shows the country under siege from giant ants. The ants were going about their daily business in the normal way until an A-bomb test accelerated their growth rate. The problem facing America's south west, where the giant ants are running riot, is that they think they are still tiny and that everything else has shrunk, so they carry on behaving as before, only now their innocent search for sugar·lumps has been transformed into elephantine rampages, crushing houses, trailers, humans and everything else in their path.

Gradually they emerge from their breeding grounds and head for Los Angeles, where they bide their time in the labyrinth of sewer tunnels beneath the city. As the war hots up, state troopers, federal authorities and scientists join forces to punish the intruders, eventually gassing them to extinction in the tunnels where they have become encircled.

Americans believed that Russia and ants had much in common, that is, they were both natural aggressors, overrunning and enslaving neighbouring colonies, whilst they themselves were controlled unequivocally from the top. What was more natural in a film which portrayed the enemy as unreasoning killers than to have the people who rescue mankind from their evil clutches as the epitome of sanity and reason, led by the avuncular Edmund Gwenn as an ant expert? It was more the modest budget levels of these sci-fi movies than the disinclination of the likes of Bogart and Gable to take part which resulted in comparative unknowns taking front-line roles. This in the end greatly benefited the films themselves.

A case in point was *The Invasion of the Body Snatchers* (1955) with Kevin

Twilight for the Pods. Miles Bennell (Jevin McCarthy) attempts to warn people that the space creatures are taking them over in *Invasion of the Body Snatchers* (1955).

McCarthy, a little-known actor, who creates no premonition of victory as would have been the case had Alan Ladd been cast in the lead role.

McCarthy's clean-cut ordinariness is ideal for the part of Dr Bennell, a small-town doctor who discovers that the reason townsfolk are acting off-colour is because they are really invaders from outer space, harvested from giant pods into perfect lookalikes and soundalikes of the individuals they have replaced. By the time Bennell realizes what is happening practically the entire town has been taken over.

Bennell and his girlfriend Becky (Dana Wynter) become fugitives and, hiding in a cave outside of town, with the aliens scouring the countryside for them, Becky makes the fatal mistake of falling asleep, which is when the pods take over their victims. She, too, succumbs, exhorting Bennell to abandon the hopeless fight, and when he refuses, she denounces him by shrilly telling their pursuers their whereabouts. In the end, only Bennell gets away, but his preposterous warnings about alien invasions get him consigned to the local mental asylum. Luckily, not everyone is sceptical, and one doctor puts a cautious phone call through to the FBI.

The film's original ending, with the near-demented Bennell staring at the audience, foaming at the mouth and shrieking that they might be next, was abandoned as being too alarmist. With hindsight, such a sledgehammer ending proved quite unnecessary. Here, the enemy is both alien and familiar, like Alger Hiss or the

Hollywood Ten, or the local druggist whose Communist sympathies are never suspected until he comes right out and says so.

The pod-people are cunning devils; they strike when people's natural resistance is at its lowest, that is, when they are sleeping (like they were at Pearl Harbour). They steal minds and discard bodies, they create havoc from within and yet remain undetected because their disguise is perfect. Their promises of equality and the absence of worry equate fairly accurately with the Free World's image of internal Soviet rule where individual decision-making is forfeited in favour of collective wisdom.

The pods self-propagate and, once harvested, systematically make it easier for fellow-pods to emerge, a factor witnessed by Bennell and Becky from their office window as dozens of pod-people unload a pod-lorry and carry the giant plants to greenhouses and other hideaways where they can mature unmolested. This rather loose reference to the brainwashing of GI prisoners in Korea makes its point effectively. Once one American soldier cracked and went to work on the others, it ceased to be a question of forcefeeding with enemy propaganda and became one of listening to friendly advice, a much more effective technique for swaying hearts and minds.

The pod-people's zombie-like efforts to convert everyone to their state, with promises of happiness which they are neither able to feel or express properly is the equivalent of the Politbureau's totalitarian dream – or alternatively Orwell's nightmare – come true.

Becky's capture by the pods represents the Big Prize for them. Sharing Bennell's disgust for them all along, she nevertheless has not the stamina to stay awake during the chase ordeal and wakes up vilifying the things which she previously defended, such as love, individualism and beauty. Rural America is being stood on its head and drained, literally, of its life-blood, and it has no defence because by the time the infiltration is discovered there are insufficient resources available to put up a fight.

The film offers some interesting observations about informing on others, and about the individual's responsibility to be eternally vigilant. It also debunks the idea that vigilance means a fixed focus, peering at the skies for invaders. These dangerous little babies are not rocketing in, but hatching under our noses, and far from threatening us with colossal firepower, they stroll down the street in broad daylight, say 'Howdy' to their neighbours and would willingly bake a pie for the church bazaar. These were cyphers for the enemies within which so bedevilled Joe McCarthy, enemies that you could not see but who were nevertheless quite capable of snatching your soul (or your country) in the space of a catnap.

Eventually, of course, the Cold War and its attendant paranoia receded, McCarthy's power crumbled and more liberal attitudes were tolerated. A new political dawn emerged which took some of the heat off the radicals, the theatre rediscovered its vocal cords again, and even popular music took on a new lease of life, deferring to hit parades and other youthful influences.

'Fifties-style proletariat male Stanley Kowalski (Marlon Brando) in *A Streetcar Named Desire* (1952).

CHAPTER SIX

BRANDO, THE NOBLE SAVAGE

*O*ne figure more than any other characterized young generation America at the mid-point of the twentieth century – Marlon Brando. In his early screen appearances Brando was an engaging mix of crazy mixed-up kid – which won him popularity among adolescent audiences – and Byronesque tragedy figure. There was excitement in his sullen looks and in every line of his sculptured body. Not even Bogart, the most accomplished of the traditionalists, could make immobility quite so poetic. Brando left people in little doubt that he was a major star in the ascendant. He was also the first of the 'fifties-style rebels, and the most impressive of the crop, not merely because he was first but also because the on-screen rebel was an extension of the real man.

Brando's non-conformity went bone-deep, a fact which the Hollywood establishment had to come to terms with after success swept him into the limelight. Showbiz writers were so used to new actors in town sucking up to them with their tails wagging, hungry for any lineage which might drop from their typewriters, that Brando's diffident 'up-yours' attitude mortified them deeply. Studio brass came in for much the same treatment. He showed right from the start that he was not the sort to be overawed or absorbed by 'the system'. Their offer of a comfortable hotel for his stay during the shooting of his first film was coolly declined. Instead he chose to lodge with an aunt, her husband and his grandmother in a tiny house in a Los Angeles suburb.

When interviewers descended on them, instead of preening himself for the occasion, Brando frequently received them without shaving, clad in the old lady's dressing-gown.

At some interviews he spent the entire time staring fixedly out the window, or picking his teeth. Sometimes he would abruptly leave without a word. Those who managed to get through to him later conceded that he was well informed on civil rights, politics, Eastern philosophy and psychiatry. If his intention was to outrage and alienate the Hollywood establishment, he succeeded magnificently. His unruly, wilful behaviour off the set was, however, counterpointed by fastidious preparation on it, and, when called to work, a harnessing of intellect and concentration which was amazing to witness. If his seriousness about being a movie 'personality' was open to question, his sincerity as an actor was never in doubt. He studied and practised to improve those already formidable powers of concentration; he even consulted analysts to unlock experiences and emotions that would help produce that all-important fusion of self and character.

Brando's headstrong maverick of early 'fifties films was a logical descendant of the breed of rebels who had gamely battled for greater freedom of expression and realism in the theatre since the 1920s.

The most influential of these experimental theatre groups, offshoots of one another in many cases, was a breakaway from the prestigious and commercially successful Theatre Guild, known as the Group Theatre, which was set up in New York in 1931 and headed by many of the Theatre Guild's alumni such as Cheryl Crawford, Lee Strasberg and Harold Clurman. A glance at some of their leading names, which included Morris Carnovsky, John Garfield, Lee J. Cobb, Luther Adler, Clifford Odets, Sanford Meisner and Elia Kazan, shows the strong Jewish immigrant presence.

The principles which they adopted were those of Constantin Stanislavsky of the Moscow Arts Theatre, which had been brought to America in the mid-'twenties by luminaries such as Maria Ouspenskaya and Richard Boleslavsky. Stanislavsky's 'Method', as it came to be known, offered an intriguing alternative to traditional acting techniques which had, for centuries, relied upon exercise, control and practice to achieve what was, in effect, an external performance.

The Method relied upon motivation and improvisation, resulting in total absorption by the actor of the role he was playing, by which means the emotional experiences of the character were matched by those of the actor during his interpretation. By forcing the actor to delve deep into the character's subconscious and seek parallels within his own experience, the Method established a fusion between player and character which made it no easy task, during a performance and often long afterwards, to distinguish where one left off and the other began. This, as its main defenders proclaimed long and loud, was what great acting was all about.

As well as their passion for realism in the theatre, with so many of the Method actors having first-hand experience of poverty and discrimination in their youth, they believed passionately in social reform and found strength in this shared idealism, which not unnaturally influenced their choice of plays and the new writings that emerged.

After nine years of critical and commercial success, the Group Theatre folded in 1940, and nothing resembling it reappeared during the war years. Afterwards, Elia Kazan's re-emergence as a leading Broadway director sowed the seeds for several other former Group Theatre leading lights to create in 1947 another radical theatre group in New York, of which Brando was among the first and most successful of the students. The diet was much the same as before, that is, Stanislavsky's Method was the only item on the menu, yet there was no shortage of keen young actors queuing up outside the Actors' Studio, as it was called, to learn their trade from the likes of Kazan, Cheryl Crawford and Robert Lewis.

Fired with a similar passion to that which its predecessors had expressed for realism and truth in the theatre, the Actors' Studio became an oasis for writers with something to say about society and about the depressing scale of its problems. In the climate of growing paranoia which seized America in the late 'forties, the stridency of their attacks on the established order unsettled audiences more deeply than either the Theatre Guild or the Group Theatre had managed to do.

In Hollywood, where McCarthyism had made it unfashionable (indeed, down-right dangerous) to support ideological rebellion as a means of attaining social reform, the major studios regarded the whole subject as a hot potato, and noisily got on with other things.

It was left to a handful of film-makers, some with political allegiances which landed them in trouble and others with no such allegiances, to carry on the impressive tradition of the pre-war social problem film. But whereas the 'thirties films were permitted to address in a refreshingly open-handed way what had then been a massive crisis of faith, the post-war versions were a lot more circumspect and fell short of indicting society as a whole, choosing instead to pick off at random previously taboo subjects such as alcoholism (*The Lost Weekend*, 1945), mental illness (*The Snake Pit*, 1945 and *Spellbound*, 1946), anti-Semitism (*Crossfire*, 1947 and *Gentleman's Agreement*, 1948) and physical handicap (*Johnny Belinda*, 1948).

Paraplegic war veteran Bud Wilochek (Marlon Brando) toasts his uncertain future with new bride Ellen (Teresa Wright) in *The Men* (1950).

Though nobody doubts the sincerity which those behind the making of these films felt and expressed through them, the massive collective enterprise of film-making meant that the front office was in a very strong position to impose strict editorial control over their properties. By confining the perspective to a single issue at a time the studios were able to deflect criticisms that the films were in any way anti-American. Another condition arbitrarily imposed was that the protagonist in social-problem films should be seen, in most cases, as neurotically at odds with a philanthropic outside world. Hiding behind that ubiquitous phrase 'the national interest' they conspired to promote the illusion that society was an o.k. place so long as the individual had the good sense not to rock the boat.

Brando's first film (*The Men*, 1950) began with a collaboration between producer Stanley Kramer, writer Carl Foreman and director Fred Zinnemann on a story about paraplegia, a subject considered to have limited, if any, box-office appeal. To compound his folly in other producers' eyes, Kramer chose the unknown Brando for the demanding central role of a war veteran adjusting to life in a wheelchair.

Sergeant 'Bud' Wilochek (Brando) begins his rehabilitation in a mood of bitterness and frustration after being paralysed from the waist down by an enemy sniper. Several hospitals and years later, pursued at a safe distance by the ever-faithful Ellen (Teresa Wright), he is still negative and self-absorbed. Transfer to a new location inhabited by a noisy, irreverent bunch of fellow-paraplegics initially fails to light a spark inside him, but slowly the defeatism and self-loathing start to subside and he begins, as they do, to re-discover his identity, though much of the camaraderie and wisecracks retain their bitter edge.

Ellen convinces him that they can have a future together, and once Bud is reassured that she is not acting out of pity, he agrees to resume their courtship, though when he is alone the nagging doubts persist. The wedding night is a disaster. Despite the optimism and understanding she has shown earlier, she is unable to come to terms immediately with having a disabled husband, and devastated by her visible uncertainty Bud storms back to hospital.

Ellen's subsequent attempts at a reconciliation are callously brushed aside, but both his fellow-patients and his doctor (Everett Sloane) conspire to force Bud to return to his wife. The film ends inconclusively as the two of them meet up again, both acknowledging the difficulties which have yet to be surmounted.

Brando accomplished in four major films following in quick succession during the early 'fifties something which no other male star, with the exception of Bogart, had done previously, namely, showed that external toughness did not mean that the character was tough all the way through. In *The Men*, the tougher Brando's rhetoric the less sure of himself he sounded, and the more he raged the more he impaled himself on his fears and self-doubts. It was a measure of the actor's skill at his job that he was capable of projecting immense suffering of spirit all the while it was being masked by defiance and bravado.

The film remains a thoughtful, sensitive production by present-day standards, and

Blanche du Bois (Vivien Leigh) spurns brutish brother-in-law Stanley Kowalski (Marlon Brando) in *A Streetcar Named Desire* (1952).

by the standards of 1950, in which context it needs to be considered, its honesty and integrity are all the more remarkable.

Remarkable, too, is the way the Brando character up-ends the age-old conception of screen masculinity. He lashes out blindly at everyone in turn, but the real target of his fury is his own handicapped body and his permanent loss of manhood. He can no more control his anger than his legs, but it is through his anger and aggression that the true depth of his terror and despair are conveyed. Before 1950 it was not considered masculine to concede to suffering, or to admit defeat. Sergeant Wilocheck is finished before he starts, and he knows it; at the end of the film the look of utter desolation on his face, as he waits helplessly for his wife to manoeuvre him up the steps of their house in order to effect a reconciliation with her, foretells the life which waits in store.

Brando's second film was *A Streetcar Named Desire* (1952), which Elia Kazan directed from a Broadway success by Tennessee Williams with three of the original cast, namely, Brando, Kim Hunter and Karl Malden. Brando's co-star on Broadway, the British stage leading lady Jessica Tandy, was not sufficiently known in films to merit the investment, so her role went instead to Vivien Leigh, who had played it in London under the direction of her husband Laurence Olivier, and who, along with Kim Hunter and Karl Malden, was to win an Academy Award.

Though not strictly a sociological statement, the film nevertheless powerfully explores the tensions that arise between individuals of differing social, cultural and educational levels forced to share a small apartment through the effect it has on the leading characters – Stanley (Brando), a brutish factory worker living in a low-life quarter of New Orleans, and his mentally unstable, alcoholic sister-in-law Blanche (Vivien Leigh), who arrives unexpectedly and causes friction in the home between Stanley and his pregnant wife Stella (Kim Hunter).

Blanche is a fragile former beauty with white-Southern aristocratic affectation who can no longer distinguish truth from fantasy. The truth is that she is a drunken nymphomaniac, but her surrealistic dreams are populated with fey admirers and olde-worlde gentility. Not surprisingly, the coarse, neanderthal Stanley is nowhere among her list of favourite men, but Stanley's off-duty diversions, such as his drinking, late-night card-games and ten-pin bowling preclude him from taking much notice of his sister-in-law, either – until he realizes that behind his back Blanche has been busy poisoning Stella's mind against him.

'Thousands of years have passed him right by, and there he is, Stanley Kowalski, survivor of the Stone Age, bearing the raw meat home from the kill in the jungle,' says Blanche maliciously. But Stella loves him and ignores her sister's advice not to 'hang back with the brutes!'

Stella's main worry is about Blanche's precarious mental state, and this sisterly concern is misinterpreted by Stanley as favouring Blanche against himself, for by then the two are openly at loggerheads. While Stella is in hospital having their baby, Stanley and Blanche have one final, tragic confrontation. Alone with her in the house, Stanley's desire to cut her down to size gets out of control, and after laughing in her face about her 'deceit, lies and tricks' he coldly rapes her.

The experience drives her over the edge, into insanity. Because of her known instability, no one believes her story of the attack except Stella, who manages to conceal her disgust for Stanley until Blanche is safely despatched to a sanatorium, whereupon her fury erupts and, snatching up her baby and a few sparse belongings, she informs him that their marriage is over. The deserted Stanley shrieks for his wife like an abandoned waif – which, in a sense, he is.

As with the central character in *The Men*, Kowalski's violent rages in *Streetcar* betray an absence of self-confidence, not a surfeit of it. When he imagines that his power-base in the home is being threatened, he can only defend it with primitive physical force, thereby clumsily destroying what he hoped to preserve because he has no other weaponry.

Outwardly he hates Blanche, but inwardly he is afraid of her, unsure of her power over Stella, terrified that her recollections of their affluent origins will alert Stella to how little he has been able to provide – the shabby apartment, cheapskate furnishings, rowdy neighbours. 'I'm king here!' he yells at Stella, but he is monarch of nothing worth having, and his need to express it in those terms merely emphasizes the hollowness of the claim.

Blanche, in her confused, dreamlike state, is not really the threat which Stanley believes her to be, yet, in the end, they are powerless to stop themselves destroying what remains of their tawdry lives: she by her desperate clinging to lurid fantasies about a bygone high-life which Stanley desecrates by his very presence; he by defending like a savage his own corner against an unwelcome intruder.

Stanley's dual roles as swaggering proletarian male and helpless boy-child are cleverly interwoven, but again Brando's virtuosity allows us to see one while we are actually watching the other. The character strikes chords on so many levels that the effect is exhausting. A man capable of raping his wife's mentally ill sister in order to engineer her removal to a mental institution deserves no popularity points, yet if his conduct is that of a ruthless degenerate, thanks to Brando's clever manipulation of our senses our enduring impression of Stanley is far more favourable.

It is while Stanley is most vigorously asserting his manhood and knocking everyone else into dazed submission by verbal assault that the little-boy-lost image of him reaches its apotheosis.

He rages at Stella, but it is out of helplessness and desperation, because he needs her, both as comforting wife and as mother-figure. Her final desertion of him is almost more than he can endure. As someone who has significance in his life and is confident in her ability to stand up for herself, knowing exactly how to respond and how to punish him when he steps out of line, Stella was a liberated lady for her time.

In their depiction of the female role in society, Hollywood and the media in general had allowed their chauvinism to make the running. The freedoms which wartime had suddenly presented to women evaporated just as abruptly as peacetime resumed. Women were once again subjected to massive discrimination, much of it subliminal, yet the end result was as if a major conspiracy had been launched by the establishment in general and men in particular, to dissuade and deprive women of the desire or opportunity to compete with men on any level whatever.

Millions of words of advice blared at them, from glossy home journals, movie magazines, movies themselves and radio stations, extolling the virtues of being more 'feminine', which between both the lines and the sheets meant keeping their minds on how to keep their husbands happy, and which tut-tutted any involvement, intellectually or emotionally, with 'distractions' from the outside world. To be truly feminine, they were told, meant making a man the focal point in their lives – dressing or undressing to please him, cooking his favourite dishes, ferrying the children to and from school, keeping the larder well-stocked and the home in good order.

Those who set their minds on a career encountered suspicion and hostility from the media, and from many of their friends. Married women, in particular, had a difficult time establishing themselves in business. Inevitably the interruptions to one's career of having and attending to a family meant, in large corporations at any rate, the closure of promotional avenues which their male colleagues followed as a matter of right. The fear that a high-ranking female executive might duck the big conference because little Johnny had gone down with the mumps was, from the chairman of the board's point of view, a very real one.

Women who fought to make a successful career for themselves, or who rose to positions of power in the business world, were looked upon by the media and by their neighbours as being somehow freakish. Heroines in popular novels, or in magazine fiction, rarely had a job or a profession or, indeed, participated in anything constructive or creative outside the immediate home or social circle — and those who did generally ended up renouncing their careers in order to find love and marriage.

Before Brando, Hollywood studios were able to ignore the younger generation completely, despite the fact that at least a half of cinema audiences in 1950 were under the age of twenty-five.

This is not to say that such a statistic would ever have turned the autocratic heads of the American film industry, who were mostly the same ones who had created the original studios. To these wizened moguls, Crosby, Bogart, Flynn and Gable must have appeared youthful and sprightly, and the idea of giving genuinely young actors red-blooded romantic roles or making them faster on the draw (both of which, medically speaking, seemed more logical) was alien to everything Hollywood stood for. The industry was in the grip of a handful of tetchy old tycoons who had made few concessions either to art or to fresh ideas since the beginning, and were not about to change the bad habits of a lifetime — indisputable proof of which can be seen in so many films of the 'forties and 'fifties which bear their signatures.

Young men were therefore depicted in film after film as spoonfed and expendable while the girls had little to do but supply love interest — which summarized precisely the moguls' own jaundiced view of the generation gap. They were, as they had always done, pumping audiences' heads full of their own prejudices, and were getting away with it because nobody had what Steve McQueen later called the 'juice', that is the power, to challenge their right to do whatever they wished.

To suggest that Brando triggered off the youth revolution of the early 'fifties might be overstating his influence — bohemians and beatniks were around earlier — but the fact remains that he was the first centre-stage actor with youth and talent on his side who refused to be taken in by all the cant and the nonsense which Hollywood levelled at every promising newcomer.

Brando's sourpuss rebel roles and his refusal to conform provided the youth of America with a model on which to tailor its own rebellion. Despite the apparent calm, rebellion seethed beneath the surface, fanned by a rising tide of dissatisfaction among the young about the pattern and quality of their lives. The tensions affecting adult society — rampant consumerism, Communist scaremongering, the threat of atomic invasion — were not of their making, yet as a direct result of what was going on around them for the first time in their lives young people began seriously to question contemporary values.

Many were appalled at the lengths to which the bourgeois classes were prepared to go to keep anyone else from enjoying any share of the cake. Middle-class narcissism and intolerance were not, on this occasion, the aberrations of a desperately weak society fighting over its last few crumbs to survive. America was indisputably the richest, most powerful, technologically superior, best-defended nation in the world – at the end of the war, for example, more than two-thirds of the entire world's gold reserves were locked away in Fort Knox.

Yet, somehow, these spectacular gains, which had been made within a single decade, resulting in immense wealth and international prestige, made little difference to the plight of millions of underprivileged Americans enduring discrimination, injustice, poverty and misery as a daily ritual. So corrosive was the climate of envy and repression that it was hardly surprising that ordinary individuals with jobs and reputations to safeguard kept quiet about what was wrong with society for fear of being branded 'un-American'.

It was not that parents did not have a conscience about social problems, but they were afraid of expressing any viewpoint which could be misconstrued as just a tiny bit radical. Youngsters, on the other hand, saw every reason to upset the applecart, for by their reckoning most of the contents were rotten anyway.

Brando became a potent hero-figure for young people because he brought their conflicts into the open. He made them realize that as long as they permitted their disaffection to be stifled, they would continue to play into the hands of the established order. The only way to shut off the bullshit was to bust loose and create their own space.

The Brando rebel pulled no punches, offered no solutions, raised no hopes and was responsible for nobody but himself. Later rebels would come along with solutions for society's ills – Steve McQueen with his blue-eyed integrity and innate sense of fair-play, Charles Bronson and Clint Eastwood as armed vigilantes meting out frontier-style justice to criminals on whom the authorities had gone too soft. The Brando rebel was content to be an outsider, and to create distance between himself and anyone who disagreed with his right to be his own man.

Distance could be achieved, for example, by dressing to outrage sober-suited fathers, by expressing oneself differently – 'hip-talk' – so that adults could overhear conversations without penetrating them, and by using souped-up motorcycles on the highway to overtake and cut in on adults in their cars, thereby scoring yet another point against the enemy.

Motorcycles gave young people an exhilarating sense of their own identity quite apart from the thrill of biking. The powerful phallic symbolism of a throbbing machine thrust between the thighs was not lost on a generation that would experience sexual licence at least on a par with that of the madcap 'twenties.

Groups of leather-jacketed enthusiasts, riding knee-to-knee, became familiar sights in towns and on highways across America, their presence often marked by rowdiness and horseplay and a letting off of youthful steam. Unfortunately, not all

Bikers' leader Johnny (Marlon Brando) believes that silence is golden after a night's revelry has ended in a killing in *The Wild One* (1953).

bikers were simply liberated youths out for a good time. A hardcore of delinquents also took to their wheels, and formed themselves into rival sub-groups or chapters who fought internecine battles on the streets, and terrorized small townships which had no way of retaliating.

A real-life incident in which just such a group, calling themselves Hell's Angels, suddenly descended on a small Californian town, Hollister, for a weekend of destruction, hell-raising and bullying, provided the basis for Brando's most definitive rebel movie, *The Wild One* (1953),

Brando agreed to do the film because Stanley Kramer was producing it, reassured as always by the feeling that when Kramer tackled a contemporary issue the outcome could scarcely fail to be interesting.

Director Lazlo Benedek later said about the film, 'The subject isn't about juvenile delinquency. It's about youth without ideals, without goals, that doesn't know what to do about the enormous energy it possesses. What I tried to do was show that if you react with similar violence, you lose, that the vigilante attitude is useless. You just end up with an even greater problem. . . It's about the dangers of the white backlash mentality.'

Brando's platitudinous voice-over sets the pre-credits scene for the gang's first appearance, during a roar-past on a deserted stretch of road. After clashing with the local police, who materialize in strength, Johnny (Brando) and his gang swarm off to a nearby town where, at first, the reception committee establishes good terms with them. When an old-timer is forced off the road by a war-whooping biker, who breaks his leg in the process, some of the townspeople who gather round are

86

prepared to concede that the car driver may have been partly to blame because of his age, though a few voices in the crowd murmur: 'What are they trying to prove?'

Their injured buddy gives Johnny the excuse he needs to 'hang around for a while', and he tries to make polite conversation with a hard-working waitress named Kathy (Mary Murphy), who is pretty enough to have the town studs sniffing around in droves, and bored enough to encourage them yet, miraculously, there is no boyfriend in sight. Unfortunately, Johnny's idea of polite conversation is to pick arguments and snarl threats ('You keep needlin' me and if I want to I'm gonna take this joint apart and you're not gonna know what hit you'), which, understandably, gets their courtship off to a slow start. The fact that her father is the local sheriff slows the affair down even further, because if there is one thing Johnny hates more than a bike which fails to start, it is a policeman. Correctly on this occasion, however, Johnny senses that this middle-aged, docile copper is no match for him.

Events begin to liven up with the arrival of Chino (Lee Marvin), an extrovert delinquent with a motorcycle gang of his own, a breakaway group from Johnny's Black Rider Motorcycle Club. Chino is ready for a rumpus ('I've been looking for you in every ditch, hopin' you was dead,' he tells Johnny). Predictably they slug it out in a ritual trial of strength, but though Johnny and Chino are old enemies, they share an intense hatred of what the town stands for, that is, conformity to law and order, and the scene is soon set for a violent clash between right and wrong.

Against his better judgement, though some townsfolk would prefer to call it cowardice, Kathy's policeman father arrests Chino after some trouble with a local bigwig, and Chino cheerfully submits, knowing that his gang will spring him at the first opportunity. Johnny's on/off relationship with Kathy takes a turn for the worse after he rescues her from the clutches of his buddies and whisks her out of town on the pillion of his bike, but he loses his temper with her when she makes a rather pathetic, hard-luck-story attempt to capture his affections.

When she is spotted running away from him, in obvious distress, a few local gallants conclude that Johnny must have molested her, and decide to 'pound a little respect for law and order into the guy's thick skull'. Abducted to a storeroom and beaten up, he manages to give them the slip, but only momentarily, for by then a vigilante group has thrown a cordon around the town and escape on his motorcycle is not possible. During his final attempt to break free someone in the crowd hurls a tyre-lever at him, which knocks him out cold, while his powerful bike careers forward, killing an innocent bystander.

While all this is going on, Johnny's motorcycle gang is nowhere to be seen. They are either sleeping it off in ditches, or, having observed Johnny in his painful throes of courtship, decided *en masse* that a therapeutic roughing up should bring him to his senses. Either way, they are powerless to help Johnny, who is marched away on a manslaughter charge by an avuncular county sheriff (Jay C. Flippen). The charge is eventually dropped when a couple of the town's worthies, mortified by their part in the previous night's tragedy, admit witnessing the tyre-lever incident.

For all its surface decoration, *The Wild One* suffers from a hollow centre, and only Brando's laconic performance keeps it alive to the end. All the mannerisms of the 'fifties hipster are there – the peacock swagger, the narcissism, the jive talk, the pre-Presley sideburns. It is as well that Brando is on form, for the unknowns surrounding him are anything but.

He bristles with rebellion, but the dumbheads and reactionaries who make up the townspeople are nothing to get steamed up about. Asked by someone what it is that he is rebelling against, Johnny's despairing reply is to ask 'What have you got?', for nothing which has caught his eye – or ours – thus far is worth a V-sign.

Disquietingly, for a film with pretensions of attacking the existing social order, the worst Hollywood traditions regarding the use, or misuse, of romantic interest are slavishly retained. Kathy could have been pivotal in getting Johnny to reveal what is bugging him, but the opportunity is squandered in a succession of trite setpieces. Denied a chance to develop any kind of personality, Kathy has neither insight into nor influence on Johnny, and the one valuable component besides Brando's involvement which could have held the second half of the film together, the key that would unlock Johnny's thoughts, is blithely discarded.

Johnny is the classic outsider, as ill-at-ease in his gang's company as when he senses traditional conformity bearing down on him. Each has become a sham, and he wants something else, but there is nothing there, and there is no clear indication as to where he must go, or what he should do, to find himself.

The gang loafs around the town's only bar waiting for something to happen. Their antics are a prelude to something happening, but the prelude never finishes. At the end of the film they ride off to another town where, one suspects, nothing is going to happen all over again.

By softening the impact which the gang has on the beleaguered town – at Production Code insistence – Johnny is a figure without real menace, and the gang itself seems no worse than an average bunch of Saturday-night revellers. But what the film captures emphatically, and Brando's performance is cleverly in tune with this mood, is that aimlessness of youth which Benedek described.

As a further concession to the moral climate at the time, a tiny note of optimism is sounded at the end, when Johnny is permitted a self-redeeming smile, his only one of the film. Thankfully Benedek leaves it at that, thus avoiding a real cop-out, and allows Johnny to rejoin his cronies for another swipe at authority.

The idea for a film which focused on gangster infiltration of trade unions on the New York docks had its origins in the late 1940s when Elia Kazan and playwright Arthur Miller – Kazan produced Miller's *All My Sons* and *Death of a Salesman* – discussed the possibility of collaborating on a story. Gangsters were known to have been dipping their fingers into union cash tills since the 1930s, and some trade union leaders were not averse to lining their pockets with the proceeds of corruption and extortion. The history of trade unionism in America makes salty reading, and the real-life saga of Jimmy Hoffa, volatile leader of the Teamsters union, whose power

Union boss Johnny Friendly (Lee J. Cobb, left) shows the young Terry Malloy (Marlon Brando) that the price of controlling the dockside can be dangerously high in *On the Waterfront* (1954).

was smashed by Attorney General Bobby Kennedy, and who later vanished without trace, presumably a gangland 'contract' victim, contained more duplicity and dirty dealings than any Warner Brothers' gangster movie script.

The Kazan-Miller partnership did not survive the House of Un-American Activities hearings, when Kazan's willingness to testify antagonized Miller. But Kazan remained on the lookout for a writer who could produce a hard-hitting script on the subject. Budd Schulberg's credentials for the job were immaculate. A screenwriter from the age of nineteen, the New York-born son of the moviemaker who had discovered silent star Clara Bow and a one-time collaborator with Scott Fitzgerald, he had taken the lid off the movie industry with his best-selling novel *What Makes Sammy Run?* and had spent the war years as a member of John Ford's documentary film unit. He had also testified, like Kazan, before the Un-American Activities Committee. Schulberg became interested in a series of articles in the *New York Sun*, written by Malcolm Johnson, which courageously exposed the corruption and racketeering on the New York waterfront, and in 1950 he began work on a screenplay based on Johnson's editorials. Three years later, Schulberg and Kazan, with Malcolm Johnson as adviser, began the collaborations which resulted in *On the Waterfront* (1954).

The film shows the regeneration of a semi-literate dockworker, Terry Malloy (Brando), from the corrupt union hierarchy's lapdog to the catalyst who finally breaks the bullies' hold on his fellow dockworkers, a result which the law and religion alike had been powerless to achieve. Malloy enjoys the favours of the union's top brass because his brother Charlie (Rod Steiger, in a small but volatile performance) is chief mouthpiece for union boss Johnny Friendly (Lee J. Cobb). Terry is popular because he is an uncomplicated guy who carries out his orders unquestioningly, knows when to keep his mouth shut and bears no obvious grudges despite the fact that Friendly and his brother torpedoed his once-promising boxing career by forcing him to lose an important, and easily-winnable, fight.

Malloy's unwitting involvement in the murder of a young docker, killed for allowing himself to be interviewed by a crime commission which is tenaciously building up a case against Friendly, brings him into contact with the victim's sister Edie (Eva Maria Saint), who at first suspects nothing, and with a tough Pat O'Brien-style Catholic priest (Karl Malden).

Malloy's hard-bitten philosophy of life – 'do it to him before he does it to you' – belies his gentler attitude towards smaller creatures, like his pigeons, and towards Edie, for whom he feels a growing attraction, but he is no more able to express this feeling than he is willing to disclose the identity of her brother's murderers. When Edie chides him for not having a 'spark of sentiment or romance or human kindness', Malloy matter-of-factly replies, 'What good does it do you besides getting you in trouble?'

The murder of another docker who outspokenly opposes Friendly and his mob marks the turning-point for Malloy. He can no longer tolerate their viciousness for the sake of 'loose change jingling in his pocket', and, accordingly, he no longer discourages questions from a crime investigator. When Friendly is tipped off that Malloy has been seeing Edie and talking to a commission investigator, brother Charlie is sent to extract assurances from Malloy that he will continue to act 'deaf-and-dumb', the mobsters' colourful way of describing someone who keeps his mouth shut. However, Malloy – in one of the most powerful and elevating scenes in the film – refuses to backtrack on his principles.

Charlie's murder, soon afterwards (punishment for breaking faith with his increasingly paranoiac boss), serves two purposes: to put the frighteners on anyone who might be considering giving evidence before the commission, and to smoke Malloy out of hiding so that the union's hired killers can nail him. But before the gangsters can finish him off, the priest manages to persuade Malloy that to 'fix' Friendly permanently he should not try to fight him in his own stronghold – 'Fight him in the courtroom tomorrow, with the truth as you know the truth!'

After giving evidence, Malloy is cold-shouldered by the dockland community *en masse*. Whatever the rights or wrongs of the union's behaviour, co-operating with outsiders contravenes the unwritten code of the workers, and they close ranks against him.

Ignoring the contempt heaped on him from all sides, Malloy stands up to Friendly and his thugs a second time, on the very dockside which is under the gangster's control, and it takes a savage beating up of Malloy by Friendly's henchmen to bring the exploited workforce to its senses and force the mobsters to withdraw.

Brando's slow transformation from gangland nobody to people's champion is elegiac cinema at its most breathtaking. As well as some heavy-handed post-McCarthyite symbolism, for example, the informer as hero, there is an interesting parallel to be drawn between Malloy and a modern-day Christ figure in a film already well-sprinkled with Irish American Catholic influences, for example, the bulldog-like priest, Malloy's boyhood coercion by orphanage nuns and the convent where Edie is being educated.

The parallel can be carried further. Johnny Friendly, the demagogue running things on behalf of a higher authority (that is, Pilate), tolerates Malloy only while he can be considered harmless. Malloy is rebuked for not taking up proper arms (that is, testifying) against them by the agent of his own orthodox religion (the priest, that is, the Jewish elders) whose own efforts, mainly rhetorical, have achieved nothing.

Later when Malloy/Christ emerges as a genuinely compassionate figure likely to bring the enslaved union (Jews) round to his way of thinking, the partisan mob spill his blood, an act of folly they quickly regret, for by doing so, they give the passive crowds a martyr figure powerful enough to restore their faith and self-respect.

The rough, masculine credentials of the character are never in doubt. Yet his vulgar egocentricity ('Me? I'm with me!') hides, like Stanley Kowalski's in *Streetcar*, an inner yearning to be loved and accepted as something other than a failure, which, in a moment of cruel self-analysis later in the film, he admits is all that he is.

The difference which Edie's love and her acceptance of Malloy, failings and all, makes to him is to transform him from acting instinctively (that is, protecting his own skin) to acting compulsively (that is, sticking his neck out) even though afterwards, as he understands only too well, his life 'won't be worth a nickel'.

His hunger for love is expressed eloquently on the tenement rooftop where he keeps his pigeons, which he admires because they 'marry just like people and stay that way till one of them dies'. That is the way he would like it to be, too, secure in the knowledge that love will at last make him feel the 'somebody' which his conniving brother and the gang boss denied him the chance to become many years before, when they fixed his one and only important fight.

Toughness and tenderness converge throughout the film, as they do inside Malloy's head, and when after her rejection of him for complicity in her brother's murder he returns to Edie's apartment and shoulders the locked door off its hinges, it is not to enforce a Kowalski-type prerogative but to hear a straight admission from her that she loves him.

It did not take the generation born during the Depression years long to acquire a taste for Brando's rebellion act of the early 'fifties. Its appetite for it, born during the years of post-war expansion, swelled as money rolled into its pockets. Freed from having to take the first job that was offered, children of working-class parents, for the first time since the 'twenties, found themselves with enough breathing space to examine what they wanted. Brando's declaration, at the end of *On the Waterfront*, that he is going to get his rights became a powerful call-to-arms to all youngsters to gather on mythical waterfronts for their rights, too – the right to be themselves as individuals, to make their own mistakes, to choose their own heroes and to create their own culture.

George Eastman (Montgomery Clift) courts socialite Angela Vickers (Elizabeth Taylor), with tragic results, in *A Place in the Sun* (1951).

CHAPTER SEVEN

1955 AND ALL THAT JIVE

Montgomery Clift and James Dean were each compulsively trying to die during the 'fifties. It was mythically appropriate that the automobile, symbol of power and sexuality among the live-fast-die-young adolescents of the day, should have been prominent in the physical destruction of both of them. Films in which fast cars were the thrill tools were popular around the time that Dean lost his life, in an auto crash on 30 September 1955. Clift's permanent disfigurement the following year, when his car plunged out of control after a party at Elizabeth Taylor's clifftop mansion, marked the beginning of his dreadful decline.

Clift was the paradox to end them all – the cultured, controlled and contemplative qualities he exhibited on the screen were an inspired fabrication. The screen rebel, the unsinkable loner, who stood his ground resolutely and with no fuss against all the odds, dissolved away from the cameras into the kind of human wreckage which audiences would not have recognized.

As squarely as Brando came to represent the brutish, misapplied aggression of the working classes, and as Dean would later express a predominantly middle-class neurosis and detachment, Clift personified the voice of upper-class intellect and refinement. His idealism came from within, his sense of estrangement and stubborn hostility for the shabby world around him grew from the cherished hope that there must be some place on this earth where a man can find peace, where there is something of which he can feel proud to be a part.

Clift was the first, and some would say the best, of the screen's all-time losers. The conflicts he engaged in with others were merely extensions of an overwhelming disenchantment with himself, and it was a measure of Clift's talent that this at times morbid self-absorption never got out of hand or appeared too self-pitying on screen. That was something he kept exclusively for his life off-camera.

Like Brando, Clift helped to dispel the cosy notion that handsome young men could sail through the difficult, paranoiac post-war years unscathed. Their rebel characters symbolized the disillusion and disorientation of young people trying to come to terms with what was seen by them, increasingly, as a shabby inheritance. Clift was a striking example of sensitivity and intellect refusing to accept the complacent solutions or simplistic remedies which those in authority doled out, like foreign aid, to their not-so-well-off allies.

Clift was on an entirely different plane from Brando. His characters had none of the arrogance, the self-assurance or the outward show which made Brando so hypnotic to watch. Clift's characters burned and fizzed inwardly like the core of a nuclear reactor. His marvellously expressive eyes were the keys to his soul, and he used them to perfection, in turn pleading, defiant, beaten and half-crazed.

During Clift's early days in films, the dividing line between masculinity and chauvinism was indistinct, and the careers of many of the great names in the cinema, including Cagney, Gable and others, were fashioned round the assumption that physical toughness and moral stength were inherent in each other. Indomitability, Hollywood-style, implied loss of innocence, and the most consistently successful screen lovers were philanderers or cads of one kind or another who made mincemeat of the guys who really cared for women.

Clift showed that pain and sensitivity and isolation in defence of principle were as much hallmarks of heroism as Bogart's laconic wisecracks or Cooper's competence with a gun. His toughness was on the inside, hidden behind the demeanour and impeccable manners of a doomed romantic, behind the sensitive mask a man who is sure neither of himself nor of what his reactions might be in crisis.

Mixed-up Private Prewitt (Montgomery Clift) releases his anguish on a bugle in *From Here to Eternity* (1953).

An interesting contrast between hero-styles old and new occurred in Clift's first Hollywood movie, *Red River* (1948), a Howard Hawks western in which he plays John Wayne's adopted son. Wayne, as always, is the tough-guy hero, aggressively masculine, commanding respect through physical superiority, a man's man. He plays Tom Dunson, an embittered cattle rancher whose fiancée has recently been killed by Indians in a wagon-train massacre which also wiped out the family of young Matthew Garth (Clift). Dunson takes pity on Matthew and agrees to rear him as his own son. Dunson is law-abiding but dictatorial, his understanding of the human race dulled by the sadness in his life, for which he compensates by driving himself and his men extremely hard.

Matthew grows to admire and respect Dunson for his integrity and his obvious qualities of leadership, but on a long cattle drive their relationship becomes strained when Dunson starts bullying the drovers like some medieval despot. Disagreements over where the cattle should be herded sour the relationship even further. Finally, when Dunson kills one of the men, Matthew can tolerate Dunson's ruthlessness no further. Supported by the other drovers, he seizes control and takes the cattle to the railhead in Kansas.

Not a man to leave old scores unsettled, Dunson waits his chance to level accounts with Matthew, and when they meet Matthew's reluctance to fight back reconfirms Dunson's view, expressed out on the trail, that the younger man is 'soft'. Matthew is finally drawn into a long, bruising but ultimately conciliatory punch-up with Dunson, which is interrupted when the girl whom Matthew rescued from Indians on the trail (and with whom he has fallen in love) angrily fires a rifle in the air and talks them into seeing sense.

The film ends with Dunson and Matthew burying their differences, to the point where Dunson agrees to add Matthew's initial to the D for Dunson on his Red River brand. The older man's underlying compassion has been brought to the surface, and Matthew's trial-by-combat has resulted in his courage and his manhood being firmly established.

Red River tosses the arguments back and forth about what it takes to be a man. Dunson puts the case for total self-sufficiency, going it alone, answering and answerable to no one but himself as at the centre of his own universe. Cussedness, brute strength and intolerance are the hallmarks of his authority, which he wields like the sword of Damocles over everyone with whom he has contact.

Lesser men are attracted to Dunson because he represents values and accomplishments beyond their grasp. He is the masculine cypher for America of bygone times, when the land was taken and held by muscle and rifle-power. Matthew represents the modern face of heroism, international in character as opposed to the exclusively American persona of Dunson. Clift's hero is one inside whom moral arguments carry more weight than physical bravado, a thinking man's hero who denigrates violence, in complete contrast to Dunson who knows no other way to settle arguments.

Although the rugged Dunson is idealized for much of the film, allegiance is later transferred to Matthew. Dunson's regression into brutality is encountered by Matthew's intervention on behalf of the deserters whom Dunson wants to hang. The more Dunson's character hardens, the more unsettling and divisive is its effect on the drovers, until the situation almost ends in disaster.

By contrast, Matthew's strength of character is constructive and conciliatory. He stands back from events and takes in a broader perspective before reacting. He does not have to dominate and bully others to assert authority. Matthew's authority is in-bred, out of sight of the likes of Dunson, who is capable of seeing others only in terms of hardness and softness, the former admirable, the latter to be knocked out of them at the earliest opportunity.

Yet for all his implied softness, it is Matthew who, in the end, earns the drovers' respect and delivers the cattle to the railhead, something which Dunson, for all his macho posturing, appears to be failing to do. Bringing the beef to market is a team effort and Matthew is a team player, whereas Dunson is captain, pitcher, batsman and ballboy all rolled into one.

From Here to Eternity (1953) established Clift as a rebel loner among socially aware younger audiences who might have passed up the earlier John Wayne western. In this film the emphasis is again on moral courage and the problems encountered by an individual who declines to back down on a fundamental principle even when it is blatantly and provocatively out of step with the society in which it flourishes. Private Prewitt (Clift), a regimental bugler, arrives at Schofield Barracks in Hawaii following a transfer request from his previous barracks because another bugler, whom he regards as an inferior musician, has been promoted over him.

The camp CO, Captain Holmes (Philip Ober), also runs the regimental boxing team. Prewitt was once champion material but vowed never to enter the ring again after accidentally blinding an opponent during a bout. Holmes is determined to have Prewitt in the team, and puts him through rough treatment in an attempt to break the soldier's resolve, but no amount of extra duties, route marches or bullying can break Prewitt's spirit.

Throughout Prewitt's ordeal his only friend is Maggio (Frank Sinatra), a diffident soldier whose careless attitude constantly gets him into trouble. The two spend their leisure time together in a servicemen's club where Prewitt meets and falls in love with Laurene (Donna Reid), a bored hostess.

Holmes's aide, Sergeant Warden (Burt Lancaster), respects Prewitt, but keeps his distance, suspecting trouble. Warden is a hard-headed professional soldier with problems of his own, the most obvious of which is the risk of court-martial which he runs by having a love affair with Karen (Deborah Kerr), Holmes's attractive but lonely wife.

The three central characters, in turn, have to face their moment of truth, and in each case it is a question of honour. For Maggio, it is the defence of the honour of his family after Sergeant 'Fatso' Judson (Ernest Borgnine), the loud-mouth, bullying

NCO in charge of the punishment block, insults a photograph of Maggio's sister. Maggio bounces a chair off Fatso's thick skull, and later, when Maggio is sentenced to a term in the stockade, for getting drunk on duty, Fatso is waiting for him.

Prewitt's ultimate fate is tied up with Maggio's, for after Fatso has brutally murdered Maggio by a series of excessive beatings, Prewitt goes after him with a knife. He kills Fatso, but is seriously wounded in the fight. Bleeding badly, he takes refuge in Laurene's apartment, and is recuperating satisfactorily when the attack on Pearl Harbour occurs.

Hearing details of the attack broadcast on the radio, Prewitt attempts to join his unit, because he is a professional soldier and it is the honourable thing to do, although he is clearly in no condition to do so. His knife wounds re-open, but he is desperate to get back inside the barracks – so desperate, in fact, that he fails to identify himself to a sentry who, fearing infiltration by enemy ground troops, opens fire and kills him.

Warden has to make a decision between starting afresh in civilian life with Mrs Holmes or renouncing her in order to continue his military career. Again, honour determines the outcome, but it is the honour of uniform which Warden decides to uphold, and any misgivings he might have about it afterwards vanish when the Japanese attack.

Of the three, Warden is the only survivor at the end, but he was survival-minded all the way through, keeping a check on the duty roster and on his emotions while his lady-friend allows hers to run riot. Prewitt is a martyr to honour, whose rejection of the violence of the boxing ring as a result of the accidental blinding subjects him to the violence of coercion.

He could have avoided persecution by putting on the gloves, but Prewitt's personal code – 'If a man don't go his own way, he's nothin'' – ruled out compromises of that kind. The more they grind him down the more resolute he becomes. His solitary attitude leads his persecutors into the same trap into which Matthew Garth's 'softness' led Dunson in *Red River* when Prewitt's refusal to box was mistaken for cowardice. Prewitt, in fact, has more moral fibre than all the others put together, because he can be loving, and loyal to his friend Maggio and loyal to the Army despite what they are doing to him.

Again, typifying the difference between traditional and 'fifties-style heroes, Prewitt had the courage to be non-violent, the guts not to fight despite appalling provocation. 'Just because a man loves the Army, it don't have to love him back,' says Prewitt after yet another attempt to break him. He clearly regards the uniform as a father substitute which he needs to please without surrendering his own identity.

Problems with father figures recurred throughout the 'fifties. It dominated two of James Dean's three films, and Paul Newman often played unstable youths rejected by angry paternal figures – for example, *The Left-handed Gun* (1958), *Cat on a Hot Tin Roof* (1960) and *Hud* (1963). Prewitt's devotion to the Army outlasts every indignity which can be inflicted on him, and that same devotion kills him when, heeding the call to arms after the Japanese invasion, he abruptly quits the safety of Laurene's apartment and runs into the defensive gunfire of his own side.

The year 1955 was a vintage year for raising hell. James Dean unveiled his tortured ego to audiences and held them spellbound, but died on 30 September that year, too early for his true worth as an actor to be properly analysed. It was the year that *The Blackboard Jungle* was released, accompanied by an eruption of violence never before seen inside cinemas, as youngsters ripped seats, jived in the aisles to the theme song 'Rock Around the Clock' and attacked policemen who had been called to restore order.

In the Deep South, Elvis Presley, a gangly trucker-turned-vocalist, was knocking 'em dead with a 'white' version of a 'forties rhythm-and-blues classic, 'That's All Right, Mama'. It was also the year that Paul Newman made his first film, *The Silver Chalice*, a glossy Roman epic which gave little hint of his hell-raising roles to come.

These diverse happenings all went to show that the youth rebellion was unstoppable. If adults had believed that youngsters of the 'fifties had been effectively anaesthetized by the McCarthy era or the clean-up which followed, they were wrong, and deservedly so. Brando had shown that authority that was unsure of itself could be swept aside by anyone prepared to take the consequences. Kowalski in *Streetcar* was a brute, but he was his own man, taking directions from an inner compass, untroubled by any kind of conscience after cruelly disposing of the woman who threatened his existence.

The divided townspeople were equally ineffective in controlling the bikers in *The Wild One*, because nothing they could throw at Johnny, not even the beating-up at the end, was worse than what he had already experienced. *On the Waterfront*'s Terry Malloy showed that a man can beat a mob if he is prepared to fight and suffer for his beliefs, because the mob mentality is fragmentary, and every piece which becomes dislodged diminishes its power.

'Fifties 'problem films' often focused on the problems generated by affluence to include the alienation of those sections of society who were either indifferent to, or largely excluded from, a rise in materialism. Adolescents, as we have seen, fell outside the net, and were swept away by the momentum of their own culture. Movies such as *The Wild One* (1953), *Rebel without a Cause* (1955) and *The Blackboard Jungle* (1955) portrayed youngsters as outcasts from mainstream establishment thought, resisting the efforts of society's 'persuaders' to take their turn on the treadmill.

Teenagers in the mid-'fifties experienced a level of autonomy which had not been possible for previous generations. As teenagers at the time realized, they were the first generation of young people who seized the opportunity to be different from their parents, but it was an act fraught with moral and psychological dangers.

Until the mid-'fifties, young people had modelled themselves on the previous generation. Fathers were the hero-figures of the next-generation fathers, and the fact that, by and large, young men were content to settle down with wives not dissimilar from their own mothers shows that the home environment was a powerful influence on the way that character and the aspirations of growing children were created.

The system worked as effectively as it did because parents and the establishment spoke with the same voice. If a young man collided with the law, he was in deep trouble at home, and if he was thrown out of school, both his parents and the law sided with the school authorities. There was nowhere to cut and run, other than outside society's perimeter fence.

The unfortunate knock-on effect of this within lower-income families had been a confinement of the potential of sons and daughters to roughly the limits and standards attained by their parents. Fathers who were professional and middle-class could by persuasion and example stimulate a taste for success in their children. Children growing up in rough districts within big cities had no obvious escape routes, so they had to look beyond their immediate families and environment for a worthwhile goal.

The youth revolution of the mid-'fifties provided just such a focal point for thousands of disaffected youths in low-income environments. It also expressed the universal desire of youth at all levels of American society to be recognized as individuals. Since the 'twenties, their raw energy had been diverted or diffused by

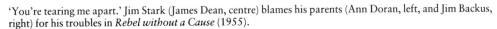

'You're tearing me apart.' Jim Stark (James Dean, centre) blames his parents (Ann Doran, left, and Jim Backus, right) for his troubles in *Rebel without a Cause* (1955).

one national crisis after another, such as the Depression, the War and its aftermath. By the mid-'fifties, America found itself with plenty of work, good wages, and no wars nor even rumblings of war to spoil the view ahead.

Despite this, rebellion and unruly behaviour were rife in schools. Kids already had spending power, thanks to rampant consumerism and its effects on wage packets. They were primed and ready to burst loose, and when rock 'n' roll, with its infectiously dismissive attitude towards adult conventions and morality, erupted in jukeboxes across America, the fuse was lit. It was still a decade or more before Kristoffersen would describe freedom as 'just another word for nothin' left to lose'. In 1955, the freedom to be oneself was all that mattered, the freedom to enjoy sex, to express individuality, to scorn the cant and the bullshit – these desires became routine expectations, and the elation provoked by the records of Elvis Presley and Bill Haley was symptomatic of a wider yearning for identity.

James Dean made an immediate impact with youth, and more than any other actor of his generation, even Brando, he influenced the way young people behaved and dressed. Teenagers of the 'fifties hungered for their own identity. Liberated by the growth in consumerism from the hardships their parents had known in the 'thirties, the boom of the post-war years had nevertheless been marred by political divisiveness and the spectre of an atomic holocaust just over the horizon.

Perceptive, literate young people on the campuses experienced a keen sense of betrayal at the shambles they were shortly going to be expected to inherit – a world of doubtful ethics, phoney respectability and vacillating leadership. Less perceptive youngsters, high-school drop-outs and the like, just wanted to raise hell and not think about tomorrow, and assumed, as a defensive skin, a collective bravado and swagger which on an individual level were in short supply.

Dean's appeal had a foot in both camps. To middle-class kids, he embodied the profound alienation, confusion and resentment over the controls which older generations, fresh from making an unholy mess of their own lives, wielded over theirs. Dire warnings about flunking exams, about pre-marital sex, about not behaving responsibly sounded hollow against the background of the adults' abysmal failure to establish social and communal values which young people could respect.

Impatient to be noticed for themselves but unsure about what lay hidden inside them, young people saw in James Dean a potent symbol for their uncertainties, their unformed desires. His anger, his bitterness and his corrosive distrust were emotions they could no more understand than the Dean movie characters could, but they could feel them. They were more real to them than the reality of living and of being thrust unwillingly into adult life in a highly complex, exhaustively competitive and potentially destructive techno-psychological age. Dean's awkward, inarticulate, volatile screen character touched a raw nerve at precisely the right time; its effect on his own generation, and on subsequent generations of young people all over the world, has been startling.

East of Eden (1954), his first major film, is the Adam-and-Eve Bible story transplanted into pre-'twenties California. The film revitalized interest in what is generally accepted to be one of Steinbeck's lesser novels, of which only the final segment was used. What the screenplay mercifully omitted was the earlier chunk of the Trask family history, where God-fearing ('trembling' might be a better word) Adam married a bundle of trouble named Kathy, who is seduced by Adam's swine of a brother, Charles, on her wedding night. Kathy later has twin sons, Cal and Aron (*vide* Cain and Abel), and the suggestion in the novel, which was perhaps thought too risqué for 1954 movie audiences, is that the twins were fathered separately.

The film takes up the story when the boys are in their late teens. Cal (James Dean) is the surly, decadent one, inwardly aching for affection from his dour, sanctimonious father, Adam (Raymond Massey). Aron (Richard Davlos) is his father's obvious favourite, diligent, neatly groomed, with a nice girlfriend, Abra (Julie Harris), with whom he expects to settle down. Aron, in fact, represents all the decent qualities which are lacking in Cal.

The model for misunderstood youth in the 'fifties: Cal Trask (James Dean) in *East of Eden* (1954).

The two boys have grown up believing their mother to be dead, because Adam cannot bring himself to disclose the truth that his wife, driven near-demented by the monotony of farm life and by her husband's cold, puritanical ways, wounded him with a gun and deserted the family while the twins were babies. Throughout the intervening years, she has run a thriving whorehouse at the nearby seaside town of Monterey. Even before he discovers that she is alive, Cal senses something of the wounded pride hiding behind his father's stern facade; he is desperate to establish a closer relationship with him, but there is no emotional meeting-point between them.

Adam dreams of freighting his lettuce crop to meal-tables in the east by means of refrigerated wagons. He sinks all his savings into the project, but the experiment flops and Adam is ruined. What is worse is that this mishap further erodes his status within the close-knit farming community. Cal sees a way to gain his father's affections by replacing, through a business venture of his own (financed by his wealthy mother), the cash which his father has lost. However, the deal which he strikes with an unscrupulous neighbouring farmer involves profiteering from World War I, and when Cal explains, with glowing pride, how the money has been earned, at a surprise birthday party which he has rigged in his father's honour, Adam is furious with him and spurns the gift.

Instead he rejoices in Aron's impromptu announcement of his engagement to Abra. After the careful planning and effort which have gone into the venture, this latest rejection hurts Cal deeply, and in a fit of jealous rage he lures Aron into Monterey to let him see their debauched mother, an experience which proves so catastrophic for Aron that he gets raving drunk, enlists in the army and goes off to active service in Europe, despite having been a committed pacifist until that fateful day.

Adam's futile attempt to remove Aron from the troop-train bound for the trenches ends with the old man collapsed on the station platform. With Adam bed-ridden, unable to flicker even an eyelid, Cal dispenses with the starchy nurse who has been keeping a grudging eye on him and settles down at his father's bedside, their reconciliation at last a probability.

Elia Kazan's thoughtful, probing study of a family in conflict depended on Dean's performance for its impact. He was the central character, and it was his relationships with the other three members of his family which mattered – given the wrong slant in any direction, the whole thing could have collapsed like a pack of cards, or worse still, turned out derisively unmoving. At the time of its release Dean was alive, though the sad facts of his early life, and the parallels between himself and the character of Cal – Dean's mother died when he was very young, and his relationship with his father was acrimonious – were unknown. One's original appreciation of the performance is therefore all the more valid because it is based on what one sees, and not on what one is subsequently able to read into it.

Kazan's interest in the story had been aroused initially by the painful and complex father-son relationship. With his finger quite shrewdly on the pulse of contemporary thinking, he elevated it to the central issue of the film, at the expense of some of the other relationships contained in the novel. Painful echoes of Kazan's own stormy relationship with his father surfaced during the making of the film. Like Dean, Kazan later admitted to knowing every feeling which the film aroused and expressed, and certainly no one can doubt its honesty and integrity. These qualities alone do not, of course, guarantee a good film, yet by any reckoning *East of Eden* is an exceptional film, with scarcely a scene which fails to work or which could be called superfluous.

Overnight, Dean became the patron saint of sad, inarticulate youngsters grown sick of parental put-downs. Cal is a logical outsider, excluded from the very beginning from the inner circle of the three A's – Adam, Aron and Abra. His intense pain and isolation after watching the young lovers cuddling in the ice-house provoke a senseless, enraged attack on his father's ice blocks, symbols of the barrier between them. Before the attack, Cal is photographed observing the lovers through a solid wall of ice.

The coldness motif is used frequently to illustrate the emotional wasteland stretching out before him, as when he rides on top of the train between Salinas and Monterey, struggling to keep himself warm by huddling, foetus-like, inside his sweater. The long, ill-lit corridor leading to his mother's room at the brothel symbolizes the chasm between them. His first attempts to bridge that gap are cruelly thwarted – she awakens from a snooze in her chair to find him on his knees in front of her, transfixed by her worn appearance, and summons a bouncer to throw him out, oblivious to his pitiful pleas to be allowed to stay and talk.

The camera remains fixed at the door, coldly, objectively witnessing his torment, as his frantic struggles to cling on to walls and waterpipes prove futile. Cal's next attempt to confront her is more successful, outside the bordello, on the hilly road from the bank which she visits each week. Tentatively, curiously, they search each other out, each sensing and being drawn to the other's loneliness. She agrees to lend him the money for the venture which will bale Adam out of his financial fix, and does it matter-of-factly, without emotion, unlike Cal's acceptance of the cheque and the intent way he watches her sign it, his whole world riding on that slip of paper.

Cal's self-consciousness with women is underlined by his obvious unease when they are around, but when Abra reveals her loveless childhood, in a delightful picnic lunch scene in the vegetable field, he is attracted to her little-girl honesty and warmth, and responds touchingly. Behind her cleverly designed plea for Cal to show more tolerance towards his father, one glimpses the dawning of a powerful sexual attraction. Through his shy smiles and playful manner, he, in turn, demonstrates a symbolic, though as yet unrealized, eagerness to supplant his brother in Abra's affections, by contentedly scoffing Aron's lunch while they talk.

Later, at the fairground, Abra is again sidetracked into a revealing interlude with Cal. They fool around among the sideshows, grimace into distorting mirrors, and ride a huge ferris wheel, in the contrived intimacy of which Abra's suppressed yearnings finally surface. Both aroused by and frightened of the truth about herself, the strength of her feelings for Cal and the discovery of Aron's shallowness, she surrenders long enough to participate in a brief, awkward kiss, dissolving immediately afterwards into stunned silence and a nagging sense of guilt.

In *Rebel without a Cause* (1955), Dean played Jim Stark (note, an anagram of Trask), a middle-class youth with a talent for attracting trouble. He is lonely and bored because every time there is an incident his parents sell up and move to another town, where his loneliness and boredom guarantee he will end up before long in another scrape.

At the start of the film, the Trask family have just arrived in a new town, and Jim is up to his old tricks, about to be hauled into the Juvenile Hall for being drunk and disorderly. At the police station, he encounters two other teenagers in trouble. Judy (Natalie Wood) has been arrested for streetwalking, but the underlying problem is a soured relationship with her father. His diffidence drives her into wild company, a tough school gang led by the flashy, self-preening Buzz (Corey Allen).

The trouble with Plato (Sal Mineo) is that he has no family with whom to have problems. His parents are divorced: his father is long gone and his mother permanently globetrotting, so the youngster is emotionally in limbo.

Teenagers Jim Stark (James Dean) and Judy (Natalie Wood) hide from their parents, and the school gang, in *Rebel without a Cause* (1955).

With the four central juveniles introduced, and their unhappy circumstances explained, the film moves on to show how their lives become inter-dependent during Jim's first day at Dawson High School. His rivalry with Buzz leads to the famous 'chicken-run', in which the youths drive stolen cars over the edge of a cliff, and the one who jumps to safety first is labelled a coward, a 'chicken'. The two arch-rivals grab a moment's calm together before their dice with death, their mutual animosity blunted by the danger which lies ahead. 'Why do we do this?' Jim wonders, peering down on to the jagged rocks at the foot of the cliff. Buzz's reply sums up the attitude of bored, thrill-hungry teenagers the world over – 'We have to do something!'

On the actual run, Buzz's sleeve gets fouled on the door handle, foiling his escape. Realizing that Buzz is dead in the wrecked car, the alarmed schoolkids take off in their own cars, leaving Jim, Judy and Plato alone on the cliff, staring disbelievingly at the twisted wreckage below.

Jim returns home, deeply agitated and confused, more desperate than ever for moral support from his parents. Once again they fail him badly, bickering feebly amongst themselves, fretting about what the neighbours will think, hostile to any suggestion that the police should be alerted. Disgusted with their spinelessness, Jim meets Judy and they head for a broken-down, deserted mansion in the Hollywood hills. They are joined by Plato, who shows up to warn them that the remnants of Buzz's gang are out for revenge, mistakenly believing that Jim has gone to the police.

The huge, empty house, lit only by candles, is the ideal fantasy home where they can pretend they are a real family, and enjoy the reassurance of physical nearness denied them by their weak, disapproving or uncaring parents. In one scene, all three are touching, Jim's head nestling in Judy's lap, and Plato's head, in turn, cradled contentedly in the crook of Jim's arm. Later, while the exhausted Plato sleeps on the ground, the other two explore the cavernous interior of the old dark house, unaware that the remains of the gang are closing in.

Plato puts up a spirited but one-sided fight when roused by them, and manages to escape clutching the jacket in which he had stuffed his mother's handgun. When they follow, he shoots and wounds one of them, and the others, brought sharply to their senses, take flight.

Observing the activity inside the abandoned house, a passing patrolman radios for help, suspecting a break-in. When he moves closer to take a look, the by now dangerously unstable Plato takes a shot at him and runs for cover into the college planetarium nearby. Jim and Judy follow, realizing that the only way to prevent further bloodshed is to disarm Plato. This they achieve by surreptitiously removing the bullets while Plato's attention is diverted, but the planned peaceful surrender is tragically bungled when a cop, spotting the now-harmless gun still in Plato's hands, misjudges his intentions.

Caught in the glare of police spotlights, Plato panics and runs, and is brought down by a police marksman. 'I got the bullets,' Jim screams amid the ensuing commotion, but it is too late to save Plato. 'The poor baby's got nobody, just nobody,' sobs his grief-stricken housekeeper, as Jim zips up the red jacket which Plato so badly wanted and an equally grief-stricken Judy replaces the shoe which Plato lost during his final, crazed dash for freedom.

Many of the film's most watchable moments are pure Deanery, hatched in collusion with director Nicholas Ray: the self-punishing, two-fisted attack on the police desk after his arrest; the sly explanatory glance he gives the Juvenile Division lieutenant after his father's placatory offer of a handful of cigars is turned down; Jim's tight, quick movements as he backs off from Buzz's challenge to fight with knives; rolling the cold milk bottle around his forehead back home after the chicken-run; the slow wounded-animal movements around Plato's body after the shooting.

All these touches add up to a remarkable, three-dimensional view of a character in acute distress. Nevertheless, by comparison, Jim Backus and Ann Doran as Jim's parents are both pathetic and chillingly plausible without ever once straying beyond their neat, cliché-ridden pigeon-holes; their one-dimensional characters represent the worst of matriarchal middle-class American society.

Jim's contempt, his near-loathing of them, is kept cleverly low-key, surfacing here and there as nothing more insidious than wry insolence, yet Jim leaves one in no doubt about his disgust at his mother's persistent emasculation of his father, and about his anger at the way his father permits it to happen. Everything in *Rebel without a Cause* is catalogued through Jim's consciousness. It is a Jim's-eye-view of the big, bad world, and this is what makes the images so potent, like Joey Starrett's vivid stocktake of good and evil in *Shane*. From where Jim stands, adults are uniformly inadequate, parading their myopia, their spinelessness, their narcissism like war decorations, and bitching endlessly among themselves about who knows best.

Adult perfidy is everywhere. Jim's problem is warring adults, and Judy's is stupid, needlessly hurtful parents. Plato has no parents at all, and lacks the emotional range that can make full-scale desertion bearable.

On a straight comparison, though bearing in mind it is Jim's viewpoint we see events from, the delinquents are practically models of good sense. Buzz's rivalry with Jim lacks personal animosity. It is the age-old ritual of defending one's territory against an intrusive male, but there is a strong kinship of like against unlike, the way, for instance, Johnny and Chino engaged in local rivalry in *The Wild One*, but were united against their common foes, authority and adulthood. Buzz's death robs Jim of a valuable friend, and his brief gesture of goodwill before they revved up the cars was, in effect, a death-bed confession of solidarity.

For Judy, too, the outer toughness is cosmetic, something to be applied before she leaves the house every morning to impress the other kids. Theirs is a world where reality and make-believe are interchangeable to suit the moment. They assume toughness for its protective shell, and act out fantasies which compensate for the happiness they lack. For example, in the deserted mansion, Jim, Judy and Plato pretend to be a family, but the game is such a poignant reminder to Plato that he has no family that he wishes Jim had been his father.

Thematically as well as structurally, *Rebel without a Cause* is a near cousin of Warner's pre-war crime movies, in which a three-cornered fight between the police, basically good gangsters (for example, Cagney in *The Roaring Twenties* and Robinson in *Brother Orchid*) and genuine dirty rats (Bogart in both the above films) usually ended up with the bad-bad guys obliterated, the good-bad guys in control of the middle ground, and the cops, too late and hampered by the rule-book to do anything, blundering in at the end with guns blazing.

In *Rebel without a Cause*, the adults and police form one group, Jim (and, to a lesser extent, Judy) is the good-bad guy trying to find the middle ground, while Buzz and the other delinquents, including Plato after his dangerous instability is established, are the bad-mad guys who have to be broken or removed before the middle ground can be claimed by its natural inheritors, Jim and Judy.

In American society, as in politics, middle ground is safe ground, and society functions best by consensus — that was the understanding which swept Eisenhower into the Oval Office in 1952. The violent deaths of Buzz, indirectly through his own reckless bravado, and Plato, through adult miscalculation, become milestones along Jim's painful road to self discovery. Like John Garfield throwing away his gun after weighing up the odds, Jim emerges from the night's ordeal a strong believer in social consensus. He is ready to abandon his strident idealism and move towards social rehabilitation, because rewards for holding out, as Garfield often discovered, are illusory, and one cannot escape from growing up simply by putting it off.

Cal (James Dean) is bookended by authority, in the shapes of Sam (Burl Ives, left) and Adam Trask (Raymond Massey) in *East of Eden* (1954).

In *Giant* (1955), Dean's third and final film, he was third-billed alongside Rock Hudson and Elizabeth Taylor, in a small but significant role of a surly ranch-hand who strikes it rich, and delights in rubbing his former employer's nose in the dirt. On a trip to Virginia to buy a thoroughbred horse, the handsome, rich Texan Bick Benedict (Hudson) falls in love with, and marries, Leslie (Elizabeth Taylor), the beautiful, wilful daughter of the wealthy family with whom he stays.

Unfortunately for the young bride, she is not forewarned about the awfulness of life back on his hot, barren Texas pile. Virginia was cool and green, and the people, even those with money, had some spark of humanity. By contrast, she finds Texas empty, hostile and phobia-ridden.

After the accidental death of Bick's domineering sister, her will reveals that a thin wedge of the Reata land has been bequeathed to the surly ranch-hand Jet Rink (Dean). Jet, who has never owned anything in his life, resists all overtures to sell the land back to the Benedict estate. It is his, and he is going to turn it into oil-dollars, he says. And, sure enough, though it takes several years to coax it out of the ground, Jet does strike oil, and his stubbornness pays off handsomely.

Now the contest between Bick Benedict and Jet has become equal in terms of material resources *and* determination.

Soon it is Jet's shadow, characterized by the grimy figure who could not wait to taunt Bick the moment oil gushed from his patch of scrubland, that is falling across everything of Bick's, instead of the other way round. As Jet gets richer and more powerful, Bick's antiquated rancher attitude becomes anachronistic even to Jordy (Dennis Hopper), his only son and logical heir, who prefers studying medicine to messing around with cows.

At the end, Jet drunkenly reveals to no one in particular the reason why the hatred between himself and Bick is so deep-rooted – it is because of Leslie, whom Jet has loved and admired since they got to know one another all those years before. Surrounded by all the wealth and power a man can have, he is still denied the one thing he wants above all else, and it is destroying him.

One marvellous scene shows Bick and his lawyers anxiously trying to buy back the piece of land Jet has inherited from Bick's sister. They reason it all out with him, emphasizing the advantages to him of selling it back to them, wheedling and cajoling and feigning goodwill while Jet vacantly twirls a lariat. He might look a dumb ol' boy but he has the situation sized up fairly well. He has no intention of making a cash settlement – he just lets them drone on for his own amusement, and then, at the end, leaves them with the nearest they will get to an affable smile. It is the smile on the face of a mountain goat who has just watched a couple of tawny cats eat each other in the dark by mistake.

The film contained some interesting contrasts – the burly Hudson and the wiry Dean; Jet's tiny plot of land set in a vast expanse of prairie; Jet's black oily handprint on the white pillars of the house at Reata; the extravagant lifestyles of the affluent ranchers and the squalid, no-hope existence of their Mexican workers. But the film was too long and too undisciplined for Dean to have the same impact as in his two earlier films, and Dean himself succumbed to boredom during its making.

He scene-steals with furtive glee, never missing a trick or a mannerism which will capture the attention, and the innate cruelty of his attitude towards his co-stars is augmented by their helplessness to stop him. His performance is practically a text-book for camera-hoggers. While others are talking, he fiddles with his hat, ducks his head under a water-tap, plays with a lariat, stares at his boots, shuffles his feet or giggles nervously. Only Carroll Baker, in the smallish role of Leslie's daughter during the second half of the film, manages to fend him off. But then they had been fellow-students at the famous Actors' Studio in New York in 1952, so Carroll had picked up a few useful tricks herself.

Director George Stevens was no admirer of Dean's feisty attitude on the set, but he was profoundly impressed by Dean's qualities as an actor. According to Carroll Baker, Stevens kept the cameras rolling for two and half days on her big scene with Dean, where Jet drunkenly proposes marriage.

Sitting at a table, Dean attempts to manoeuvre the scene his way, lolling back and forth, stirring his drink, coughing, toying with his sunglasses (although it takes place indoors during a thunder-storm) and deliberately forcing the audience to watch him while Carroll is talking. But she responds intuitively to the situation, using a rose from the table decoration as a metaphoric sabre to cut him down to size.

A couple of days after completing his role in *Giant*, Dean died in a car crash en route to a race meeting where he was scheduled to drive his new $6,000 Porsche Spyder. The hysteria and exploitation which followed his death meant a dispassionate assessment of him as an actor and innovator had to be postponed. Even now, it is difficult to judge where the myth begins and the reality ends. The truth seems to be that Dean approached his film roles as nothing more than a logical extension of his theatre experience. He could not suspect that he would have such a short time to prove himself, or that for reasons not specifically connected with his acting but arising directly from that short, rebellious life, he would pass into history as the patron saint (or possibly sinner) of disaffected youth.

Had he lived, it might have been a vastly different James Dean whom we would now be discussing. The potency of his rebel image could have been damaged by later events, obscured by too much success and wealth. By dying young, Dean never betrayed either the promise he showed as a brilliant, intuitive actor, or the generation for whom he spoke. He never demanded millions of dollars for tedious, meritless performances in over-dressed movies, the way Marlon Brando, his one-time idol, did. Neither did he fade slowly and grotesquely before his fans' disbelieving eyes the way Elvis Presley did.

In all his three films, but most effectively in the first two, the painful, passionate search for identity obscures everything else, and since he died before answers could be found, before the conflicts could be reconciled, the search goes on, unresolvable, eternal, yet as fresh, tantalizing and disturbing as it was all those years ago.

Billy Bonney (Paul Newman) disarms the opposition in *The Left-handed Gun* (1957).

CHAPTER EIGHT

CREAM AND OTHER BASTARDS

*P*aul Newman is associated more closely with the 'sixties, the decade which gave him his best roles, than the previous one. Nevertheless, his artistic origins were steeped in the Method, and when James Dean died he became the natural inheritor of Dean's rebel crown.

Unlike Dean, whose iconoclasm all too often had neither cause nor purpose, Newman represented the ambitious side of raising hell. His characters had an overpowering drive to have more than they started out with, and it was a drive which fanned out in many directions, lured onwards by the promise of wealth or sex or power. In *Sweet Bird of Youth* (1959), he has a line which is practically a Newman character reference: 'Only cream and bastards rise!'

The repressive atmosphere of the 'fifties really did create the widespread feeling that ruthlessness was a necessary, if not a key, ingredient, alongside guts and ambition, to achieve success. As the decade progressed and the spectre of McCarthy faded, Americans began to live with the notion that Russia might want to co-exist peacefully. Suspicions of Soviet motives were countered by a growing confidence that their leaders could handle any crisis. Stalin's death in 1953 plunged Russia into a mood of uncertainty which further reduced its likelihood of taking on America.

In 1955, Bulganin and Krushchev, the two Russian leaders who had succeeded Stalin, met the American president in Austria to put their signatures on a peace treaty, and optimism rose even higher, helped in no small way by the contrasting physical appearance of B and K, as they were amusingly tagged by Western correspondents. Neither could be described as visions of terror: Bulganin with his academic's goatee beard and Krushchev looking for all the world like an over-the-hill wrestler.

While it lasted, the Red scare had given America something to worry about at a time when its economic strength seemed to be sweeping social inequality to one side. The War had made America stronger than any nation in the world, and that strength had been converted into more employment, better wages, better working conditions and a real sense of prosperity throughout the industrial heartland of the country. Inequality in some regions was still appalling, mainly in the non-industrial South and in areas of high ethnic migration.

Elsewhere, millions of ordinary Americans were encouraged to work towards, or if they had already gone a way up the ladder, to regard themselves as, middle-class. Factory parking lots gleamed with shiny automobiles. As prosperity increased, so did the top income-tax levels, but at 90 per cent it was a far cry from the days during the 'thirties when 54 per cent was considered outrageous. Consequently, the after-tax incomes of low-wage earners rose faster than those in middle- and high-income categories, which created a fairer distribution of the nation's wealth.

The elimination of class was not, of course, a realizable ideal, yet the illusion that equality was attainable was good for national morale, and one which found equal favour among bosses and unions, liberals and conservatives. It was particularly popular with the media, who saw the alleviation of inter-class antagonism as a key to the establishment of a fair society.

Utopianism, however, with its socialist overtones, tends to frighten capitalists and entrepreneurs to death, and the desire to beat the hell out of everybody in sight remained as strong as it had been during the Yukon gold rush. Far from making everyone feel relaxed and contented about the general rise in living standards, oddly enough the mood of apprehension and the desire to get ahead of the pack became intensified.

People on the upward spiral took themselves and their appearance very seriously. Advertisements for toothpaste and deodorant warned of the consequences of not having a 'winning' smile or smelling good, that is, lost promotion opportunities and sexual and social ostracism. The pursuit of money, possessions and the glamorous lifestyle which went with being a member of the board of a thriving corporation was all-important. People were encouraged to emulate the American dream, wherein the guts and the determination to succeed could diminish every obstacle in their path. They were also encouraged to believe that a man of humble origins need not be deterred from striving to reach the top because he stood as good a chance as anyone as long as his attitude was positive and he had a clear head for heights.

The films of the 'fifties were similarly preoccupied with individuals triumphing against heavy odds, defending their rights or seeing off the competition. Many of the conflicts depicted were to do with rivalry within the organization, disputing the ownership of land or settling arguments about who was top dog among the gangsters. The success motif reached across all genres.

In *Al Capone* (1955), for instance, the gangland killings result from one faction trying to take over the territory of another. *Shane* (1953) and *Jubal* (1954) were only two of dozens of westerns in which men killed each other over land rights. The conflict in *The Quiet Man* (1955) was over a wedding dowry, while in *Not as a Stranger* (1955) an unscrupulous medical student marries a well-to-do nurse in order to fund his studies. Power, its pursuit and its corrosive effects on both those who wield it and those who suffer through it, are starkly exposed in *The Sweet Smell of Success* (1959), in which an egocentric gossip columnist tortures and finally destroys a slick press agent who gets enmeshed in his domestic problems.

Paul Newman epitomized the 'fifties go-getter who dreams of reaching the top but is held back, and often ultimately thwarted, by a morbidly stubborn instinct for self-destruction. Only the substitution of honest goals and a rediscovery of the character's finer instincts save him from disaster. Newman was redeemable, but never without a fight, for his desire to be top dog clashed with his conscience.

In this, Newman succinctly represented both sides of the great moral arguments of the period. The twin goals of power and materialism still beckoned alluringly. The individual with precious little sees the attainment of more as a logical objective, and envies those who stop at nothing to win. But once attained, success has its other side, too, and a price has to be paid for this in terms of happiness lost.

Newman's characters revelled in waging war within themselves, on the one hand selfish and ruthless in their pursuit of power and sexual rewards, whilst on the other wearing an inner stray-dog humanity which made them interesting. In certain obvious ways, Newman represented the accepted traditional Hollywood values of glamour, wealth and power, yet he also stood for the opposite view, that a man's merit should be judged by qualities other than his material possessions, social stature or physical beauty.

He could, of course, afford to take the latter view because he had what made up the former in impressive doses, or so, at least, numerous critics of Newman have been heard to say. The cross-over between Newman the screen character – and despite the variations in pitch and performance a Newman character recognizably exists – and Newman the man has been obscured by what one suspects is a cunning camouflage to keep the punters at a safe distance. His known aversion to signing autographs, apparently triggered off by being asked to sign a piece of paper in a public toilet at a time when, understandably, neither hand was free to honour the request, seems petty when weighed against the pleasure it gives. But it is a Newman rule and is applied unequivocally.

As a rebel character, the early Newman is more closely related to Garfield's wild-boy-off-the-rails than either Brando or Dean. Garfield could play misunderstood nice guys, but he was also an arrogant heel with a murderous temper, and accompanying the character's unpredictability was a real whiff of meanness. Newman was colder and more calculating than either Brando or Dean and had no conscience about trampling on others, especially women, to get where he wanted.

The struggle for the central character's soul, which was in essence what most of Garfield's films had been about, was paralleled more closely in the early screen work of Newman than in that of any other actor of the 'fifties or 'sixties. Despite this, his début film *The Silver Chalice* (1955), at precisely the time Dean died, and the obvious influence of the Method in his early work, associate him more closely with the Brando-Dean image than with that of Garfield. His second film, *Somebody Up There Likes Me* (1956), the rough-and-tumble biopic of post-war middleweight champion Rocky Graziano, was originally scheduled for Dean, and it is clear, with hindsight, that the role was about as right for Newman as it would have been disastrously wrong for Dean. Graziano was an extrovert hoodlum-turned-slugger-turned-honourable-champion, the kind of part – indeed, the kind of man – which Garfield had been all his life.

Coincidentally, though it must have been known to Newman at the time, Brando had used the real-life Graziano as his model for Terry Malloy in *On the Waterfront*, so that he was forced into giving a vivid Brandoesque performance as Graziano. Later, he was heard to complain, 'When is someone going to say Brando reminds them of *me*?' By coming along after Brando, and giving, in his first performance of merit, a near-as-hell simulation of Terry Malloy, Newman crystallized an identification in the public's mind between the two of them which has proved impossible to shift.

Somebody Up There Likes Me begins with an incongruous title song by Perry Como, full of lush Hollywood strings, as the cameras fix on the grubby slums of New York. In a sleazy gym, a has-been boxer is thumping a leather glove into his young son's tearful face. The kid is Rocco Barbello, whose refusal to hit back angers his father enough to make him really punch him. As Rocco races into the arms of a policeman after breaking a window, the cop mutters to his partner, 'Ten years from now, he'll be in the death house at Sing Sing.'

The prediction is not so far off-target. Running wild with tenement street gangs, Rocco (Paul Newman is sent to correction centres, reform schools and prison with hardly a break in between to catch his breath. Sentencing him to reform school, one judge says hopefully, 'Maybe they will be able to break his spirit', to which Rocco replies defiantly, 'We'll see whose spirit gets broke!'

Rocco's attitude to life is summed up neatly to the governor just before he is despatched to somewhere tougher: 'There ain't no place I can't lick.' His release from prison in 1942 coincides with the Army draft, but Rocco is a problem soldier. On his first morning, ignoring the reveille call, he sleeps until eleven and then floors the corporal who suggests he ought to pick up a discarded cigarette butt. This leads to a wigging from the CO, and Rocco, further incensed by being tagged a 'wiseguy' dumps the captain on his can, too.

On the run, he remembers a one-time prison pal who mentions a New York boxing gym where he might find 'quick dough' for the services of his equally quick fists. But after several fights, under the assumed name Rocky Graziano, the Army picks him up, and he ends up with a dishonourable discharge plus a year in Leavenworth Jail for absenteeism.

But salvation is around the corner for Rocky. A successful boxing career follows his release from Leavenworth, and guided by an astute manager (Everett Sloane) and the calming influence of a fragile sweetheart (Pier Angeli) he battles on until he is champion of the world. His newfound legitimacy and hard work are duly rewarded, while his past mistakes are joyously forgiven.

Somebody Up There Likes Me is a socially conscious film whose obvious antecedents are the 'thirties gangster films. Newman's Rocky and Cagney's Rocky in

Angels with Dirty Faces (1938) have identical backgrounds, share the same immigrant pugnaciousness necessary for survival, and practically share the same fate – it is pointed out that several of Graziano's contemporaries ended up in Death Row. Graziano is saved because his fists take him to the top of the stinking pile, and the crossover to upright citizen – in the ring, no one was more upright – is just a short step once the inner conflicts created by poverty and a bad father/son relationship are resolved by success and the admiration of the crowd.

Rocky is a good-bad guy who suppresses his basic instincts in order to be 'somebody'. He continually puts his aggression to useful purpose, like sticking up for his weaker buddy against prison-yard bullies. He is loyal to his friends and refuses to rat on his enemies even though the price of silence is the removal of his legitimate livelihood. Also he treats women with respect. In other words, the redeemability of Rocky is never in doubt, because even in trouble he has a basic honesty and integrity.

The film, of course, makes a strong effort to take Graziano's side. His dishonourable discharge from the Army is made to seem almost as if it is the military's fault, and later, when newspaper accounts of the event appear, we are invited, somewhat sanctimoniously, to share Rocky's outrage.

Dispirited boxing champ Rocky Graziano (Paul Newman) faces a charge of desertion from the US Army in *Somebody Up There Likes Me* (1956). Manager Irving Cohen (Everett Sloane, left) and street pal Romolo (Sal Mineo, right) commiserate as rookie MP (Robert Duvall, in an early role) makes the arrest.

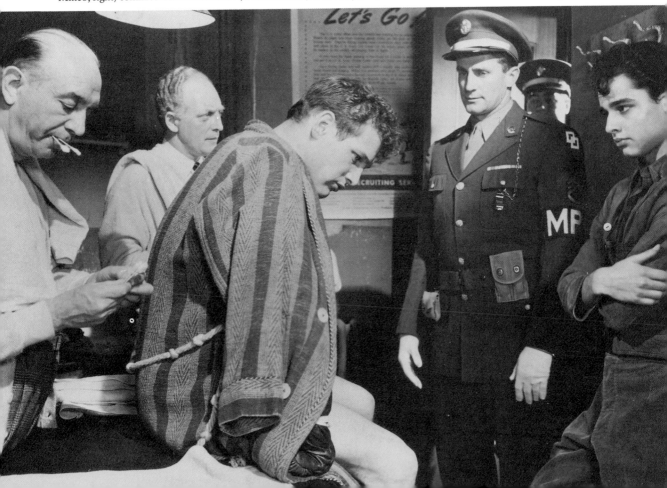

The romance between Rocky and Norma is pure corn, but Newman carries it off manfully as, one after the other, sweet nothings freeze on his tongue because love and tenderness are alien to him. His hunched, hands-in-pockets walk, his helplessness with words which contrasts with his lion-hearted ring performances – these factors, in addition to the physical prowess and demeanour of a fighter (which Garfield did not have in *Body and Soul*), make it a memorable performance. What James Dean would have made of it remains an intriguing question.

Rocky is saved because his willingness to be a good citizen, that is, to function inside society, is stronger in the end than his desire to self-destruct. He had to become a successful boxer before the burdens which prevented him becoming a successful human being were lifted, in much the same way that Miller in *The Blackboard Jungle* had to see a way forward out of the ghetto before he stepped into line.

Here, again, society is shown to be tolerant and ever willing to forgive – at least, to forgive a winner – and it is Rocky's refusal to mend his ways, not society's indifference, which keeps him on the outside for so long. At the end he is rewarded with a world championship, a sweet little wife, an adoring family and the adulation of his neighbourhood, whose swarms of thieves and muggers gladly forgo their night's takings for the thrill of listening to the fight commentary. Subscribers to the theory that a nobody could become somebody simply by trying devilish hard could not have had their case put more vividly, or endearingly. All that was missing was the President trotting down the White House steps to shake Rocky's hand, to the accompaniment of the Boston Symphony Orchestra.

In sharp contrast, *The Left-handed Gun*, a psychological western with Newman as Billy the Kid, the law, that is society, is as ham-fisted and intransigent as those who oppose it and in the straight fight between them the casualties are high.

Billy encounters a friendly rancher, Turnstall (Colin Keith-Johnston), who is taking his herd into New Mexico. The two strike up a friendship on the trail, during which Turnstall, a gritty Scotsman, encourages Billy to learn to read and to respect the teachings of the Bible. Turnstall is a peace-loving man who forbids the drovers to wear guns. In considerable awe of his benefactor, Billy obeys without a murmur, but when Turnstall is ambushed and killed by rivals hiding behind the law, Billy is unable to pursue them because his gun is hidden in one of the wagons.

The identity of the four bushwhackers is not difficult to discover, and with the backing of two more of Turnstall's men Billy begins his dispassionate mission of revenge. None of the targets has a chance against him, and the law seems powerless to stop him despite the fact that two of Turnstall's murderers were lawmen.

Hiding out in Mexico, Billy becomes acquainted with Pat Garrett (John Dehner), a sombre ex-marshal who has quit law enforcement to get married and live within the law-abiding Mexican village community. Invited to Garrett's wedding, Billy arrives with his buddies in high spirits and respects Garrett's appeal not to start any trouble, but while posing for a photograph Billy spots the only surviving member of the group who killed Tunstall.

Instinctively, he goes for his gun and the town square erupts with gunfire and panic as the townsfolk scatter for cover. Outraged, Garrett vows revenge. He accepts the townspeople's offer to become their sheriff and heads the posse which eventually corners Billy. It is Garrett himself who shoots the fugitive dead, though afterwards he is stricken with remorse for having done so.

As westerns go, the action on *The Left-handed Gun* is rather restrained, leaving lots of time for studying the manic-depressive Billy as he drifts from one crisis to another. Newman's taut, brooding performance suggests a man on the fringes of insanity, impulsively playful one moment and capable of a cold-blooded killing the next. All of Billy's instincts are negative in *The Left-handed Gun*, as Rocky's were for the first half of *Somebody Up There Likes Me*, but there is no way out for Billy after killing his fourth victim in front of Garrett, who, apart from his personal animosity towards Billy, is a stickler for justice and cannot allow the killing to go unpunished, especially when he had heard the victim declare his innocence in the Turnstall murder.

The Left-handed Gun is a difficult film to analyse, because it rests on shifting sand and Billy is villainous or virtuous depending on one's perspective. Turnstall's death is cold-blooded murder, and had Billy been able to gun down the killers at the scene of the killing, presumably he would not have had a price on his head. Killing them afterwards, one at a time, does not change the moral argument, so Garrett's determination to kill him seems even rougher justice than that which Billy hands out.

Politically, the film seems to adopt a right-wing stance. Billy is left-handed, for which we can read left-minded. The murder of Turnstall is arranged to protect the stability of local beef-market prices, and to protect the economy on which the town survives. Dumping large quantities of beef on to communities already struggling to balance their books parallels the Russians' way of coercing small neighbouring countries by choking their economies with gift supplies.

Billy's response to Turnstall's death, like his behaviour on other occasions, is irrational and self-destructive. Friendships, other than his loyalty to the dead Turnstall, mean nothing and the revenge motif cripples his mind. Garrett revenges the revenged, as implacable in his mission as Billy was in his, and as motivated as Turnstall's killers had been, by an identical desire to preserve the status quo. They did not want their economy turned on its head by unwanted beef. Garrett does not want the peaceful Mexican community in which he has chosen to settle down disturbed by Billy's brand of violence. Garrett wants him out of the way because he is too vivid a reminder of Garrett's own violent past, and because that past can never be forgotten while Billy lives.

The homosexual undercurrents in Billy's character in *The Left-handed Gun* were tastefully camouflaged because homosexuality was not considered a subject for the screen in the mid-'fifties, though it had been hinted at in a discreet nudge-nudge manner in films such as *The Maltese Falcon* (1941) and *Strangers on a Train* (1951). *Tea and Sympathy* (1956) depicted a sensitive schoolboy (John Kerr) being cured of his effeminacy by a tactful housemaster's wife (Deborah Kerr, no relation), an awkward little stage play which was unsensationally handled in the screen version by director Vincente Minnelli.

Back in the 'thirties, the implicit lesbianism of Lillian Hellman's stage play *The Children's Hour* was removed when it became the basis for *These Three* (1936). The film escaped Hays Office censure by converting the love affair between two female teachers into a story in which one of them steals the other's fiancé. A 1962 remake under its original title in the USA and as *The Loudest Whisper* in the UK reintroduced the lesbian theme but failed through inept casting.

The playwright Tennessee Williams, himself homosexual, had several plays featuring homosexual themes made into films. *Cat on a Hot Tin Roof* (1958) was a powerful Southern-family drama centred on the last days of rich tycoon Big Daddy Pollitt (Burl Ives), who is terminally ill but from whom the bad news has been purposely withheld. Among those who have been let into the secret are his wife, Big Mama (Judith Anderson), his eldest son Goober (Jack Carson) and buxom, fertile daughter-in-law Mae (Madeleine Sherwood).

Also staying at the mansion are his younger son Brick (Paul Newman) and his wife Maggie (Elizabeth Taylor), who have arrived to help celebrate Big Daddy's sixty-fifth birthday, an event which the old man evidently loathes. The film charts the progress of two major conflicts. The first is the classic sibling rivalry for Big Daddy's affections and, since he is dying, over his fortune. Secondly, Brick is fighting against nervous collapse and alcoholism following the recent suicide of Skipper, a sportsman with whom he had become infatuated.

At first he refuses to fight back, preferring instead to wallow in drunken self-pity and to blame himself for Skipper's death. Nothing which the seductive Maggie can suggest or flaunt can compensate for the loss of Skipper. 'I'm on a hot tin roof,' she complains, to which Brick's solemn advice is 'Jump off, Maggie, jump off!' He wants nothing more to do with her because he suspects that in breaking Skipper's sexual interest in him, by seducing Skipper, she inadvertently broke his spirit and thus led to his suicide.

Realizing that Goober is being manipulated by his scheming wife to soften up Big Daddy into handing over to them Brick's share of the fortune – in which Brick, incidentally, has no interest – Maggie decides to do a little scheming of her own. She lies to Big Daddy about being pregnant, which brings an immediate denunciation from Mae who insists that she can hear Maggie's pleas for love every night through the thin walls that separate their respective bedrooms.

The commotion has brought Brick back from his self-imposed exile upstairs, and overhearing his wife being humiliated by Mae in front of the others makes him realize that they are both being destroyed by his obsession for Skipper. Yes, he declares, Maggie is pregnant, and the reason Mae did not overhear them is because not everyone makes love as noisily as his sister-in-law. All that is left to do, once Mae's angry protests have been silenced by a born-again Goober, is for Brick to convert Maggie's claim that she is pregnant into reality, and this, as the credits roll, he appears to have every intention of doing.

It was entirely consistent with Newman's playing of the character, to which he had clearly devoted much thought and preparation, that Brick should be infatuated with another man whilst remaining indifferent to his sexy wife. It was a stunning demonstration of sexual ambivalence, matched blow for blow by Elizabeth Taylor's feline aggression as she strives – unsuccessfully for nine-tenths of the film – to arouse the tiger in his tank. Yet despite the sultry Southern atmosphere and the booze-sodden invective, Newman manages to give Brick a refreshing innocence, as if the relationship with Skipper were more on the lines of Butch's affection for Sundance than Oscar Wilde's hunger for Lord Alfred.

Brick was a long way from Marty, the dreary Italian-American butcher who dreams of love and escape in *Marty* (1953), and from the doomed George Eastman in *A Place in the Sun* (1951), yet each in his own way personified the 'fifties male, awkward, uncertain and guilt-ridden. In Britain, kitchen-sink drama made the theatre come alive to ordinariness in a way which would have been impossible for the likes of Noel Coward and Ivor Novello. Rock 'n' roll made ordinary youngsters stars overnight. The emphasis was not only on youth but on the ordinariness of

Drink to me only. Brick (Paul Newman) needs booze and a crutch for support in *Cat on a Hot Tin Roof* (1958). Big Daddy (Burl Ives) clearly disapproves.

youth, and the fact that being ordinary was no longer something of which to be ashamed.

The sexual timidity of Marty, who is afraid to kiss his girl in case she is offended, matches the self-consciousness of Cal in *East of Eden* (1954) when he is alone on the fairground wheel with Abra. Sexually timid, indeed deprived, males were very much the norm in 'fifties movies, from the moonstruck Marty to the catastrophic Richard Sherman (Tom Ewell) in *The Seven-year Itch* (1955), who discovers a blonde bombshell (Marilyn Monroe) living upstairs after wife and kids are conveniently packed off on vacation. Sherman's agony is palpable as he dreams up excuses to visit her apartment, and when he glimpses her knickers as she warms herself over a subway warm air grille (a situation recently revived in *The Woman in Red*, [1984]) his guilt complexes ruin the enjoyment.

Post-adolescent timidity was a feature of all Elvis Presley movies, and most obvious in the early ones, such as *Loving You* (1957) and *Jailhouse Rock* (1958). *Loving You* is practically the singer's own biography, in which his own dirt-bowl origins were transformed by the sudden rise to record and movie stardom. Deke Rivers (Presley) is an orphan who has borrowed the name from a gravestone in his favourite churchyard. Listening to a touring hillbilly band, he is snatched from the crowd by the band's wily promoter Glenda Markle (Lizabeth Scott) and offered a chance to sing. He causes an immediate sensation.

Scott puts him under contract, dresses him up in hillbilly clothes and gives him the star vocal spot in the band, and the barnstorming style which put the real Elvis ahead of all the competition brings him rapid fame. As Presley's biographers have pointed out, in grim detail, success is not without its difficulties, and the unfortunate Deke has, to paraphrase one of the movie's many musical hits, 'a lotta livin' to do' before he can swallow the liberal doses of hype and bullshit which go hand-in-hand with music stardom.

In a juke-box joint, where Deke is enjoying a quiet night out with one of the band, he is first of all menaced by a fan's boyfriend into singing 'Mean Woman Blues' and then clobbered because of the effect it has on her. When crusty adults try to outlaw his swivel-hip movements, Deke is genuinely confused by all the fuss. It is something which happens naturally when he sings, he says. In the end, he goes on TV to demonstrate that there is no harm in wearing out one's denims from the inside. And having won the argument he quits the business to take up with sweet farmgirl Susan Jessup (Dolores Hart), who has been waiting patiently in the background for Deke to come to his senses.

The contrast between Deke's raunchy singing style and his backstage innocence is one of the more intriguing aspects of the film, and, indeed, forms another parallel with Elvis's real life — until, that is, later in his career, drugs, sycophancy and boredom wrought its deadly toll. In *Loving You*, Deke addresses every woman over the age of 25 as 'Ma'am', and keeps his hands to himself. While the girls go into a frenzy in front of him, Deke is thinking about apple pies.

Interesting, too, is the two-tier romance which became a feature of many Elvis films, in which a virginal young thing and an 'older', more worldly, woman compete for his attentions. Lizabeth Scott's scheming Svengali-like press agent was the equivalent of the gang-moll of the film noir period, a dame who means trouble. She already has one broken marriage and an emasculated hanger-on husband (Wendell Corey). When she sees that Deke is taking too big a shine to Susan, Glenda connives at her dismissal. But purity wins in the end, and Glenda has to settle for the washed-up old bandleader she dumped during better times.

The older woman has a rougher deal in *King Creole* (1958). Ronnie (Carolyn Jones) is a sad-faced gangster's moll who is regularly slapped around by her boss Maxie Fields (Walter Matthau) and insulted by his henchmen. Danny Fisher (Presley) moonlights as a waiter at Fields' nightclub when school is out, and gets his chance to sing at the club. As well as infuriating his school authorities and entertaining the mob, he runs wild with a street gang, diverting the attention of his victims with some good ol' singin' while their pockets are being picked.

For Dolores Hart, cast again in *King Creole* as the whiter-than-white popsie who takes Elvis's fancy, it was business as usual. She plays Nellie, a shopgirl who cottons on to the fact that the other members of the gang are robbing the store while all eyes are on Danny singing 'Lover Doll'. Again the emphasis – for the benefit of the fans – is on the purity of their relationship, despite Danny's shady gangland associates. When an attempted robbery of the drug-store where Danny's father (Dean Jagger) works ends with the old man getting badly hurt, Danny turns the screw on the mobsters, but in disposing of the thug who attacked his father Danny is badly hurt. Ronnie helps him get away, but their hideout is discovered and she dies shielding him from Fields' gunfire, leaving him free to take up again with Nellie after the Fields bunch have been safely accounted for.

Though *The Graduate* (1967) is an influential 'sixties movie, its hero's agonizing, post-adolescence timidity belongs to the earlier decade. In *The Graduate*, Benjamin Braddock (Dustin Hoffman) experiences both the anxiety and the woman-handling from a bored, middle-aged sexpot, Mrs Robinson (Anne Bancroft), a friend of the Braddock family suffocating within the gloss-and-glitter of middle-class Californian society.

For Benjamin, an over-suckled adolescent newly home from college and nail-biting over his future, the fawning attitude of parents and friends alike embarrasses him acutely. After a party at his house, he is cajoled into driving the predatory, hard-drinking Mrs Robinson to her home, where, in the absence of her husband, she makes no secret of her lustful feelings towards Benjamin, who is both excited and appalled by her behaviour.

Complications arise when Ben is railroaded into dating her daughter Elaine (Katherine Ross), much to the older woman's (jealous) fury. He becomes persona non grata when the romance takes off, and for a while it seems that her obstructive attitude will ruin the relationship. Ben is increasingly desperate to prevent Elaine from marrying a plummy college kid aborts the hastily arranged wedding ceremony with only seconds to spare. In the end they make their getaway to a new life together by forcing their way aboard an old people's excursion bus, Elaine still in the wedding dress she was wearing when Ben crashlanded the church and abducted her.

The Graduate is also interesting for the perspective it gives on how the 'sixties' new-look leading men were developing. Hoffman was refreshingly different from the brawny, self-assured heroes of earlier times. He padded through life with an air of fazed exasperation, repulsed by the phoney middle-class values and the double standards of adults. Mrs Robinson was quite happy to have him as her lover so long as he recognized that her daughter was off-limits, a condition of their relationship which he abides by until his love for Elaine overwhelms all other considerations.

Love proves to be both his social undoing and his salvation. His climactic swoop on the wedding ceremony and triumphant abduction of Elaine are his most positive accomplishments in life, in comparison with, for example, his fumbling attempts at a hotel-room seduction of Mrs Robinson earlier in the film, and the way he allows himself to be lionized and at the same time humiliatingly brow-beaten by his awful parents. Ben becomes a man because the alternative is to lose everything, including his self-respect, and for 'sixties heroes, self-respect came high, sometimes highest of all, among their priorities.

Self-respect was important, but often proved elusive, to many of the controversial characters played by Paul Newman during the 'sixties. The good, awkward guys like Benjamin proved the exception rather than the rule in socially-alert productions of this decade. For the most part, it was the cream and the bastards who made the running, with Newman up among the stars who were forcing the pace. In *The Hustler* (1961), Eddie Felson (Newman) earns the nickname 'Fast Eddie' because of the speed and accuracy of his cue action at the pool table.

He is a vain, amoral character who cheats suckers in pool-halls, letting them win the opening challenges until the stakes rise; then, when the big money is placed, he cleans up. Away from the pool table, his life is desolate until he encounters the lonely, crippled Sarah Packard (Piper Laurie) at an all-night restaurant. A mutual attraction based on the emotional emptiness of their lives keeps them together long enough for Sarah's dependence upon him to grow to dangerous proportions. When he finally deserts her, the way he earlier deserted his small-time manager Charlie (Myron McCormick), her shame and despair become unbearable and she kills herself.

A ruthless gambler, Bert Gordon (George C. Scott), sees there is a fortune to be made out of Eddie's pool-room talents, and arranges a series of upmarket competitions which lead to a showdown with the best pool-player on the circuit, Minnesota Fats (Jackie Gleason). Eddie has lost to Minnesota in a previous encounter, but now he is fired with hate for himself, for Gordon and for the mistakes he has made which cost him his friendship with Charlie and caused Sarah's death.

The contest is toughly fought, but Eddie forges ahead, wiping the slate clean with

'Fast' Eddie Felson (Paul Newman) in a tight spot in *The Hustler* (1961).

Gordon, whom he bitterly denounces after winning. With his future as a pool-player jeopardized by his break with Gordon, Eddie hits the road back to nowhere, to more grimy pool-rooms where, one suspects, he will continue to hustle for small wages, and risk back-alley beatings from the suckers he has fleeced should his identity be discovered.

The Hustler is a grim film to watch, with everyone in it – apart from Minnesota Fats, who takes everything in his smooth, pampered, tomcat stride – corrupt or lame in some way. Eddie's jungle world is no place for a weakling, as the tragic Sarah discovers. It is a jungle in which Eddie finds, somewhat too late, that all victories lead to defeat, and that success is forever illusory. He ends up on top of the pile, but none of it has any meaning, for on the way up he has destroyed the only things which might have given it value – his relationships with people who cared for him, and who needed him badly.

Hud (1963) was Eddie Felson in a Texan hat, the unfeeling, no-good son (again Newman) of Homer Bannon (Melvyn Douglas), a wealthy cattleman. Hud's main interests are womanizing and dodging his responsibilities at the ranch. Everyone is fair game to Hud, even the decent but world-weary housekeeper Alma (Patricia

123

Neal, in Oscar-winning form), on whom he forces his drunken attentions one night.

Alma's protector on that occasion is Hud's teenage nephew Lon (Brandon de Wilde), who while idolizing his feckless uncle draws the line at attempted rape. When one of the Bannon cattle is found to have foot-and-mouth disease, Homer and Hud clash over what to do next – Hud wants to hush it up and sell the entire herd as quickly as possible, despite the danger of sparking off a major epidemic. Homer insists on co-operating with the government inspector (Whit Bissell), who has no option but condemn the herd. The physical destruction of his life's work, carried out under his dignified orders, proves too much for the old man, and shortly afterwards he collapses and dies.

At the end, Hud has nothing but shattered dreams to comfort him. Alma has been driven away by his boorish behaviour, and Lon, no longer starry-eyed or under Hud's influence, decides to make his future elsewhere. But as he contemplates his future, and uncaps another beer can, Hud is sourly unrepentant: 'There's so much crap in this world, you're going to wallow in it sooner or later,' he tells the departing Lon.

In an intriguing harkback to 'fifties motivation, Hud's lack of feeling is ascribed to a motherless childhood. 'My Momma loved me, but she died,' he declares after returning home drunk to a scathing denunciation of his evil ways from his stern-faced father. But everything else is uncompromisingly 'sixties in feel and flavour, including the graphically depicted assault of Alma, which took the permissive cinema an important step forward.

Hud portrays the conflict between old, honour-bound ideas and the new, scornful, fast-lane attitudes of youth. Hud was to Homer's olde-worlde idealism what John F. Kennedy was to Eisenhower's consensus politics. Hud might just have gone on to create another Bannon dynasty – he certainly had the brains and the audacity for it. Kennedy, too, had brains and audacity, and the dynasty was ready-made and breathing fire, but unlike Hud he was accountable to a hidebound Congress and to a political party similarly steeped in Homer Bannon-style traditions. For example, Kennedy's proposal to establish a health service for the old was vetoed, along with his plans to increase dramatically the funds available for improvements to the education system. But there were also other than domestic problems to be dealt with. There was the U2 spy flight incident involving Gary Powers in 1960. The Berlin Wall caused consternation and alarm. So, too, did Fidel Castro's overthrow of the evil Batista regime in Cuba in 1959. This was not because Batista was admired in the United States but because Krushchev supported Castro, and Castro's victory added a Soviet perspective to the already volatile politics of the Caribbean.

However, the two other issues which dominated the 'sixties were the growing demand for black civil rights and America's deepening involvement in the Vietnam War. Blacks represented around 15 per cent of the American population. At the beginning of the twentieth century, around 90 per cent of all American Negroes lived in the South, but the massive migration to northern industrialized cities such as

Detroit, and Chicago during the 'twenties and 'thirties, had shifted this balance so dramatically that by 1960 only 60 per cent – a reduction of approximately one-third – continued to reside in the South.

The position of the black minority in the South had not been helped by the centuries-old tradition of slavery. Southern-based white reactionaries bitterly opposed Kennedy's steam-roller tactics to combat discrimination. In the North, progress towards racial equality of a kind had been more visible. For one thing, the blacks were better organized, and for another, the comparatively small numbers of them posed less of a threat to the white majority. But in the South the segregation mentality still ruled, and was not going to disappear on the say-so of a smart Massachusetts politician who had suddenly got too lucky for his own good. Ironically, it was Kennedy's keenness to boost his image in the South during the run-up to the 1964 election which persuaded him to visit Dallas, Texas in November 1963.

The growing controversy over black civil rights spilled over into the cinema of the 'sixties, and whilst many of the resulting films which gave black actors meatier roles were a direct reaction to the mood of the Americans generally, Hollywood was responsible for at least part of the initiative. Prior to the mid-'fifties, either the colour question was ignored in films, or Negroes were depicted as humiliating stereotypes. Occasionally, in a musical, a black performer would demonstrate a particular talent, for example, Bill 'Bojangles' Robinson or Lena Horne, but mostly it was a case of fixing on the superficial smile to take somebody's coat or pour a drink.

Dooley Wilson's Sam in *Casablanca* was the exception rather than the rule, a character whose influence on the hero, and on the film, was significant. So, too, was Canada Lee's washed up Negro boxer Ben Chaplin in *Body and Soul* (1948), who is manoeuvred by an unscrupulous promoter into a defence of his title despite suffering brain damage. His opponent, Charlie Davis (John Garfield), knocks him senseless and becomes the promoter's new golden boy, unaware of either Ben's medical problem or of the true nature of the racket he is getting into.

Davis's boyhood pal and long-time manager Shorty (Joseph Pevney) tries to warn him about the mob and is silenced. It finally takes Ben's death to turn Davis against the racketeers who own him, literally, body and soul, and by refusing to take a dive when ordered, he makes himself a target for their hit squads. Sickened by the ugliness and the corruption of the big-time boxing game, Davis quits as champion, and is unfazed by the threatened day of reckoning. 'What're you gonna do, kill me? Everybody dies!' he sneers at the furious promoter.

During the 'fifties actors like Sidney Poitier were given the chance to be people instead of black people. A key movie, and Poitier's first important screen role, was *The Blackboard Jungle* (1955). In this film Poitier was a delinquent first and a black character second. This was an important breakthrough because it put a black character on the screen on a par with Jim Stark in *Rebel without a Cause*, and made his actions more important than his colour. It is no longer necessary to think of

Gregory Miller, the character Poitier played in *The Blackboard Jungle,* in terms of race any more than one is consciously reminded throughout *Rebel without a Cause* that Jim is white.

In *The Blackboard Jungle* (1955) Miller is a hell-raising black boy from the ghetto who hates school and controls the classroom in opposition to new teacher Rick Dadier (Glenn Ford). Miller's sidekick is the deranged, subnormal West (Vic Morrow), living proof that the advice which Dadier gets on his first day from an older teacher – 'never turn your back on the class' – is justified.

Together Miller and West represent a solid coalition against the forces of authority. Dadier's teaching style is conciliatory, he refrains from cracking heads when missiles fly at him, he believes in teaching by consensus, which the kids take to be evidence of weakness. Dadier is the Juvenile Division officer of *Rebel without a Cause* with an English degree and a sense of vocation, both bizarrely misplaced at this seat of learning. From their first encounter, the kids have the upper hand; it is their jungle and Dadier has just dropped in from a posh uptown school where the lawns and the exercise books were both neatly tended. He is ignorant of the way the jungle works, and of the danger staring at him from those uninterested, wild and apparently mindless goons slouched at their desks.

In teaching terms, Dadier favours the middle ground, debunking anything which sounds like 'fight-fire-with-fire' conservatism as being outmoded, or worse still, counter-productive, because the kids get clobbered far too much at home and on the streets as it is. According to Dadier, they get so damn much of it, more will simply have no effect. Likewise, he rejects the tame approach of another teacher (Richard Kiley), whose efforts to introduce culture into their tatty lives, by giving them an earful of good jazz from his own prized record collection, ends with the unruly class smashing his discs and behaving like animals.

Dadier is no softie, but he wants to be liked, and this means weeding out the real enemies in the class, who also happen to be the worst enemies of the class because they inhibit the process of education which is the only true ally these youngsters will have in the outside world. Miller and West form an implacable alliance, but Miller is shrewd and articulate behind the dumb insolence, whereas West is a crude moron without a grain of decent feeling; they are allies through circumstance, not by choice.

As with *Rebel without a Cause,* the process of splintering Miller from the ugly little group of which he is the natural leader begins to show up the discord between himself and West. Dadier plays up to those leadership qualities, and strikes the responsive chord he was hoping for – Miller's chip-on-the-shoulder begins to disappear as the promise of scrambling out of the ghetto and being something more than a two-bit mechanic, his original ambition, take hold.

As Miller moves towards Dadier's middle ground, West goes the opposite way, piling on the non-cooperation and terrorizing Dadier's pregnant wife. West has to be purged before the middle ground can become habitable again, in the same way that the unfortunate Plato had to die in *Rebel without a Cause* before Jim could grow up.

When Dadier finally moves against West, the powerful Miller-West double act is in shreds. Also, the other pupils have by now had time to pass a favourable judgement on Dadier, so that whilst their loyalty to the Miller-West coalition may be unquestioning, there is no longer any certainty that they will canter down the road to ruin on West's say-so.

In the eventual confrontation, West mistakenly believes he has the class in his pocket, but Miller comes down hard on Dadier's side, by whacking someone who tries to attack Dadier from behind. He, in turn, is assisted by another black youth who is not going to stand by and watch a blood-brother poleaxed by any white trash. The new commonsense coalition of Dadier and Miller wins the remaining hearts and minds, and West is assisted on his way to jail by several willing pairs of hands.

In *The Defiant Ones* (1959), Poitier plays Noah Cullen, a Negro on a chain gang, who escapes with a bigoted white fellow prisoner, 'Joker' Jackson (Tony Curtis), when the prison van they are being transported in overturns. Despite being chained together, they manage to elude their pursuers, hiding in wet undergrowth and crossing swollen rivers. When Cullen nearly drowns in some rapids and Jackson saves him, the black man's expression of thanks is angrily rebuffed. 'I didn't pull you out — I just stopped you pulling me in,' snorts Jackson.

With the police hot on their trail, and continuously menaced by the people they encounter (at one point they narrowly escape being lynched) their mutual hate and distrust mellows gradually into a grudging respect. Either they survive together or not at all — that is the horrible truth on which their wafer-thin tolerance of each other exists.

When a conniving woman latches on to Jackson, removes the chains which tie the two convicts, and tries to murder Cullen by leading him, on the pretext of showing him an escape route, towards some quicksands, Jackson realizes what is going on and rescues Cullen from certain death, this time offering no glib excuse for his actions. Continuing on their way, Jackson falls ill, leaving Cullen with the choice of deserting him or jeopardizing his own chances of freedom.

In the end, Cullen sticks with the ailing Jackson, and with their last-ditch chance of leaping aboard a freight train thwarted because Jackson is too weak to make the jump, Cullen settles down to nurse his sick buddy until the police arrive.

This was the first film in which the white and black sides of the racial divide were almost equally balanced. Tolerance, we learn, is a bilateral arrangement, and only when it is reciprocated has prejudice a chance of being licked.

Had *The Defiant Ones* been a post-Civil Rights movie of the 'sixties, it would still have been commendable and courageous, but unexceptional. The fact that it was made at a time when Hollywood chose to remain silent about the black question, afraid to risk upsetting ten million Southern whites, certainly makes it remarkable. Sidney Poitier is probably the only black actor who could have got away with playing the role, and the performance he gave has never been bettered.

Southern sheriff Bill Gillespie (Rod Steiger, right) makes certain that visiting Northern cop Virgil Tibbs (Sidney Poitier) catches his train home on time at the end of *In the Heat of the Night* (1967).

As Poitier's career developed, he distanced himself more and more from roles which were ostensibly black in the way they were written. In *The Bedford Incident* (1965), for example, there is no reference to race at all. But sensing that he might have alienated many of his black audiences by appearing to shrug off his colour, he returned to strongly anti-racist roles in *In the Heat of the Night* (1967) and *Guess Who's Coming to Dinner?* (1967).

In the Heat of the Night dumps a black policeman into the steamy South in the middle of a murder investigation – *Coogan's Bluff* in Tennessee Williams-land. Lieutenant Virgil Tibbs (Poitier) is minding his own business in a deserted railway station late at night in a small Mississippi town when he is arrested by a sneering deputy (Warren Oates). An influential white man has been killed, and Tibbs is fitted for the crime – until he reveals to the redneck sheriff Gillespie (Rod Steiger) that he, too, is a cop.

The two form an uneasy relationship. Tibbs stays on to help Gillespie solve the mystery, and Gillespie, whose respect for the law is stronger than his dislike of

Negroes, obligingly rescues Tibbs from a savage beating by three racist thugs. At the end of the film, Tibbs is back at the railway station where he was arrested, but with a more sanguine view of Southern justice, while Gillespie grudgingly concedes that Tibbs is okay. It is not in any way a reconciliation of attitudes. Tibbs leaves with the same anger about the harsh treatment of blacks in the South that he felt when he was on the receiving end of it at the start of the movie, and Gillespie has not shifted a metre towards softening his prejudice. This is where the strength of the film lies, by making each man remain true to his beliefs.

Guess Who's Coming to Dinner? should have been a 'fifties musical, with Doris Day as the daughter who wants to marry a black Nobel prizewinner, played by Sammy Davis Jr, and Jay C. Flippen as the outraged father croaking soliloquies when his prejudices ran into overdrive. Louis Armstrong could have been added to croak the narrative – the way he did, quite unnecessarily, in *High Society* (1955) – possibly revealing, at the end, that he was really the groom's father, which would immediately reconcile everyone and they could all jitterbug happily to the maestro's cornet as the titles rolled.

Instead, what happened was a desperately serious attempt to put over a turgid anti-racist message, with Spencer Tracy and Katharine Hepburn as the stuffy white parents, and Sidney Poitier as the prospective son-in-law. There was not a tune in sight, nor much realism either, as Tracy and Hepburn woodenly, and predictably, come around to the idea that having a Nobel prizewinner in the family has its compensations. *Guess Who's Coming to Dinner?* is a film of lost opportunities. Why could the black boy have not been a garage mechanic or a fugitive from Attica, that is, someone who might have really tested the fibre of the white middle-class family's bigotry? Why could the Tracy character not have been a real inflexible schmuck whom no amount of cajoling would have changed? Why did the producers not study a modest British movie called *Flame in the Streets* (1961) in which John Mills as a tub-thumping union official has an identical problem which he resolves with a lot more credibility?

The difficulty about making films about blacks is that there is only one Sidney Poitier, and busy bee though he is, he cannot be everywhere. In the past, other black actors have shown potential, such as Billy Dee Williams, Roscoe Lee Browne, Al Freeman, Calvin Lockhart, Richard Roundtree, James Earl Jones, Jim Brown and O. J. Simpson, and more recently Richard Pryor and Eddie Murphy, but nobody rings the box office chimes like Sidney and it is a real problem for the film-makers.

At the tail end of the 'sixties , it looked as if a black movie industry – films written by blacks about blacks and starring blacks – might get off the ground. This meant that black people were not only sharing power behind and in front of the cameras, but having a real part to play in the decision-making. The signs began to look encouraging when films like *Sounder* (1972) and *Lady Sings the Blues* (1972) became surprise box-office successes. *Cotton Comes to Harlem* (1969), directed by Ossie Davis – who played the black military prisoner who goes off his head and dies

129

in Sidney Lumet's *The Hill* (1965) – had Raymond St Jacques and Godfrey Cambridge as two amiable detectives taking on the law to snatch a cotton bale containing stolen money. Calvin Lockhart and Cleavon Little also appeared, and it was the first ever box-office success by a black director.

Davis was narrowly beaten to the starting gate on a life story of Billie Holliday. His *Gordon's War* (1973), a sociological drama about a returned Vietnamese veteran who declares war on the drug dealers responsible for his wife's death, was observant but unsuccessful. *Shaft* (1971) ushered in black tough-guy movies, memorable as much for the pulsating score by Isaac Hayes as for Richard Roundtree's performance as the James Bond black-alike. It was a case of anything Bond could do Shaft could do cleaner, and it made enough money to propagate a couple of sequels, *Shaft's Big Score* (1972) and *Shaft in Africa* (1973).

The hero – if that's the word – of Mel Brooks' *Blazing Saddles* (1974), a so-so western spoof, is Bart (Cleavon Little), a black railroad worker elevated to town sheriff because no one else will take the job. As he is about to be hanged when the job offer is made, his acceptance is a formality, but the task awaiting him is formidable. Aided by the Waco Kid (Gene Wilder), an ex-alcoholic gunfighter (shades of *Rio Bravo* here), he faces the threat of a marauding gang of outlaws clustering in the nearby hills. Stumped for inspiration, he begs the townsfolk for 24 hours to work out a defence plan, but his appeal gets an angry thumbs-down – they want to be saved there and then!

'You'd do it for Randolph Scott!' he reminds them, and thus chastened by having their double standards rammed down their throats, they relent; the sheriff saves them by constructing a replica town nearby and filling it with cardboard cut-out townspeople, which entirely fools the robbers.

Watermelon Man (1970) offered the satirical idea of an insurance salesman with a strong streak of racial prejudice waking up one morning to discover that his skin has changed colour overnight. He is now as black as Godfrey Cambridge. His horror is palpable as first he tries to scrub it off, and later finds no respite from a world which evidently delights in his discomfort. Even the innocent habit of a dawn jog takes on a sinister perspective. As a white man no one took any notice, but when he starts jogging as a black man he is promptly arrested. *Landlord* (1970), with Diana Sands, Lee Grant and Beau Bridges, was the story of a wealthy white kid who buys a Brooklyn tenement and becomes involved with his black tenants. Underrated at the time, the film has belatedly acquired a measure of status.

The success of *Lady Sings the Blues* (1972) encouraged several other biopics about black personalities, including *Leadbelly* (1975) with Roger E. Mosely as the famous twelve-string guitar player who spent seven years on a chain gang for murder. *Cool-hand Luke* never had it so bad. *Greased Lightning* (1977) charted the career of one-time Virginia moonshiner Wendell Scott (Richard Pryor), who became a champion stock car racer, the first black racer, in fact, to surmount the colour bar in that most Southern of all sports, jalopy-racing. Another black sporting giant

Police lieutenant Tibbs (Sidney Poitier, left) finds himself fighting racism as well as lawbreakers in *In the Heat of the Night* (1967).

resurrected for the screen was boxer Jack Johnson, in the enigmatically named *The Great White Hope* (1970), with James Earl Jones as the broody champion and Jane Alexander as his white girlfriend, the cause of much bitter controversy.

California Suite (1978) is four separate stories about hotel residents enjoying a holiday, or splitting up, or staying over during Academy Awards night. Two excitable black doctors, Panama (Bill Cosby) and Gump (Richard Pryor), and their wives are vacationing, but the trip is a disaster. They have forgotten to book and have to tolerate deplorable conditions. Needling and up-staging each other all along the way, they finally revert to fisticuffs with moderately amusing results.

In recent times, Eddie Murphy's *Beverly Hills Cop* (1984) has broken a few box office records, but the sad truth is that the black movie industry has currently faded to near-nothing, and its sociological influence, regrettably in an area where the need for constructive dialogue has never been greater, was absolutely nil.

Ratzo (Dustin Hoffman, left) and Joe Buck (Jon Voight) say hello to hard times in
Midnight Cowboy (1969).

CHAPTER NINE

YOUTHANASIA

*U*nlike their 'fifties counterparts, 'sixties youth possessed a strong sense of self; and the acutely repressive atmosphere which had curtailed both cultural and spiritual self-expression among young people in the 'fifties had vanished. The youth movement of the 'sixties was shattering in its impact, and far-reaching in its effects. 'Fifties rebels could, and did, take aim at any number of false gods – but they encountered the heavy hand of conformity everywhere. The problem for 'fifties protesters had been that protest was new, and had therefore been sporadic and disorganized. It took until the mid-'sixties for protest to come of age, to become articulate and to be in with a fighting chance of affecting society.

In America by the mid-'sixties, youth was involved in the nation's politics to a far greater extent than ever before. Protest had been muted during the Kennedy years because Kennedy had restored a fair measure of confidence, but after his death, Lyndon Johnson was a prosaic and unglamorous replacement, with none of the buccaneering spirit of JFK. Gerald Ford was accident-prone and Richard Nixon was already, in liberal eyes, discredited for his pro-McCarthy activities. Young people saw the gap opening yet wider between their expectations of the kind of society they wanted and that which the politicians, legislators and the multi-national corporations were creating.

What the Watts and Berkeley University riots and, later, the anti-Vietnam protests added up to were, in effect, attempts by groups of angry young people to obstruct what they saw as a series of attacks on individual freedoms. For them, protest went far beyond growing their hair long, wearing freaky clothes or smoking pot. It was their way of disassociating themselves from the way society was being steered, or being manipulated, for the sake of narrow, vested interests.

The cinema of the 'sixties underwent more change, and embraced a greater variety of controversial themes, than that of any previous decade. It began the decade prudishly, and ended it orgiastically. In between, many sacred cows went to the slaughterhouse, and new ideas swept in to fill the void. Uncharacteristically, much of the new thinking had its source in Britain and the cinema there went through one of its best renaissance periods since Alexander Korda's pre-War days.

The mood had been prompted by John Osborne's *Look Back in Anger*, first staged at London's Royal Court Theatre in 1956. In it, a 'fifties smart-ass, echoing in many respects – or disrespects – the early Brando model, raves against the Establishment and the awfulness of his life. It was strong stuff for the genteel theatre audiences of the 'fifties. Its influence was soon felt in the literature of the day and writers echoing this theme, including John Braine, Colin Wilson and Alan Sillitoe, soon became household names.

Room at the Top (1959), the film version of Braine's no-nonsense novel, is about an amoral social-climber from the Yorkshire dales who uses his good looks and ambition to get ahead. This film set the tone for several other Northern-based heel-as-hero films, most notably *Saturday Night and Sunday Morning* (1961), *A Kind of Loving* (1962) and *This Sporting Life* (1963). Albert Finney, Alan Bates and Richard Harris starred respectively, and all became famous overnight.

Alfie (1966) was a London variation on the same theme. With the Swinging 'Sixties by then at its height, and London the centre of 'sixties fashion and music, its handsome Cockney star Michael Caine could hardly fail to become a major attraction. Caine's impish, tongue-in-cheek portrayal makes the character a lot more acceptable than he was written in Bill Naughton's novel. His eventual comeuppance – a fate shared with many of Paul Newman's unscrupulous characters – though richly deserved, is a hollow victory for morality.

Biologically, at least until the Pill came to her aid, there was not a lot that a woman could do to improve her lot as portrayed in films. In this respect British films of the immediate pre-Pill era such as *Room at the Top*, *Saturday Night and Sunday Morning*, *A Kind of Loving* and *Alfie* – and some Hollywood ones, too, such as *Love with the Proper Stranger* (1963) – were, at least, honest in their portrayal of who stood to get the worst deal when pregnancy resulted.

For women generally the liberating effects of the Pill were enormous. Female passivity in sexual relationships gave way to new dimensions of desire and experimentation. For those who sought it, women had suddenly acquired the means to become the predators, and, more importantly, the ones who now more frequently took the initiative to end a relationship when it either became unsatisfactory to them, or had served its purpose.

Openly asserting their new-found freedoms, girls smoked pot, burnt their bras and hoisted their hemlines. The mini-skirt had a much deeper social and sexual implication than the transient fashion it was. For one thing, it told male chauvinism where to get off in no uncertain language. Women could be proud of their bodies, and of their sexuality, and egged on by the popular media a new, exciting generation of women appeared – Jean Shrimpton, Twiggy, Julie Christie and Sandie Shaw among them – modish creatures, often from working-class environments. Yet despite their everyday names they were dazzling.

From 1960 onwards, female roles in American movies went through a bad patch. This was partly the response of male-orientated Hollywood to the threat of feminism. The gains which feminism had clocked up in other segments of the entertainment media never happened in the movies. Apart from the handful of female superstars like Barbra Streisand and Jane Fonda who possessed the talent, the guts and the tenacity to reach and remain at the top, women were worse off in films of the 'sixties and 'seventies than they had been for several decades.

For example, cruelty to women has traditionally been depicted as a brutal crime, and audiences were spared the shocking detail. When Howard da Silva uncoiled his whip in *Unconquered* (1947) and prepared to flog the delectable Paulette Goddard, the audience hissed its disapproval. But far from denting their popularity, movie heroes like Clint Eastwood and Lee Marvin boosted their box-office ratings by treating women like dirt, and showing everything which happened in graphic detail. Male audiences loved every minute of it, which seems to endorse the view that from 1960 onwards young men were floored by an epidemic of sexual inadequacy, and that watching their favourite macho men in action was the best tonic on the market for their condition.

That they did not have far to go, or long to wait between doses, suggests that Hollywood shared its audience's fears that feminism might get out of hand. War movies had always been a male-society stronghold, but before the Pill women in war dramas fared rather well. In *From Here to Eternity* (1953) both Deborah Kerr and Donna Reed had strong romantic roles, and their involvement affected in a fundamental way the tragic course of events. British films such as *The Way to the Stars* (1945) and *A Town Like Alice* (1956) were as much love stories as war dramas. But 1960 changed all that. *The Long and the Short and the Tall* (1960), *The Longest Day* (1962), *The Great Escape* (1962), *Battle of the Bulge* (1965) and *The Hill* (1965) represent just a snatch of the war film titles screened during the 1960s which reduced the level of female participation to mere observation.

The only time they seemed to have some passing relevance was when someone found a reason to shoot them. Even superstars of the calibre of Sophia Loren were expendable – in *Operation Crossbow* (1965), as an innocent Italian mother married to a Dutch engineer, she is shot to prevent Allied plans for raiding the underground V-bomb factories being passed on to the enemy. The hapless Loren is caught up in it all by some ghastly mistake. Gia Scala suffers a similar fate in *The Guns of Navarone* (1961), though she deserves it for having betrayed the Allied assault team to the Gestapo.

In *The Dirty Dozen* (1967), the twelve criminals all have some redeeming feature, except Private Maggott (Telly Savalas), who believes that all women are sluts. Offered the chance to knife one during the raid on the German chateau, he delivers a sneering sermon before slitting her stomach. The shower sequence in Hitchcock's *Psycho* (1960) deserves its reputation as one of the most shocking scenes in screen history, but the knife assault contains a rape motif which actually excites – and that was exactly what Hitchcock had in mind.

No such subtleties intrude in *A Clockwork Orange* (1971), in which the Cat Lady

(Miriam Karlin) and Mrs Alexander (Adrienne Corri) both die as a result of injuries incurred during violent rape attacks. The film is crammed with grotesque anti-feminist images, from the nymphets who while away Alex's dull afternoons, to the sculptured furniture – life-size naked girls in Kama Sutra postures – in the Droog's favourite soda joint, where even the drinks are dispensed from flabby, tit-shaped containers.

Nudity on the screen, banned before 1960, had become commonplace before 1970, though male stars neither volunteered, nor were expected, to remove their underpants however torrid the love scene. Sean Connery as James Bond and Clint Eastwood as Harry Callaghan emerged as the great, super-cool heroes, whose selfish, gratification-seeking conduct and callous disregard for women was seen by many as a panic reaction to the spread of feminism.

'Who are those guys?' Fugitive robbers Butch Cassidy (Paul Newman, left) and the Sundance Kid (Robert Redford) have problems shaking off the posse in *Butch Cassidy and the Sundance Kid* (1969).

136

Emasculation was the ultimate male nightmare of the 'sixties. Male buddy movies removed that threat by relegating the female role in the affair – and quite often the male relationship assumed the spirit and the texture of an affair – to a sideline position. She needed to be around to reaffirm the heroes' heterosexuality – Katherine Ross's schoolmarm role in *Butch Cassidy and the Sundance Kid* (1969) is a classic example of this – and with that function fulfilled, had little else to do.

Butch and Sundance's wry personalities and the humorous digs at western lore kept the film in a high gear. In scores of westerns, the hero sneaks up on the bad men's horses, unties them all from the hitching rail and stampedes them simply by waving his hat. When Butch tries it, no amount of yelling and fluttering his arms has any effect. The nags stare at him bewilderedly and refuse to budge.

Midnight Cowboy (1969) was a male buddy film with nostalgic western undertones. Its hero, Joe Buck (Jon Voight), is a modern cowboy freak who dresses in fringed buckskin and flexes his muscles in front of a poster of Paul Newman as Hud. He quits his job as a dish-washer in a dead-end Texas town and travels to New York in search of the good life. All that he encounters is poverty, discomfort, rip-offs and Ratzo (Dustin Hoffman), a terminally ill conman who both adopts and feeds off Joe.

The film's strength lies in its characterizations, and the gritty realism which director John Schlesinger manages to inject into the scenes. The rotten core behind Manhattan's gloss finally makes Joe decide to take his tubercular buddy to the fresh air and clear skies of Florida, but Ratzo dies on the bus shortly before they reach their destination. Joe is left cradling his friend's dead body in his arms – a genuinely moving moment which studiously and unerringly avoids being sentimental.

Male buddy movies were usually saddled with thin storylines, so, in the main, their saving grace was the characterizations. *Butch Cassidy and the Sundance Kid* and *Midnight Cowboy* were poles apart thematically, yet their central characters were distinctive and human, due to excellent performances and realistic dialogue. In most male buddy films, the characters are what matter: Burt Reynolds and Jon Voight in *Deliverance* (1972); Walter Matthau and Jack Lemmon in *The Odd Couple* (1968) and *The Fortune Cookie* (1966); Lee Marvin and Jack Palance in *Monte Walsh* (1970); Marvin, again with Paul Newman, in *Pocket Money* (1973); Newman and Robert Redford in *The Sting* (1973); Gene Hackman and Burt Reynolds in *Lucky Lady* (1975); Hackman and James Coburn in *Bite the Bullet* (1975); John Cassavetes, Peter Falk and Ben Gazzara in *Husbands* (1970) are among the male buddy titles which spring to mind immediately.

Hot on the heels of the male buddy movies – at the box office, at any rate – were the male enemy films, which pitted two stars of equal drawing power against each other, and whose bitter rivalry usually climaxed in a violent trial of strength. A number of early male buddy films, for example *Boom Town* (1939) with Clark Gable and Spencer Tracy, and *Wild Harvest* (1947) with Alan Ladd and Robert Preston, had an interlude in the middle of the film in which the male protagonists are at odds with each other. In both these films, the buddies fall out and become deadly rivals because of a woman, but old enmities vanish when a much bigger threat to their existence appears on the horizon. Interestingly, in most male buddy films where a woman sparks off the trouble, she appears to be not up to much, and the conflicts are resolved, often after a fight, when common sense is restored.

The genuine male enemy films offered no simple resolution, and though a woman might be caught up in the conflict – as in *Prime Cut* (1972), for example – the hatred was more likely to be based on some unsettled score which ran deeper than sexual rivalry.

A recurring theme, one which was behind many of the most watchable movies of the 'sixties, was the fight by an individual either to preserve or to regain his personal rights against heavy odds. Whereas during the 'forties and 'fifties the largely omnipotent forces which harassed the individual, usually making him back off, were for the most part unidentified – you could make of them what you wanted – by the 'sixties, they bore the distinctive labels of higher authority, for example, politicians, police, military, big business and organized crime.

James Bond was a powerful cypher, but nothing more, of the omnipotence of the State in running the affairs of society. He exhibited neither spiritual nor moral sensitivity, and never questioned the wider implications of his actions. He was simply a robotic extension of the advanced gadgetry put into his hands by the people who controlled him. Beautiful girls meant nothing. They were simply bodies to be enjoyed and discarded. Even the humour he exhibited was black, mostly cynical throwaway comments as he doled out death to those in his path.

Sex is the dominating feature of the Bond movies. Apart from the numerous flurries of action, Bond spends his time either having sex or setting up the next encounter. The dames he lays mostly have names that go with being laid – what, for instance could be more explicit than Miss Pussy Galore or Miss Plenty O'Toole? His enemies know where to hurt him, too. When the wily Goldfinger wishes to extract answers from him, a deadly laser device is harnessed to split him up the middle commencing with his male tackle. Not surprisingly, the unflappable James gets hot under the collar as, helplessly, he watches the beam advance on up between his legs.

If Bond and his numerous imitators provided reassurance for males whose sexuality was under threat, they provided even greater reassurance that those who ran the country were up to the task of looking after the security and welfare of ordinary folk. Backed by superior technical wizardry, and the inexhaustible resources of the State, Bond represented the machinery of government at its most terrifying. There was never any suggestion that he was either unique or alone as a secret agent – the number '007' implied that there were others equally proficient, equally dedicated to the cause, ready to pack a toothbrush alongside the Smith & Wesson and jet off to some tropical paradise to tweak the Russians' whiskers – a conveyor-belt of resourceful Jerries, in fact, willing at a moment's notice to put the boot into any number of KGB Toms.

Civilized man *versus* the elements. It is no weekend picnic for, left to right, Bobby (Ned Beatty), Ed (Jon Voight), Drew (Ronny Cox) or Lewis (Burt Reynolds, far right) in *Deliverance* (1972). The body is that of an attacker (Billy McKinney) whom Lewis has killed in self-defence.

Bond owed his original popularity on the screen, in America in particular, to the Cold War intensifying during the 'sixties. The U2 spy flights, Kennedy's blockade of Cuba, the Russian crackdown on Czechoslovakia, all added to the distrust that people had of the Russians. It was easy to believe that they had a massive spy network working ceaselessly to cripple and subvert the free world. Bond was a reaction to all that, a superman armed to the teeth with slick gadgets, final proof of the omnipotence of the State.

Indirectly, of course, Bond was also telling us how futile it was to either resist or oppose the State, whose access to finance was unlimited, whose control of technology and weapons was infinite and who could blitz all before it, as its faithful instrument James Bond did, without batting an eyelid. The State existed to preserve our freedoms, but it also had a duty to keep us in line, that is, salvation through coercion. To fail to recognize the hype about the all-powerful, unstoppable organization that was working for us was to miss the whole point of the Bond films.

No criticism was ever made of the fact that Bond used gangster methods to achieve his goals. The parallel here between fiction and fact is quite interesting. During the 'sixties and 'seventies, a remarkable coalition developed between organized crime and the US Government. President Kennedy's assassination was widely supposed to have been the result of a right-wing conspiracy using highly-trained hit-men. The elimination of his brother Robert in California during the run-up to the 1968 presidential campaign, the unsolved disappearance of powerful union boss Jimmy Hoffa (who had been Robert Kennedy's prime target in a series of acrimonious Senate hearings to investigate Hoffa's links with organized crime), and the assassination of Martin Luther King have also given rise to a flood of conspiracy theories.

Systematic murders of black and white militants have been more widespread than many people imagine. The international activities of the US Central Intelligence Agency (CIA) have provoked accusations of the organization making up its rules as it goes along, and that behind the so-called information gathering agency committed to the preservation of national integrity is a perverse right-wing elite accountable to nobody but itself, dedicated entirely to the elimination, or at least, the discrediting, of any opposition.

Such organizations obviously cover their tracks rather well. Nevertheless the CIA has been accused of behind-the-scenes propping up of unwholesome right-wing juntas such as the one in Chile and some equally unsavoury dictatorships closer to home. Its involvement in Vietnam appeared to range from supporting the unstable South Vietnam government to having an interest in the lucrative drugs traffic. As these involvements gained prominence in the US media, paralleled with a growing dissatisfaction with the handling of the War itself, from the mid-'sixties onwards, a sense of outrage and distrust over the way social and foreign affairs were being conducted began to emerge.

Long before Watergate, the American public's view of the authorities had shifted from the kind of gratitude which the Bond films attempted to prop up to a nagging suspicion that things were going badly adrift. The idea that individuals were powerless to affect the course of events had been well and truly ingrained, not just through Bond and his ilk, but by the way the system had worked since World War II. The futility of trying to hit back against people who insisted in wielding the wrong kind of power had been well learnt during the McCarthy era.

Film-makers of the McCarthy period had resorted to using alienated heroes to express their distaste at what was happening in society. So, too, from the mid-'sixties onwards, a new breed of screen hero emerged who refused to accept that the State, or authority, was always right. This type of hero, who would see out the 'seventies, came in roughly two versions, characterized by Steve McQueen in *Bullitt* (1968) and Clint Eastwood in *Dirty Harry* (1971).

It is interesting to see that Bond himself began to loosen up as the decade progressed. The overt right-wing politics was remodelled along more liberal lines, and Roger Moore's appointment as Sean Connery's successor blunted Bond's cutting edge by transforming him into a more flip, fun-loving character, rendering the movies which Moore made a lot more escapist than several of the spin-off parodies.

Moore's Bond was still an instrument of the State, but the waspish, masochistic 'watch-the-poor-bastards-squirm' attitude which Connery had represented had gone. In its place was the MI5 equivalent of a head prefect from a public school, full of pranks and healthy gamesmanship, who gave the impression that he couldn't hurt a fly and was only in the department to play with the expensive toys. This shrewd shift in the character's motivation safeguarded the popularity of the Bond cycle of movies at a time when appearing as a cold-blooded hit-man for dubious right-wing interests would have put him badly out of step with the mood of society.

Virgil Hilts, 'The Cooler King' (Steve McQueen), in *The Great Escape* (1963).

CHAPTER TEN

THE MALADY LINGERS ON

Steve McQueen's craggy, triangular face, all-seeing eyes and toilet brush haircut made him just right for the 'sixties. No other star transmitted the wary sensitivity and the easy-going mentality of 'sixties youth more eloquently than McQueen. The characters he played were always cool and direct, disinclined to hide behind long words or bullshit, or to get involved in tedious moral arguments. He was grown-up and positive as a personality, yet he could turn on that sweet, misunderstood-little-boy act with heart-melting results. The abrupt, shy smiles, thoughtful stares into space, puckered frowns and nervous, cat-like blinks were part of the armoury of an actor who knew instinctively how to serenade audiences of the 'sixties.

McQueen was alert and knowing even in repose; he commandeered attention even when he was doing nothing in particular, as, for example, stroking the steering wheel of a jalopy, or staring thoughtfully over the top of his knuckles. The wry detachment which he displayed in the presence of women, a combination of natural shyness and devastatingly effective body language, had a powerful effect on female audiences. They could imagine him being like that with them, and, in essence, he probably would have been, for McQueen never quite got the hang of being a phoney. He could be infuriating, unreasonable and at times as cussed as a mule, but he was never a phoney.

He was inevitably compared with Dean because rebellion was unmistakably his big number, and because he raced fast cars. McQueen's obsession for speed was thankfully devoid of the self-punishing impulses which Dean had, and his rebellion was cerebral rather than flashy, truth-seeking instead of self-gratifying.

Appropriately, he became the first major star of the decade, in *The Magnificent Seven* (1960), following supporting roles in *Never Love a Stranger* (1957) and *Never So Few* (1959). His role of Vin, the enigmatic hired gun in *The Magnificent Seven*, was theoretically a featured role along with those of Robert Vaughn, James Coburn, Charles Bronson and a few others. Yul Brynner was the star, but after the film's preview, McQueen got co-star billing.

Chris (Brynner), an out-of-work gunslinger, and Vin (McQueen) meet in a dusty, nowhere town where fear of reprisals by the racist townsfolk is delaying the burial of a dead Mexican in a white folks' graveyard. Chris and Vin volunteer to drive the funeral wagon, an act of bravery – or foolhardiness – which is witnessed by another group of Mexicans who provide an intriguing offer of work. They want their village to have an armed defence from marauding bandits. Chris and Vin round up several other trouble-loving souls who are handy with guns and knives to do just that but the bandits outmanoeuvre them, confiscate their guns, and dump them miles from anywhere, as a summary warning.

A few want to quit, but Chris welds them together as a fighting unit again whilst at the same time improving the village's natural defences. When the bandits return, Chris and his men are ready for them, and the previously timid villagers eagerly pitch in with sharpened sticks, farming tools, anything that can inflict damage. The bandits are decisively routed, but of the seven, only Chris, Vin and an inexperienced young gunman – who, anyway, takes a shine to one of the peasant girls toiling in the fields and decides to stay on with her – survive.

In the Kurasawa film, *The Seven Samurai*, on which *The Magnificent Seven* was based, the samurai warriors were bound together by tradition, honour and a strict code of ethics. This makes their sacrifice plausible, even proper, at the end. Chris's gunmen seem attracted to the caper simply as an escape from tedium; not one of

The gunslingers on their way to meet the bandits. Left to right: Vin (Steve McQueen), Britt (James Coburn), Chico (Horst Buchholz), Chris (Yul Brynner), Harry Luck (Brad Dexter), Lee (Robert Vaughn) and O'Reilly (Charles Bronson) comprise *The Magnificent Seven* (1960).

them appears to be doing anything very much when Chris's offer of work turns up. Their lack of any real purpose, almost a unifying negativeness, makes their sacrifices seem curiously out-of-character. Vin is the exception.

It is here that the McQueen character pays dividends. He really does come across as a wryly-indifferent, danger-loving rebel scouring the countryside for the seductive rap of gunfire. You can accept that he is just crazy enough to want to be there when the shooting and the dying starts, irrespective of the rights or wrongs involved. It seems credible that gun battles are his private aphrodisiac and that when he rides off over the ridge at the end, he is in pursuit of more of the same.

Similarly, in *Hell is for Heroes* (1962), it is the lull between the counter-attacks which upsets World War II infantryman John Reece (McQueen). He also hates Army regulations enough to have been demoted from master-sergeant to buck private (for stealing a jeep and driving it at a colonel). Reece is a loner, a trouble-maker, a psychopathic misfit who thrives on the mad conditions of war. In a normal, civilized society he would be behind bars or cooped up in a death cell. When a French bar girl warns him that drinking off-limits will mean trouble from the military police, Reece's reply is, 'Lady, the whole world is in trouble!' He despises his own officers as intensely as the Germans, but the company to which he is assigned is all he has got, there is nowhere else to go, and no one else to serve under.

Entrenched in the scrubland near the Siegfried Line in 1944, the company withdraws several platoons for another engagement, leaving only a handful of American soldiers to hold off the Germans. When Reece discovers that the enemy knows how puny their defences are and is planning an attack, he believes that their only chance is to destroy the heavily-fortified pillbox from which the German assault is likely to be launched.

Sergeant Larkin (Harry Guardino) insists on obeying standing orders, which means staying put until the rest of the company returns. When mortar-fire puts Larkin out of action, Reece ignores the order and leads a couple of men in a crazy, ill-fated attempt to snatch the pillbox. When the company does return, instead of being thanked for his courageous initiative, Reece is threatened with another court martial for disobeying orders. Before that can happen, the full-strength company mounts its own assault on enemy positions, and Reece dies knocking out the pillbox on which he had set his mind.

Marriage is the enemy out to vanquish Rocky Papasano (McQueen), the roving-eyed jazzman-bachelor of *Love with the Proper Stranger* (1963), and though he puts up sturdy resistance, the opposing forces, like those guarding the German pillbox in *Hell is for Heroes*, prove too much for him. Trying to bluff his way into the choicest gigs at a musicians' exchange, Rocky is confronted by signorina-in-distress Angela Rossini (Natalie Wood), a sales assistant at Macy's department store, who wants a date with a reliable abortionist. Her story places Rocky as the father-to-be, the result of a one-night seduction, of which he has no recollection, after an out-of-town gig.

Baffled but ever-helpful, Rocky secures the appointment plus half the money she needs to have the operation. But the sleazy surroundings where the abortion is due to take place, and Angela's obvious distress, make them change their minds. From then on, the film is a sophisticated and engaging battle of wills, as Rocky fights against falling in love, and Angela resists pressure from her volatile Italian family who want her to marry a respectable but dim-witted restaurateur. Love, of course, triumphs in the end, as Rocky straightens out his priorities and opts for the 'bells-and-banjos' style of romancing which he knows Angela enjoys.

Director Robert Mulligan cleverly compares the plusses along with the disadvantages of Rocky's alley-cat lifestyle. In one scene, he encounters an old flame who has married his former school chum. Both are tongue-tied and embarrassed, and Rocky finds the gulf between them inexplicable. As he later explains to Angela, 'We used to break a lot of bread together, and now we look at each other and we've got nothin' to say!' The difference between them is that she has a fulfilled life and a family of her own, while Rocky has never grown up, which is why his relationship with the doll-like Edie Adams is adequate before Angela arrives. When Edie remarks dreamily that they are in love, Rocky replies 'Yeah, you with yourself and me with myself!' For the equality-conscious, off-the-peg sex-loving 'sixties that just about says it all.

Despite wicked distortions of the truth and an attempt to burlesque the hardships of wartime prison camps, *The Great Escape* (1963) has a sweep and style which rarely falters. Hilts (McQueen), a daredevil flyer, is also a determined break-out artist, veteran of eighteen failed solo attempts. He has tried to get under the wire, over it and through it, and no sooner is he incarcerated in the notorious Stalag Luft North, a can for dedicated escapers, than he is scouting the perimeter for possible exit points – an infringement which lands him in solitary confinement. 'You still be here when I get out!' he says to the po-faced commandant as the sentries lead him away.

Hilts remains aloof from the main escape effort being planned by British officers, pursuing instead oddball schemes of his own which inevitably fail. The British watch his antics with bemusement, grateful for the diversion he creates. When Hilts is asked to sacrifice his freedom, should he ever achieve it, by returning with details of the surrounding countryside, he scornfully refuses. It takes the machine-gunning of his 'stir-crazed' cellmate to bring Hilts to his senses. He does, in fact, return with the information which the British prisoners need for the planned mass breakout to succeed in the immediate vicinity of the camp.

Almost everyone in the escape is either recaptured or killed. Hilts gets as far as the Swiss frontier on a stolen motorbike, but is forced to surrender after a spectacular, bone-jarring attempt to leap his bike across the heavily fortified border. His return to Stalag Luft North coincides with the removal by the Gestapo of the disgraced commandant. 'So, the job just didn't work out,' Hilts says to him, flashing that tight, dry smile, as both men are led off in different directions.

Although it is a wartime setting, the Hilts character is rooted in 'sixties defensiveness. He says little; he does his own thing; he is preoccupied with self and is wary of first-name relationships ('Just make it Hilts') which might trap him into compromises. Appeals to his team spirit fail because Hilts is not a team man – he is a loner, unaffected by movement within the crowd, suspicious of the value of collective decisions.

Thus, instinctively, McQueen hit all the right notes with young 'sixties audiences, overcoming their natural lack of interest in a war-games movie by playing a character to whom they could so obviously relate. Hilts's personal vision transcends the discomfort and the confinement of prison-camp life. It is the vision of a man whose spirit cannot be captured, who expects adversity and is ready for it, who will take no nonsense from any source.

Translated into contemporary attitudes, McQueen's laconic indifference to authority came in the form of a conscientious disavowal of authoritarian mumbo-jumbo. It was just what the young audiences had been waiting to hear, and coming from a man whose own childhood had been chequered by reform-school attendances, it certainly sounded authentic. And even if it wasn't, his screen character had enough style and charisma to become a symbol for youthful individualism.

After the escape comes the Great Recapture. Virgil Hilts (Steve McQueen) heads back to the cooler in the final minutes of *The Great Escape* (1963).

Winning through against tough odds was also the theme of *The Cincinnatti Kid* (1965). Set in New Orleans shortly before the war, the Cincinnatti Kid (McQueen) is a talented, ambitious poker player who desperately wants to beat an ageing cardsharp, Lancey Howard (Edward G. Robinson), who has confidently humiliated every challenger for the past twenty years. Their contrasting lifestyles explain the Kid's determination to be 'The Man' who deposes Lancey. While the Kid earns a meagre and risky living in low dives, Lancey is a national celebrity, moving elegantly from city to city, in demand at swanky parties to give demonstrations of his prowess, fawned on by well-to-do admirers.

Their marathon showdown is a beauty. Lancey's viperish charm fails to trap the Kid during the interludes between playing, and with the stakes at $8,500, the final square-off occurs – Lancey wins by a Royal Flush to the Kid's Full House. Shocked and demoralized, his one and only chance of the good life gone, the Kid withdraws to an uncertain future while Lancey packs his suitcase and moves on to another lucrative payday in another town.

As a straightforward rags-to-more-rags tale of a poor guy from the slums destined to remain there, *The Cincinnatti Kid* contains enough energy and realism to hold the attention. Card-playing is a cerebral business, and both stars use eye muscles and blank stares to considerable effect.

There was a certain irony in the fact that McQueen was up against such a fluent scene-stealer as Robinson, having so effectively in his early films used superficially innocent little mannerisms, like the cat-like blinks and the puckered frowns, to distract other players. During the making of *The Magnificent Seven* Yul Brynner became sufficiently outraged at McQueen's camera-hogging tricks, like toying with his hat while he spoke, or fidgeting while others were speaking, that he asked director John Sturges to restrain him. To keep the peace, Sturges told McQueen not to 'busy it up all the time – for Chrissake, don't do anything, just stand there.'

In *The Cincinnatti Kid*, it was McQueen's turn to defer to a superior scene-stealer. Edward G. Robinson's game-weary air, the mournful, rhino eyes, the immaculate manners are used with great finesse to camouflage Lancey's rotten, predator's soul. It was a performance to be savoured, particularly since it was his last memorable screen appearance.

Comparisons with Paul Newman in *The Hustler* are inevitable, and to a point revealing, for though only four years separate them, during those four years America had matured – or aged, as some might put it – as a result of the events in Dallas. Eddie was spiritually on the wrong side of 1963, his grim, nihilistic world as prematurely dead as Sidney Falco's (Tony Curtis) in *The Sweet Smell of Success* (1959). Though the Kid loses, he still has his girl, and the black shoeshine boy who pitches dimes against him, and both rally round him in his desolation, giving him hope for tomorrow.

Bullitt (1968) was basically a story of conflict between cops and politicians, with the streets of San Francisco as the battleground. At a more substantial level, it

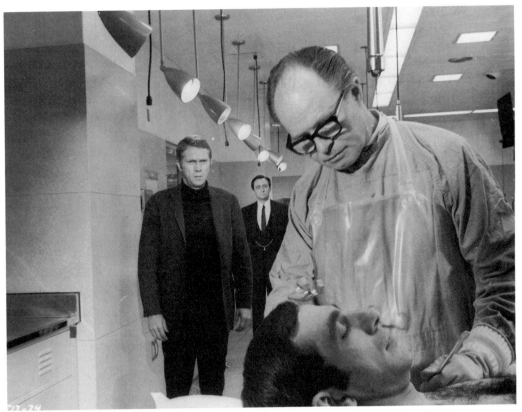

A dead hoodlum or an innocent fall guy? Detective Frank Bullitt (Steve McQueen) isn't telling all he knows to troublesome Senator Chalmers (Robert Vaughn), in *Bullitt* (1968).

redressed the dreadful imbalance of Bond and the super 'tecs. Police lieutenant Frank Bullitt (McQueen) has a conscience, while all round him his politically motivated superiors and a slippery, vindictive senator (Robert Vaughn) threaten to have his ears for breakfast unless he obeys their orders. Bullitt's problem is that he disagrees fundamentally with those orders. Even with the whole department on his back, suspension in the air, gangsters trying to kill him and an unhappy love-life, Bullitt must solve the case his way.

The senator has drafted a top-notch Chicago hoodlum to give evidence before a Congressional hearing on crime, a move guaranteed to advance the senator's political career. Police Lieutenant Bullitt is assigned the task of keeping the witness alive, that is, clear of the Mafia's death squad, until his testimony can be heard. When the gangster is murdered at the secret hideaway – and one of Bullitt's men dies, too – the battle lines are drawn.

Bullitt suspects the senator of duplicity, while the senator accuses Bullitt of incompetence. When the senator attempts to pull rank, Bullitt advises him to 'work your side of the street, and I'll work mine!' In an attempt to draw the killers' firepower, Bullitt at first conceals the gangster's death, and later, his corpse, from the senator, a potentially disastrous ploy which nevertheless works.

The dead man, he discovers, is not an underworld big-shot, as Bullitt was conned into believing, but an innocent lookalike, killed so that the real villain, who has swindled the Mafia of a fortune in protection money, can skip the country. Bullitt intercepts him at Los Angeles airport, before he can take off for Rome, and ignoring the senator's urgent demand that the man must be kept alive to testify — 'We must all compromise' — Bullitt guns him down inside the air terminal in front of hundreds of alarmed witnesses. The car which spirits the furious senator back to his office, where doubtless he will formulate his plans to get Bullitt thrown off the force, bears the ironic motif 'Support Your Local Police'.

Bullitt's conscience is, again, that of young America at the height of the Vietnam War, faced with the impossible choice of having to jeopardize their lives for a cause which many perceptive people found repugnant, or to 'spit on the flag' as the hawks used to say. In the Bond films, when the top brass said jump, Bond jumped, there was no argument, no safe middle ground. Bullitt was his own man, he only jumped when the reasons for doing so were acceptable on moral grounds. He was as unlike Bond as chalk is to cheese. Our first glimpse of him, being woken by his partner, confirms the difference. He stirs to life inside his grubby apartment like someone being aroused from rigor mortis, bad-tempered, grit-eyed and unshaven. Later we see him stocking up with solo dinner packs at his neighbourhood supermarket, stealing a newspaper from a kerbside autostall, driving like a lunatic, deaf to promises about promotion and unrepentant about upsetting the powers-that-be.

Bullitt stoically fights his corner by ignoring everyone in turn. When the alleged gangster objects to Bullitt discussing him on the phone, he stares right through him and carries on as before. When a young policeman asks if working through the weekend on guard duty will mean he gets other days off in lieu, Bullitt mutters 'So long' and departs. A police chief who is about to read the riot act after he has failed to deliver the gangster safe and sound gets the phone slapped down on him.

After realizing that his star witness is dead, the senator's demand for a signed statement that the killing occurred while he was in police custody brings no response whatever — Bullitt conducts a short conversation with a policeman standing behind the senator as if he had ceased to exist, and it happens again at the airport where Bullitt waits to nail the real Mafia fugitive. When the senator concedes that integrity is something he occasionally parades in front of the voting public, Bullitt moves away from him as if to avoid contagion.

Lee Marvin was a sturdy anti-establishment figure of the 'sixties, too. After an apprenticeship — which took him into middle age — as a supporting roughneck, his breakthrough movie was *The Killers* (1964), a tense crime thriller directed by Don Seigel which contained many of the fluent hallmarks of Seigel's later work with Clint Eastwood. In *The Killers*, Charlie (Marvin) and Lee (Clu Galagher) are two syndicate hit-men who arrive in a small town to dispose of Johnny North (John

Cassavetes), a former racing driver who has cheated the mob out of the takings from a robbery.

Even though North is forewarned of their arrival at the blind school where he works, he makes no effort to save himself and clears his classroom in order to wait

The chase hots up for a small-time crook (Norman Fell, centre) as contract killers Lee (Clu Galagher) and Charlie (Lee Marvin) wring the information they want out of him in *The Killers* (1964).

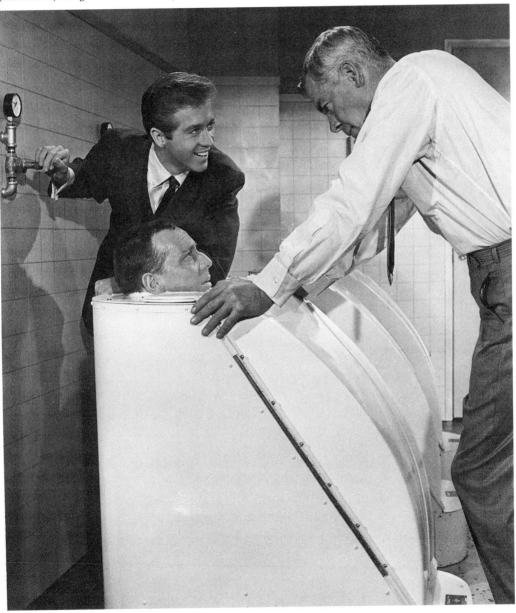

passively for his killers. Puzzled by their victim's apparent death-wish, the two killers decide to find out why, suspecting that their investigations could uncover enough money to retire on.

Told through a series of flashbacks, the story they piece together shows North's infatuation for the willowy mistress (Angie Dickinson) of a crooked business tycoon (Ronald Reagan) who involves him in a payroll robbery which goes badly wrong. Discarded afterwards and cheated of his money by the woman with whom he has fallen deeply in love, North loses his taste for living and readily submits to being murdered when his killers show up.

The Killers broke new ground in two significant directions. It superimposed for the first time on a gangster movie the loose, hip attitudes of the 'sixties. It was also one of the first of the male-buddy films which became very popular towards the end of the decade. Charlie hates authority, goes his own way and remains true to his code despite the corruption he encounters. Life for Charlie is a violent conundrum which can only be solved by total immersion in it. He is both fierce and despairing in a world where morality has disappeared.

Winning is all that matters to him any more. He is contemptuous of the losers who clutter up the background, crying into their beer or lying down in front of his gun, and they are losers because they are trapped by feelings which, by contrast, do not hinder the winners. The 'sixties male hero was often saved by his detachment from the world around him, a world in which emotions made people vulnerable.

Point Blank (1967) had a similar theme, that of a lone outsider taking on big-time criminals who hide behind the telescopic rifles of their killer bodyguards and the impenetrable trappings of their business empires. Walker (Marvin) is a small-time crook who acts as a courier for the syndicate, picking up and delivering money dropped by night on to the ruins of Alcatraz. Unknown to Walker, his accomplices, his wife Lynn (Sharon Acker) and Reece (John Vernon), are lovers. They decide one night to kill him and snatch the money for themselves, making it look as if Walker has ratted on his bosses.

Though badly shot up, Walker survives the ordeal, but the betrayal leaves psychological scars as deep as the bullet wounds. The film follows his obsessional trail of revenge, which ends with Lynn's remorseful drug suicide and the dispassionate killing of Reece, who is thrown from a high window after confessing he used the stolen money to buy into a powerful crime ring. Then begin the opening moves in a deadly battle of wits and guns to recoup the money from high-ranking criminals. But it is an impossible mission, the syndicate's chain of command reaches infinitely upwards and outwards and the hierarchy proves impenetrable, even to the ruthless and resourceful Walker. Comprehending finally that the odds are impossible, Walker abandons the contest and attempts to pick up the shattered fragments of his life again.

Like the Cincinnatti Kid, Walker is another embodiment of the post-Kennedy cynicism and disorientation. His first name is never mentioned, which is itself a revealing comment on the superficial and dispassionate nature of his relationships. As in *The Killers*, the key moments in the film are provided by double-dealing women, as, for example, when Lynn joins up with Reece to kill Walker, or when Lynn's sister Chris (Angie Dickinson) seduces Reece, whom she hates, to give Walker an opportunity to catch him off-guard.

The film combines a nostalgic film noir flavour, that is, an embattled central character fighting unknown forces, betrayed by one woman and saved by another — the precarious sexual balance familiar in many film noir classics — with the graphic violence which characterized gangster movies of the 'sixties. This merging of styles is only part of the fascination of *Point Blank*.

Walker's virtual return from the grave, his go-it-alone harassment of the power-brokers in smart suits and chauffeured limousines typifies the unequal struggle of ordinary individuals against the huge, impersonal business empires and conglomerates which grew up during the 'fifties and 'sixties. As companies grew and the people running them became remote, legitimate avenues of complaint became sealed off. Similarly, the high costs involved in taking legal action against corporations which retained high-powered lawyers on the payroll made a mockery of the old idea that justice was for everyone.

Prime Cut (1972), again with Lee Marvin, explores similar territory. A Kansas City-based, Mafia-funded meat-packing business, run by a smiling villain with the unlikely name of Mary Ann (Gene Hackman), fails to honour the debts it has incurred with its Chicago paymasters. Mary Ann's hamburger factory is a front for a drugs and prostitution racket where young girls are selected from orphanages for the skin game. In a horrifying scene, the prostitutes are penned naked for inspection like cattle at an auction.

Nick Devlin (Marvin), a spunky Irish gangster, takes on the assignment of corralling Mary Ann and teaching him the error of his ways, a job which proved too tough for his predecessor, who ended up as sausagemeat. As in *Point Blank*, the odds are heavily stacked against the outsider as he tackles the cautious, ruthless breakaway gang in its own heavily fortified backyard. Devlin wins, destroys the rotten Kansas set-up, releases the children waiting to take their places in the cattle pens, and leaves the dying Mary Ann to expire slowly and agonizingly from a wound in the groin. 'You'd do it for an animal,' pleads Mary Ann, to which Devlin coldly replies: 'You ain't an animal,' and calmly steps over him.

The film, directed by Michael Ritchie, appears to pay tribute to Hitchcock in several places: for example, in the down-and-out hotel where Mary Ann's equally murderous brother gawps at TV while gnawing canned meat, and most memorably in the scene where Devlin and Poppy (Sissy Spacek), one of the girls he rescues from the farm, are pursued across a ripe cornfield by a demonic baler-machine. To save them, Devlin's men ram the baler with their limousine, which is gobbled up and spat out in square bales as effortlessly as a pile of wheat. In the human confrontation which follows, the city-dweller dispassionately avenges the insult.

Harry Callaghan (Clint Eastwood) brings the city to a violent halt apprehending thieves at the start of *The Enforcer* (1976).

CHAPTER ELEVEN

GUN LAW

Steamrolling urbanization, which paralleled the growth of large corporate organizations, led inescapably, it seemed, to a decline in traditional American values. The old West met the burgeoning East, and what happened was not an absorption of the older ideals of honour and fairplay but, to a large extent, a surrender of them. Many films of the 'sixties and 'seventies attempted to resolve the conflicts between the obsolescent idealism of a man doing what a man must do, as enshrined in the frontier code, and the social realities of urban existence with its dependence on compromise.

The screen character of Clint Eastwood was a perverse yet timely reminder that the individual's fight against bureaucracy or intransigent authority was never lost as long as he could hold on to what he believed. Eastwood brought the simple, and to some admirable, ethics of the mythic West to the urban jungle. He represented a rolling back of the emasculating pressures of having to be a phoney in order to keep one's job, of kowtowing to a system which put personal honour and dignity at the bottom of the pile.

During the 'forties and 'fifties John Wayne's brand of crude, unquestioning patriotism was enough because nobody wanted to blitz a system which was in theory keeping enemies out and feeding everyone reasonably. By the late 'sixties, however, due to the increasing political and social turmoil, people could no longer naïvely accept that everything the government said was the truth. The general mood of betrayal, of distrust of government motives, of unease at the civil authorities' ineffectiveness in controlling criminal and terrorist activities had soared to an all-time high, especially among young people.

On the streets, law-abiding citizens fared no better against the crooks and muggers than individuals who had been ripped off by large corporations. Red tape and the ponderous processes of law were easily exploited by sharp lawyers, who earned large fees keeping criminals out of jail. There seemed no viable way of making the law work against wrongdoers, and on all sides the ordinary citizen was under siege, from the violent criminals against whom he had little or no protection, or from the law which was slow, complicated and prohibitively expensive to crank into motion in defence of basic rights.

Eastwood's monosyllabic No-Name in Sergio Leone's trilogy of 'spaghetti' westerns, the films which established him internationally, was the opposite side of the coin to John Wayne's extrovert heroism. Wayne was the centre of his circle, whereas Eastwood had no circle, and no objective other than to win and to go on winning. The method of winning was unimportant, and the rights and wrongs of the argument meant nothing. Even when he no longer played No-Name, Eastwood's screen character in the Harry Callaghan films brought an identical grit and single-mindedness to bear on the problems facing modern-day cops. Despite the irritating over-simplifications and insensitivity of these films, they provided a depressing view of modern justice invariably favouring the criminal.

Coogan's Bluff (1968) brought No-Name to New York, in the guise of Deputy Sheriff Walter Coogan (Eastwood) from Arizona. Coogan believes in simple equations – criminals must pay their dues and the law must be respected. After rounding up a surly Indian who has broken out of the Navajo reservation, and handcuffing him to a verandah post while he cavorts with the lady inside, Coogan is sent to New York by his exasperated senior police officer to retrieve a violent prisoner, James Ringerman (Don Stroud), who broke jail in Arizona.

Clad in cowboy hat and fancy boots, Coogan causes quite a stir wherever he goes. He has a neat line in put-downs. When a cabbie enquires if everyone back in Arizona wears 'them clothes' Coogan replies, dryly, 'No, lifeguards wear swim trunks and nurses wear white dresses!' Reporting to the 23rd Precinct building, where he expects to take delivery of the wanted man, Coogan learns from Lieutenant McKilroy (Lee J. Cobb) that it will take a few days to complete the handover because Ringerman is in the prison wing of Bellevue Hospital, after a disastrous LSD trip.

Angered by the delay, he attempts to secure the fugitive's release by pretending that he has Kilroy's authority, a ruse which goes badly wrong when, at the Pan Am heliport, he is attacked by a couple of Bannerman's cronies and left unconscious while Bannerman skips into hiding.

McKilroy is unimpressed with Coogan's police methods – 'This isn't the OK Corral, this is the city of New York. We've got a system. It's not much but we're fond of it!' – but Coogan is undeterred. He traces Ringerman through his girlfriend, and chases him on a borrowed motorbike: a modern-day equivalent of the bad guy being roped by the good cowboy. But even with Ringerman on his knees, Coogan still cannot claim a victory – nothing happens in New York legal circles until the paperwork is done. Finally, compelled to defer to the authority of the Courts, Coogan cools his heels until the official handover.

The character of Coogan is a forerunner of *Dirty Harry*, in the way that No-Name precedes Coogan. They are all branches from the same tree, a tree that flourished during the 'sixties in the atmosphere of distrust and emasculation created by political brouhaha and the rise of feminism. He represents the clash between western decisiveness and eastern pragmatism, between prairie freedoms and city curtailments, between wild justice and civilized methods of dealing with criminals.

All Coogan wants to do is bag Ringerman who, to him, is just another species of wild animal. 'Animals and people, they don't act much different when you're hunting them,' he tells McKilroy. Promotion, too, is something he chases without let-up, though his method is to step over the incumbent sheriff and not seek favours. Asked why he is in hot water with his home-town sheriff, Coogan answers simply, 'He looks at me and sees the man who's going to take his job someday!'

Coogan is already a law unto himself, convinced that easy-going city policing is only a short step away from the criminals having the cops on the run instead of the other way around.

Sexually, he is both moralistic and libidinous, and convincing in both roles. When a prostitute along the hall in his shabby rented room offers him sex, Coogan turns her down, first slapping her rump and later booting her out of his room. With Julie, the social worker, he is equally direct – 'You're a girl, aren't you? Sit back and act like one' – by which he implies that he judges her to be a reasonable lay. Like Hilts in *The Great Escape*, first-name relationships impose commitments which he would prefer not to have to honour, so to Julie he is 'just Coogan, without the mister'. That is about as far as he will go, leaving the way clear later in the film for him to steal a look at some documents in her filing cabinet while she is out of the room.

With Ringerman's girlfriend Linnie, too, he is poison. Despite her drug-induced instability and pleas for help behind the bravado, he leaps into bed with her at the first opportunity, then dispassionately beats her up and throws her to Ringerman's wolves in cold retribution for her having lured him into a going-over by the same people.

Everyone Coogan encounters is used and discarded in turn: the blonde bed partner back in Arizona, Ringerman's pathetic mother, Julie, Linnie, even McKilroy, whose authorization he pretends to have for springing the prisoner from Bellevue the first time. In Coogan's bitter, one-eyed world the end always justifies the means, and if being a bastard is the only way to achieve results, then be one and enjoy it.

Similar avowals reside in *Dirty Harry* (1972), in which Clint Eastwood plays the eponymous San Francisco cop who makes Bullitt seem like a Seventh Day Adventist. San Francisco homicide detective Harry Callaghan is Coogan with the excuse that wide open spaces or 'too much sun' are responsible for his trigger-happy ways. His main opponent is Scorpio (Andy Robinson), a deranged sniper who balances his demand for $100,000 from the police against the threat of killing either a Catholic priest or a Negro – neither of whom appears to figure very high in Harry's reckoning since the likelihood of the ransom being paid brings the angry demand, 'Are you going to play this creep's game?'

But, as Harry learns, they are: the entire San Francisco police force, the Mayor's office and possibly the military might of the USA are about to compromise with a mad murderer rather than put one more priest or black man in jeopardy.

Several obstacles prevent Harry from nailing the killer – loopholes in the law, which, cunningly exploited by smug defence lawyers, enable Scorpio to walk free after his arrest, to fulfil Harry's grim prediction that he will kill again 'because he likes it!'

When a busload of school children is hijacked by Scorpio and threatened with death unless the police hand over another $200,000 and provide an escape airplane, Harry decides that the 'messing around' has to stop. Acting completely contrary to orders, he succeeds in getting Scorpio within range of his Magnum revolver, and this time there are no cosy escape clauses to hide behind. After killing Scorpio, he disgustedly dumps his police badge in the river. To Harry, honest isolation is more honourable than sucking up to a hamstrung police system.

Dirty Harry is not a particularly good sociological film. Its over-emphasis on cinemagenic diversions, such as the inevitable nude disco – one also featured in *Coogan's Bluff* – distract rather than add to its social relevance. Its anti-liberal stance at times verges on the hysterical, bagging together all those who either oppose or try to control Harry as either evil or stupid. Scorpio wears a huge anti-war buckle on his belt, which during less politically charged times could be dismissed as random character colouring. At the start of the 'seventies, the implication is more sinister.

Equally, the legal brain which confirms that the prosecution has no case to answer because Harry took the murder weapon from Scorpio's hiding-place without official authorization is a university professor. There would have been nothing unusual about that in calmer times: objective advice often makes more sense coming from an independent source. However, in the early 'seventies the objectivity of university teachers was not only called into question, but they were often accused of misguided liberalism. In these circumstances, a peace-symbol maniac being let off the hook by a dove-like academic contained political overtones which were too unsubtle to be overlooked.

Ironically, many of Harry's traits are paralleled in the killer. Both are racist (Harry's racism is only hinted at, but clearly admitted by the man himself with a consenting wink); both are skilful with firearms; both are egotistical and both are loners. One is criminal and the other straight, but events prove that they are reasonably matched as adversaries – much more evenly than, for example, Coogan and the loutish Ringerman.

Harry has so many enemies in *Magnum Force* (1973) that they seem to be popping out of the woodwork everywhere he goes. The film, however, brought a perceptible softening of his granite heart, and moved him slightly to the left of a bunch of rogue traffic cops.

The film opens with a motorcycle policeman wearing dark shades signalling a limousine with four flashily dressed occupants to stop. The cop admonishes them for crossing a double line and demands to see their credentials. Then, coolly, he draws his pistol and shoots them all through the rolled-down window of the car, at point-blank range. Harry (Eastwood) arrives at the scene of the crime, but runs into a superior officer, Lieutenant Briggs (Hal Holbrook), and from their first words it is obvious that the relationship is a cool one. Briggs has removed Harry from homicide patrol because 'We can't have the public crying police brutality every time you go out on the street!' Harry has been cooling his heels on surveillance duty since Briggs demoted him for the public's good.

When the brutal murders continue, and the victims are all discovered to be leading gangland figures ('Someone is trying to put the courts out of business,' says one senior detective), Harry is reinstated on the homicide squad on condition that he behaves. His eagerness to get back among the bullets wrings a salutary promise from him, though it is never his intention to obey orders.

Convinced that the murders are being committed by a vigilante group, Harry remembers four young traffic cops whom he vaguely knows who could easily fit the bill. For one thing, people expect to see cops at the scene of a crime so there would be no getaway problem, and also their prowess on the shooting range is extraordinary for police academy rookies. He sets a trap for them, and sure enough they topple into his hands, but the surprise is that their leader is Lieutenant Briggs, a right-wing bigot who believes in vigilante justice. At the end, he gets a taste of Harry's vigilante justice, and is killed by a time-bomb which he intended for Harry.

Deranged murderer Scorpio (Andy Robinson) pays the price for getting on the wrong side of San Francisco cop Harry Callaghan (Clint Eastwood) in *Dirty Harry* (1972), first of the Harry Callaghan quartet of movies.

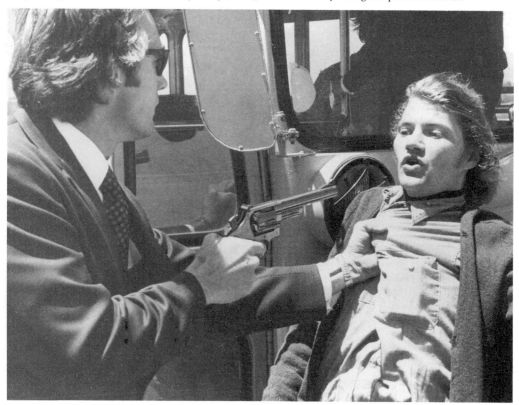

In *Magnum Force*, Harry is still in command of his reflexes, still the energetic crusader against evil and the gutless attitudes of his superiors. However, he displays considerably more method and less rancour than he did in *Dirty Harry*. In the earlier film, he had no friends, no time for niceties and no sexual activity. Nailing Scorpio was a full-time job and Harry devoted all his time and energies to it. *Magnum Force* gives him opportunities for sexual dalliance, but these encounters never amount to anything as deep as a relationship.

Politically, he seems to the right of Briggs, but the ending changes all that. Briggs' leather-clad disciples are a variant on Hitler's stormtroopers, maniacs pursuing impossible dreams. When Harry reminds them that one week's work adds up to a dozen dead people, they coldly predict the following week's bag will be a 'dozen more'. This bizarre conduct makes Harry, by comparison, an angel of mercy. What is more, it blinkers the film's social observation by nullifying any objective examination or criticism of Harry's actions, or his racism, or his chauvinism. When Briggs talks coldly about 'execution' and 'retribution' for anyone jeopardizing the security of the people, sentiments lifted squarely from *Mein Kampf*, Harry is let off the hook, because the opposition is so depraved that defeating it becomes all-important, and nobody who values democratic ideals is going to quibble about how he achieves it.

The Enforcer (1976) brings Harry (Eastwood, for the third time) face to face with another Scorpio – this time, a vicious ex-Vietnam combatant named Maxwell (DeVeren Bookwalter) who leads a group of long-haired revolutionaries into robbing a military rockets shipment, having first brutally disposed of the night security guard. What precisely these aimless thugs want the deadly weapons for, other than the bravado of having stolen them, is not made clear. It is certainly not to further any political ambition, for they have none despite the fancy title they give themselves. Instead, they kidnap the Mayor of San Francisco, hide him away on the deserted ruins of Alcatraz prison and demand a $5 million ransom, failing receipt of which he will be returned a small piece at a time.

Before the final shoot-out with the Maxwell gang – a re-run of *High Noon* with Harry ducking and diving amid the deserted buildings, picking off the opposition with the same steely determination as Gary Cooper – the various incidents in *The Enforcer* are strung together more loosely, and more humorously, than in the previous Callaghan/Eastwood epics. Harry starts off being demoted to behind a desk in Personnel after his blood-and-guts rescue of a woman hostage in a supermarket robbery ends with the store nearly demolished and the villains littered around in ungainly heaps.

The familiar accusations of having used 'excessive force' reverberate around him, but this time his police captain, McKay (Bruce Dern), has had enough. Harry regards his transfer to Personnel as being several notches below the humble stake-out work which is his usual purgatory.

Greater horrors await him in the bowels of City Hall. The Mayor has a new gimmick to boost his re-election chances – to appease liberal and female voters, he decrees that women are to be given better promotion prospects in the police force. Those with special qualities are to be selected for street duty. Equality must permeate every corner of the precinct.

The audacious kidnap of the Mayor, the ransom demand and the threat to his life restores Harry to his patrol car, which due to the City's new liberal policies, he is now obliged to share with a lady cop, Kate Moore (Tyne Daly). Kate's desire to impress him backfires badly, and Harry tolerates her the way a shepherd might put up with a dog which cannot tell a sheep from a telephone booth. But his real aggression is reserved for the mayoral decree which lumbered him with such a slapdash woman partner. However, she shapes up to become a competent partner and even manages to save his life a couple of times before she is killed rescuing the Mayor. Never one to mouth compliments when a kick in the shins will do, Harry glumly concedes that he could have done 'a hell of a lot worse'.

Vigilantism was not the sole province of screen cops during the 'seventies. The same oppressive social factors, the besieged economy and worrying inflation which drew ordinary people, even young dissidents, to identify with Clint Eastwood's highly personal form of protest made them look inside themselves to see what hidden strengths, if any, lurked there.

The protagonist in *Death Wish* (1974) is a mild-mannered, middle-aged architect, Paul Kersey (Charles Bronson), who lives in the fashionable Riverside area of New York with his wife Joanna (Hope Lange). At the start of the film they are on holiday in Miami, and obviously very much in love. Back home, a grey, drab, ill-tempered, traffic-jammed city is waiting for them, and the gossip at Kersey's office is not very cheering, either. While he was away, thirty-six people were murdered in New York. 'What this city needs is more cops than people,' suggests a colleague.

After Joanna and their married daughter Carol (Kathleen Tolan) are violently attacked and raped in their apartment by three young intruders, which results in Joanna's death, the detective in charge of the case admits to a distraught Kersey that only a slim chance exists of apprehending the culprits. For self-protection, Kersey starts to carry a bag of coins, and walking home late one night he escapes being mugged by striking his attacker in the face with the weighted bag. Later, on a working holiday in Tucson, Arizona, Kersey admits to his client, Ames (Stuart Margolin), that he was a conscientious objector during the Korean War.

Ames tells him, 'Unlike in your city, we can walk our streets and through our parks at night and feel safe!' Back in New York, Kersey decides that he can no longer enjoy the luxury of being a passive observer. Armed with a revolver, he prowls the streets late at night, killing anyone who menaces him. The press starts applauding his actions, and suddenly other law-abiding citizens begin to fight back. Mugging statistics are halved and it is the criminals' turn to fear attack.

For his part, Kersey makes no effort to avoid detection, and eventually is traced through his supermarket receipts. Fairly certain of his identity but reluctant to pull

Paul Kersey (Charles Bronson) makes it one mugger less in *Death Wish* (1974).

him in because it will mean an upsurge in the mugging rate, burly police lieutenant Ochoa (Vincent Gardenia) tries to pressure Kersey into leaving town. In the end he succeeds, and Kersey agrees to a transfer, which his firm arranges, to Chicago. To keep the mugging rate where it is, Ochoa tells news reporters that the Vigilante is still loose but that every available patrolman is on the lookout for him.

The overt right-wing bias of *Death Wish* – more heavily slanted than in any of the Eastwood/Harry Callaghan films – oddly enough did not impair its popularity with young audiences. Every time Kersey bagged a mugger, a cheer rose from the cheap seats. That this segment of the audience could identify so completely with a middle-aged moneybags who is killing disadvantaged youths confirms the anxiety which young people themselves shared about the apparent breakdown of law and order in inner cities.

The director, Michael Winner, abandons objectivity early on in the film. The thugs who violate Kersey's home are vicious animals. No redeeming qualities are shown but, then again, no information is given about them. We see them in no context other than when they are behaving like maniacs. No opportunity is offered to analyse why they have grown up into monsters; they are merely used as cyphers for the kind of mindless violence which anyone in their right minds would wish to see stamped out.

Winner loads his arguments carefully, even in the choice of Charles Bronson to play Kersey, an actor with a long list of violent films to his credit, the last name likely to conjure up conscientious objection. Kersey is middle-aged, but before his wife's death, he is depicted as young at heart, an overgrown romantic. When Joanne fancies a tumble in bed in broad daylight at the start of the film, Kersey would be happy to oblige, there and then, on the holiday beach. 'We're too civilized,' she says chidingly, insisting on hotel-room privacy. 'I can remember when we weren't!' sighs Kersey, thereby establishing his credentials as a bit of a tearaway in his own time, a Sylvester Stallone of the architects' college.

The loss of Joanne affects him deeply, and the manner of her death affects us. Old-time tearaways deserve to grow grey in peace. His sadness, and the despair of knowing that the thugs who ruined his life are unlikely to be caught, adds to our revulsion. Yet Kersey does not rush into violent action. He broods in his empty apartment, watching another gang looting parked cars in the street below. The world is going mad and all he can do, all any citizen can do, is watch helplessly through a window. Son-in-law Jack confirms as much when he meets him after flying in from Tucson – there is nothing anyone can do but 'cut and run!'

But back in Tucson, Kersey reflects grimly, muggers get their 'asses shot off'. The streets are safe, women can walk around unmolested, order prevails. There are no 'knee-jerk liberals' to impede justice.

An interesting contrast with *Coogan's Bluff* occurs. Coogan visits New York from Arizona and brings a whiff of the mythical West along with him. Kersey visits Arizona and discovers the mythical West in himself. It was there all the time, just like Coogan's, but small-c conservatism, affluence and the city life have obscured the fact. The shock of Joanne's death, together with a reminder of how appealing the primitive values of frontier life can be to an oppressed city-dweller, expose the man of action behind the one who was prepared to cut and run.

The central question which Winner's film raised, and which Winner himself felt impelled to answer with lapel-seizing vigour, repeated that of the Eastwood/Harry Callaghan films, namely, whether or not a man is morally justified in taking the law into his own hands to punish criminals who would otherwise get away. Kersey, after all, goes far beyond avenging the assault on his family. Several of his victims are actually fleeing from him and no longer pose any sort of threat when he callously shoots them in the back.

Echoes of Dirty Harry's flat warning to Lieutenant Briggs – 'Where's it going to end? Pretty soon you start executing people for jaywalking . . . or traffic violations, and then you end up executing your neighbour because his dog pisses on your lawn!' – surface towards the end of *Death Wish*. Kersey's solution is as nightmarish, as violent and as repugnant as the offences which cause it – all that is new is that the pursuers and the pursued have changed labels.

163

Colonel Kurtz (Marlon Brando) is a little bit too crazy for the US military's peace of mind in *Apocalypse Now* (1979).

CHAPTER TWELVE

VIETNAM

*F*ormer Secretary of State Henry Kissinger has described the Vietnam War as a tragedy in four acts. The problem had its origins back in the 'fifties, when fourteen nations had arrived at a settlement in Geneva over the future of South East Asia. Independence was formally bestowed on Laos and Cambodia, and Vietnam was divided horizontally along the 17th Parallel. In the south, the USA-supported regime of Ngo Dinh Diem took control while the northern half was ruled by President Ho Chi Minh and the Communists.

South Vietnam's problems were soon compounded by Communist infiltration and coercion, and corruption within the Diem government which lined its pockets with free-flowing American aid. By 1958 the situation in South Vietnam had deteriorated into civil war, with Viet Cong rebels overrunning the countryside and the Diem government controlling the towns.

With its unsavoury ally clearly outmanoeuvred and in danger of collapse, America trebled the number of technical and military advisers to fifteen thousand. Diem's murder in 1963 – believed at the time to have been CIA-inspired because of its disenchantment with the regime's conduct and its ineffectiveness against the Communist offensive – drew America deeper into the conflict.

The scale of the Communist insurgency left the USA with no illusions about what would happen if the South fell. Laos and Cambodia, already heavily infiltrated, stood no chance alone. Their defeat would leave the entire peninsula including Thailand, Burma and Malaya cruelly exposed to the Communist threat. In retrospect, these fears probably seem a bit overwrought, but at the time there was little evidence to suggest that, if America surrendered South Vietnam, the Communists would reciprocate by ending their plunder of South East Asia.

America's only answer was to apply rigidly its policy of containment, but this inevitably led to a serious escalation of its involvement. Kennedy's assassination in 1963 did nothing to weaken America's commitment. Lyndon Johnson felt obliged to continue the counter-offensive, urged on by the leading members who remained of Kennedy's administration. Johnson suffered no qualms of conscience at committing over half a million US servicemen to what was, by 1965, a full-scale war far more deadly and psychologically more debilitating than Korea had been fifteen years previously.

Historically, American strategy in war has always been a process of attrition, the deployment of organized units across a defined battle line. What the Americans faced in Vietnam were guerrillas with no territory of their own to defend, who knew the terrain well and were indistinguishable from the people the US forces were there to protect. Moreover, the Viet Cong operated from sanctuaries in neighbouring countries, so that their ferocious hit-and-run assaults were virtually unstoppable.

It was the first war of which Americans back home were able to watch the progress night after night in their living rooms. The barbaric – to Western eyes – pictures of wholesale destruction and suffering fuelled the demand for a political solution. By 1966, opposition to the War became a rallying cry which united students, press commentators, media figures and politicians. Lyndon Johnson responded to the change in public opinion by ending the bombing of North Vietnam in 1968 and calling for peace talks to begin the year after. His successor Richard Nixon announced a policy of 'Vietnamization', which meant a strengthening of the South Vietnamese army from within its own ranks, so that the USA could effect an orderly withdrawal without precipitating a North Vietnamese offensive.

A hiccup occurred in 1970, when Laos and Cambodia seemed ready to fall. To prevent this, Nixon ordered the military invasion of both countries. In 1971 he was forced to resume his attacks on Laos to destroy the supply routes along which military aid was being ferried to the Communists fighting in the South. These actions, which were almost certainly precipitated by the dreadful stalemate in which America found itself, were unpopular back home because people were frightened of any development, irrespective of its strategic importance, which might expand or prolong the hostilities.

By 1972, the choice facing President Nixon was whether to negotiate an honourable settlement or withdraw unilaterally. His reluctance to withdraw without guarantees from the other side prolonged the issue for what seemed an interminable period, yet valuable concessions were secured for the eventual 'peace with honour' agreement signed in Paris in 1973, when all military actions ceased and troops prepared to leave. Unfortunately, the Watergate scandal overlapped the programme of withdrawal and ruined the chances of the concessions being implemented.

Once the troops were moving out, Congress acted with swift determination to close the dependency loopholes. From June 1973, direct US military intervention on behalf of any country in Indo-China was ruled out, and severe defence budget cutbacks were introduced in 1973 and 1974, of the order of 30 per cent and 50 per cent respectively. With the Administration in obvious disarray – Nixon resigned in August 1974 owing to Watergate – Congress got its way, and an emboldened Hanoi sensed correctly that America would decide against retaliation if another major offensive was launched.

Whether or not more resolute or generous support would have kept the South in business for itself is debatable. Most observers believe it highly unlikely because, at best, the South was on a life-support machine and had lost its will to live. American losses totalled 58,000 dead, with many more thousands either maimed or psychologically scarred for life, and all that had been gained was a little extra time: time for neighbouring countries to look and learn, perhaps, but the cost to America had been grievous. The assault by the North drew no corresponding fire from the Americans, and following a seven-week blitzkrieg, Saigon was finally overrun in April 1975. Alas, the physical tailing-off of the War did not bring an end to the genocide, in either Vietnam or Cambodia. It merely triggered off another harrowing episode in the region's unending ordeal.

Hollywood had been a lot more circumspect about getting involved in Vietnam than the government's military advisers. This was not entirely due to political nervousness. The box-office case for making a war movie along traditional lines had weakened during the 'sixties as the anti-War lobby gained strength. In film after film during the 'sixties, rebellious attitudes towards military commanders, the triumph of conscience over duty, came into play. A good example of this was Sidney Lumet's *The Hill* (1965), with Sean Connery as Roberts, a tough NCO serving a sentence in a sweltering North African detention camp for refusing to obey an order. Despite the hellhole conditions and the appalling cruelty meted out to offenders, Roberts still refuses to abandon his principles and becomes the catalyst in a move to introduce more humane thinking into the prison after a fellow inmate is pushed over the edge into insanity and death.

In *Hell is for Heroes* (1962) McQueen's contempt for authority in uniform extended to everyone wearing pips, his own officers included. Similar emotions erupt in *The Dirty Dozen* (1967) between Colonel Reisman (Lee Marvin) and the twelve criminals awaiting execution whom he rescues and moulds into an effective fighting unit. Their initial scorn and indifference become transformed, not because they want to kill Germans – killing Reisman would be enough for them – but because Reisman is a rebel, too, contemptuous of niggling regulations, and they see that by following him they are putting one over on the idiots who love brass bands and bullshit.

With the War's dip in popularity, Hollywood was in no hurry to issue films which related specifically to the fighting, especially since the prospect of a military victory seemed remote. *The Green Berets* (1968) was the only Vietnam film of any significance produced during the War. It purports to show the war through the eyes of a journalist, Beckworth (David Janssen), whose trip to the fighting zone is arranged by courtesy of a gruff Green Berets commander, Colonel Kirby (John Wayne). This is the same Wayne character who blitzed the Japs and ran the Commies out of Hawaii, which means that any pretence at objectivity is just that – pretence.

Beckworth fulfils the same function in *The Green Berets* as those soft-bellied rookies in his earlier war movies who learnt by the final reel that Big John Knows

Best. Beckworth goes to Vietnam at Kirby's invitation after expressing uncertainty about the War. As a journalist, an observer, he becomes a cypher for all those chair-bound Americans who are denied Beckworth's opportunity to see for themselves. But they can all rest easy, because they have a free-thinking reporter to nose out the facts, right? Wrong. Beckworth is there to be brainwashed, so that he will go back and attack the critics of war.

Any reporter witnessing the same events as Beckworth would probably form the same impression he does. There is nothing dishonest in that. The dishonesty occurs in the choice of incidents which the impressionable Beckworth is free to observe. The Viet Cong are worse than animals – atrocity and rape appear to be the sole reasons they are there, whereas Kirby's men are the same lovable roughnecks and innocents whom Wayne has led in every war film since *Back to Bataan* (1944).

When Beckworth abandons his tame-rabbit liberalism at the end, because he has weighed the evidence of his own eyes, and because his eyes are also ours, we are invited to follow suit. That is the somewhat crude rationale of the film, and in 1943 it would have worked, but a quarter of a century later people no longer had their views fashioned to the same extent by the cinema. Vietnam was fought every night on TV newscasts, the arguments were more complex and, who knows, maybe right was more equally divided between North and South than any TV news report would dare to suggest while the fighting continued.

The Green Berets can just about pass itself off as a harmless chunk of low-brow fiction. Its problem is that it tries to be more than simply a war comic printed on

Colonel Mike Kirby (John Wayne) shares his view of the Vietnam campaign with sceptical journalist Beckworth (David Janssen) in *The Green Berets* (1968).

celluloid. Worse still, it is desperate to be taken seriously. To Wayne, at least, it had a purpose, which was to glorify America's involvement in the War by the simple – indeed, simple-minded – expedient of daubing stars and stripes on every frame.

It was not until the War officially ended, and sufficient time had passed for the events to be reviewed dispassionately, that films began to deal with what had happened with anything like the clarity and honesty which the subject demanded. Their reticence was understandable, in view of the angry reactions to *The Green Berets*. This was no bad thing, for the resulting breathing space allowed a degree of objectivity to filter through into the minds of both film-makers and audiences.

Of the later films made by Hollywood about Vietnam, three are probably most vividly remembered – *The Deer Hunter* (1979), *Coming Home* (1978) and *Apocalypse Now* (1979). Of the three, only *Coming Home* was reminiscent of earlier war films, such as *Pride of the Marines* (1946) and *The Men* (1950), which dealt with the problems of rehabilitation for disabled soldiers. The others, and indeed Vietnam war films generally, tended to see war and its diabolical effects on the personalities of the soldiers caught up in it in a perceptive and unflattering new light.

Only about one-third of *The Deer Hunter* (1979) actually focuses on the War itself – the beginning and end of the film shows the build-up to the protagonists' enlistment and their painful rehabilitation afterwards. It is, however, the war sequences in the middle of the film which most people remember for the horror and realism which director Michael Cimino injects into them.

The film opens in a small Pennsylvania immigrant town whose skyline, like the inhabitants' lives, is dominated by a huge iron foundry. Most of the young men in the town work there, including Michael Vronsky (Robert De Niro), who is footloose, shy with women, cool-headed and unattached; Steven (John Savage), who is about to marry Angela (Rutanya Alda); and Nick (Christopher Walken), who is engaged to Linda (Meryl Streep). Michael is the odd-man-out romantically, and, as the war sequences show, he is also the most resilient of them, the only one of the three who survives the War with his mind and body intact.

The early part of the film shows the run-up to Steven's wedding and the actual wedding itself, a joyous, bracing affair which sweeps the whole community into a wild farrago of dancing, drinking and horseplay. A touch of Hitchcockian portent is introduced into the gaiety when Steven and Angela link arms in a toast to their future, and a drop of red wine splashes on to Angela's white wedding dress. Unnoticed by any of the guests, the camera nevertheless zooms in on the red mark until it fills the screen like a jagged gash, a fateful hint of the slaughter to come.

Michael, Nick and their close-knit group of friends, who include the woman-chasing Stan (John Cazale), John (George Dzunda) who owns the local saloon, and the strong, silent Axel (Chuck Aspegren), depart for the deer hunt, a ritualistic pilgrimage high in the mountains which is both a homage to nature – clear skies and clean air miles away from foundry smoke, picturesque vistas – and an attack on it, that is, on the deer. Michael is the champion deerslayer of the group, the one against whom all the others measure their hunting prowess, the one who always despatches his prey with a single shot. For Michael, making death a clean, one-shot business gives it honour and dignity. He respects the dignity of the hunted, too, for the deer's noble bearing and no-fuss acceptance of its fate.

Their outing in the mountains ends with a nightcap in John's bar, from which the movie dives abruptly into the Vietnam fighting. Cimino employs a clever link-up device, focusing briefly on the rotating ceiling fan in John's saloon, the gentle whirring noise of which appears to get louder and change tone, then cutting suddenly to a US Army helicopter in the heart of the combat zone. The helicopter is flying over a Vietnamese village under siege by the Viet Cong. Cimino wastes no time in turning our stomachs. A huddled group of terrified women and children are discovered under a makeshift bamboo shelter. A Viet Cong soldier calmly lifts the lid and drops a hand grenade in among them. Seconds later, the shelter and its occupants are blown sky-high.

Michael and his two friends Nick and Steven are captured by the Viet Cong and imprisoned in a bamboo cage in rat-infested water. After being forced to play Russian roulette by their sadistic captors, the three manage to escape down-river. A passing US helicopter hoists Nick aboard, but Michael and Steven are left dangling from the runners as enemy fire forces it airborne before all three can be rescued.

Michael clings on to Steven's body with his legs but the bigger man's weight is too much and they both plunge into the river again, Steven fracturing both legs in the shallows. Michael is luckier; he lands in a deeper part of the river, and carries Steven on his back through the jungle until the wounded GI can be off-loaded on to a South Vietnamese jeep.

Meanwhile, at the US Military Hospital in Saigon, Nick's profound shock is not helped by his balcony view of dead GIs being loaded into coffins for shipment home. Confused, agitated, unable to compose himself enough to telephone Linda, who accepted his marriage proposal at Steven's wedding, he wanders disconsolately downtown among the clip-joints and gambling dens which will ultimately claim his soul.

The third and final segment of the film traces the homecoming. Michael attempts to piece together the torn fragments of his life. Several lives along with his own are on the edge of despair. Linda is distraught because Nick has made no contact with her. Steven broods in a hospital for the disabled, his shattered legs having been amputated, and his estranged wife Angela has a drink problem. Michael is in no mood for a hero's welcome and ducks the celebration arranged in his honour, preferring instead to be alone in a modest motel room overlooking the Pennsylvania River, the dark, restless waters of which mirror his thoughts exactly.

Later, he joins his friends on another deer hunt high in the mountains. He starts off enthusiastically enough, but when he finally gets a handsome buck in his rifle sights, a sudden revulsion at the thought of killing makes him deliberately fire wide.

When Michael learns that Nick has been sending money home to Steven from Saigon, he returns immediately to the South Vietnamese capital, which is about to fall to the Communist armies. After scouring the city's seedy nightspots, Michael eventually finds Nick in a crowded gaming house playing Russian roulette, heavily drugged; his arm is riddled with needle scars. Before Nick can be persuaded to accompany Michael home, he snatches up the revolver, points it at his own head and pulls the trigger. A moment later, he is dying in Michael's arms.

After Nick's funeral in Clairmont, over a modest funeral breakfast of scrambled eggs and coffee, Michael proposes a toast to Nick and, as the stunned knot of mourners raise their glasses, the film freezes on that final, choking moment.

Cimino's three-hour-plus film is long by motion-picture standards, yet the hyperactive camerawork, emphasis on close-ups, blurred movement and fast cross-cutting soak up the minutes. People keyed up by the advance publicity to expect a long, brutal dissertation about the War were probably surprised to find hardly any combat scenes, yet the impact of the War and its ghastly shadow is stamped on every frame, even the beginning section where preparations for the wedding and the lusty male camaraderie of Michael and his friends otherwise dominate.

Enjoying themselves before tragedy strikes: left to right, Nick (Christopher Walken), Mike (Robert de Niro), Axel (Chuck Aspegren), Steven (John Savage) and Stan (John Cazale) in *The Deer Hunter* (1979).

If the spilt wine episode augurs badly for Steven, Michael's encounter at the wedding with a returned soldier, who maintains an icy silence rather than offer any clues about what lies in store, is even worse. Unlike Beckworth on his homecoming in *The Green Berets*, the soldier who has lived through the hell of Vietnam cannot be persuaded to give any details, and soon afterwards we understand why.

Large-scale torture of American prisoners undoubtedly went on, though the Viet Cong's preference for Russian roulette, a laboriously slow method of disposing of enemies, is, by Cimino's admission, unauthenticated. It is, however, a perverted version of the deer hunt, in which the deer dies from a single bullet in the head, and it explains why Michael originally views dying at Russian roulette as dying with honour, and why he urges Steven to play the game courageously because an honourable death is all any of them can hope for. The alternative is to be eaten by rats, and the intensely patriotic Michael cannot stand the thought of an American choosing that fate.

Ironically, it is Nick's rescue by helicopter which proves to be his undoing. Separated from his friends, he drifts into Saigon's nightmare world of vice and drugs and into the hands of the evil men who later control him. Nick's death is symbolic of the fate of America in the War, a nation trying to be honourable in appalling circumstances. Cimino makes an acid point about the imperialist French, by making the cynical opportunist who lures Nick to his death a Frenchman.

The final segment of *The Deer Hunter* has echoes of *The Best Years of Our Lives* (1946), in which three discharged servicemen reorientate their lives from the estranging experiences of war. The earlier film was preoccupied with showing national values returning, and offered reassurance that the nation's reassertion of its true character would not be long delayed. Despite its harrowing middle section, *The Deer Hunter* has an unquenchable optimism which an impromptu and emotional chorus of 'God Bless America' just before the end of the film soberly underlines.

The America whose virtues the singers are extolling, the America of their experience, is a small, steelworks-dominated, rough-and-ready immigrant community which is a long way from the America shown in the pages of *Harper's Bazaar*, yet it is all they need and desire, a safe haven for outsiders that offers work and wages and the freedom to observe cultural traditions. Though possibly the lyrics of 'God Bless America' are more in step with the simple emotions of *The Best Years of Our Lives* than the complex ironies of *The Deer Hunter*, they nevertheless sum up what patriotism meant to Americans after Vietnam.

The War was not fought in pursuit of fancy ideologies, or to augur the spread of Coca-Cola imperialism, but in the words of John Kennedy, to 'assure the survival and success of liberty'. The legacy which the Americans were forced to leave behind, for example, the hundreds, possibly thousands, of Vietnamese boat people lost at sea when their waterlogged and hopelessly overcrowded vessels sank, the thousands of Vietnamese lost forever in concentration camps, the overflow of genocide into Cambodia, in no way nullifies what America sought to achieve by either its presence

Officer's wife Sally Hyde (Jane Fonda) helps paraplegic ex-Viet soldier Luke Martin (Jon Voight) to forget his troubles in *Coming Home* (1978).

or its self-sacrifice in Vietnam. It is to that understanding as much as to Nick's memory – for the two are inextricably tied together – that Michael and the others raise their glasses in *The Deer Hunter*. The farewell motif is a unifying one, a toast to the future as well as to the dead.

The subject of *Coming Home* (1978) is the rehabilitation of a disabled Vietnam veteran, Luke Martin (Jon Voight), whose injuries leave him with a one-sided and bitter view of life. A pretty hospital visitor, Sally Hyde (Jane Fonda), accidentally collides with Luke's stretcher in a crowded corridor and upsets his urine bag all over the floor. From such unpromising beginnings, a friendship develops which is initially more guarded on Sally's part. Her husband Bob (Bruce Dern) is a Marine Captain serving in Vietnam, and Sally visits wounded patients at the military hospital where she met Luke as a rewarding way of passing the time until Bob returns.

The separation, Sally's loneliness and her uncertainty about the future combine to intensify her feelings for Luke who, like herself, feels lonely and abandoned. When his condition improves enough for him to get around in a wheelchair, they go out together, and Luke visits her at her apartment. Although at first she ticks him off for suggesting they start an affair, she is clearly not repelled by the idea and allows him to see a glimmer of promise in the playful way she says 'no'.

Luke's bitterness finds an outlet in his hatred for the military, and to publicize his anti-War sentiments, he chains himself to the iron gates of a Marine Corps recruitment centre and rants into a TV news camera about the futility of the War. Sally watches the interview and afterwards rushes defensively to his side. That night they make love for the first time, and from that point on Luke's dangerously non-conformist attitude begins to affect her.

After years of being the model wife of a rulebook Marine officer, she starts taking an interest outside her claustrophobic, lack-lustre existence, swapping her prim blouse-and-skirt outfits for trendy denims and trading in her neat and tidy hairstyle for a jaunty frizz. She even starts to agree with Luke about the obscenity of war, a viewpoint likely to put a greater strain on her marriage than her increasing affection for him.

As in *The Deer Hunter*, the final segment of the film focuses on the resolution of their problems after Bob's sudden repatriation following a serious leg wound. Luke and Bob are physical and mental opposites, a factor stressed at the beginning of the film when shots of Luke, cursing and helpless in his hospital bed, are intercut with glimpses of Bob jogging to keep fit, preparing himself for his mission overseas, which he really does see as a mission, not a chore to be accomplished half-heartedly.

Afterwards, Bob is a changed man, his spirits reduced to breaking-point by what he has seen. The discovery of his wife's infidelity is more than his already disturbed mind can take. In a kind of ritualistic acknowledgement of the futility of his life, a grim admission that everything which mattered finally has no meaning, Bob kills himself, at the same time that Luke, miles away, is lecturing students on why the killing has to stop.

It is Bob's self-willed death rather than Luke's fiery rhetoric which carries the more potent message. Our glimpses of Luke's pre-draft lifestyle – the raunchy sports car, the poolside bachelor's pad – puts him in the Benjamin Braddock, over-indulged, rich-kid class, a likely one-time fun 'n' surf enthusiast, popular at beach parties, and needing no thought for tomorrow because in wealthy Southern California, good looks and affluence buy everything.

Luke's rancour over his disablement comes across, perhaps unfairly, as the reaction of a spoilt brat to having his fun curtailed. He has to ask for help when he wants something instead of being able to buy it or simply take it. The anger he expresses seems more juvenile and superficial than Bob's, whose ultimate derangement and desolate suicide powerfully denounce the myth that heroes cannot cry. Bob went to Vietnam believing in what America was doing and he came back with none of that belief, nor his sanity, intact. Here was a man steeped totally in the proud traditions of his regiment and dedicated to serving his country. Yet Vietnam had broken him completely. It had turned the stomach of a professional, and that, surely, was the acid test.

Apocalypse Now (1979) was a garish-coloured nightmare, in which few of the military personnel depicted are sane. Captain Willard (Martin Sheen) is retrieved from the claustrophobic madness of his hotel room – where, in a remorseful fit, he is seen smearing himself with his own blood – and sent into Cambodia on a wildly improbable mission to assassinate an 'unsound' high-ranking deserter, Colonel Kurtz (Marlon Brando), who has established some kind of colonial dictatorship over the natives there. Military intelligence, with CIA collusion, has a trumped-up murder charge on Kurtz, which Willard contemptuously dismisses on the voice-over –

'charging a man with murder in this place is like handing out speeding tickets at the Indi 500!'

Willard loathes the assignment, but accepts it. A small motorboat is placed at his disposal and a four-man crew assigned to take him up the Mekong River into Cambodia, a section of which needs to be flown over due to concentrated enemy activity in the region. To escort him on this section of the journey Willard has the dubious company of Lieutenant Colonel Kilgore (Robert Duvall), who commands a squad of napalm raid helicopters.

As a passenger in Kilgore's helicopter, Willard witnesses at first hand a savage raid on a Vietnam village, during which napalm bombs are dropped indiscriminately. 'I love the smell of napalm in the morning – it smells like victory!' enthuses Kilgore, whose deadly sorties are made to the strains of loud Wagnerian music.

Kurtz's island stronghold is finally reached, and the 'pagan idolatry' which Willard was forewarned about is no myth. All around, the corpses of punished natives hang from trees. Rotting, severed heads lie everywhere. Kurtz knows instinctively why Willard has arrived, for a previous 'errand boy' – Kurtz's description of would-be assassins – decided to become a disciple instead. Invited into

Captain Willard (Martin Sheen, foreground) arrives on Kurtz's territory with orders from the CIA to kill him, in *Apocalypse Now* (1979). Kurtz's disciple (Dennis Hopper, left) tries to put him off the scent.

Kurtz's pseudo-Buddhist temple overlooking the village, Willard discovers that Kurtz is a sad, obsessively guilt-ridden character who is less concerned about dying than having the truth about him conveyed back to his son in the States.

Sensing in Kurtz's manner that he really wants to die, 'to go out like a soldier, standing up, not like some poor, wasted, rag-assed renegade . . .' Willard dispatches him with a jungle knife. Outside the temple, the natives shuffle to one side to honour their new conqueror, but all Willard cares about is reaching the getaway boat and getting the hell out.

In *Apocalypse Now*, unlike *The Deer Hunter*, there is no escape from the horror of Vietnam. There are no diverting pauses or interludes for humour. The film weighs its arguments behind Kurtz, whose grand, perverted, despotic behaviour stems from an insanity that has presumably been brought on by the belief that the human race is fundamentally rotten. No such thoughts affect Kilgore, each syllable of whose name appropriately conjures up death and mayhem. Smelling napalm exhilarates him the way the aroma of columbine affects others. He is General Custer reincarnated, substituting 'The Ride of the Valkyries' on the armed chopper's loudspeakers for the cavalry's bugle-call as he charges the enemy, during one of the movie's most gripping scenes, a helicopter sortie on a village. Kilgore's madness can be interpreted as that of the warmongers back home, blinkered by a hawklike, scorch-the-earth mentality; incapable of seeing beyond the next unfortunate Vietnamese in his gunsights.

Director Francis Coppola dishes out some choice ironies which sharpen the film's impact but are made at the expense of reality. The abrupt rescue, for example, of a troop of Bunny girls, snatched to safety by helicopter not from a Viet Cong raid but from attack by sex-starved GIs, is a grotesque parody of the Ascension, the tasty fruits of a life-after-Vietnam being returned to their Vegas heaven for safe-keeping. Kurtz's assassination coincides with the ritual killing of an ox, which is hacked to pieces by the natives before the camera's nerveless eye, climaxing the mindless butchery of earlier scenes. Men have been shot, burned, speared and decapitated in order to kill a man whose greatest wish, all along, was to die.

National Guardsmen were the victims in *Southern Comfort* (1981), an interesting and unusual Vietnam allegory, set in Louisiana in 1978. The Louisiana National Guard prides itself on fitness and reliability, so that when Hardin (Powers Boothe), a competent loner transferred from Texas at the start of a routine toughening-up exercise, declares his preference for 'watching a ballgame on TV, shooting dice and sleeping' to going on manoeuvres in the Louisiana swampland, the others take a dim view of him.

His soul-mate on the trip is Spencer (Keith Carradine), a cynical city boy who assures him that with the Louisiana bunch, he will find himself taking part in some really important tasks 'like beating up on college kids'. The exercises get off to a bad start, and the greenhorn platoon quickly loses its way in the forest. To cross a river the youths steal some small fishing boats owned by local Cajun trappers, who observe them from the riverbank but make no move to reclaim their boats.

One of the Guardsmen jokily sprays the Cajuns with a stengun loaded with harmless blanks, but not realizing it is a joke, the Cajuns retaliate with real bullets, killing the platoon sergeant. In the panic which follows, the boats capsize and their compass, maps and radio are lost. Helpless, frightened and hounded by the Cajuns, who pick them off with ease, the besieged platoon stumbles deeper into the treacherous marshes, further and further away from possible rescue.

Coming across an isolated shack, the platoon extracts revenge for its sergeant's murder by destroying it and capturing a huge, one-armed Cajun trapper for trial. From then on, it becomes a vicious, demoralizing battle for survival, with the platoon out-manoeuvred at every turn, and being given only momentary, tantalizing glimpses of their merciless attackers. When one of the platoon, a half-crazed sadist, nearly drowns the Cajun in an attempt to extract information about the others, Hardin intervenes and saves the Cajun's life, but is obliged to kill his fellow Guardsmen in the knife-fight which his action sparks off.

With the platoon eliminated except for Hardin and Spencer, the Cajun whom Hardin saved returns the compliment by giving them an avenue of escape, but an error of judgement lands them back in trouble, when the ride they hitch on a passing farmtruck takes them right to the encampment where their would-be killers are waiting. After a desperate, primitive fight to stay alive, the two Guardsmen beat it back into the swampland; before long, through the undergrowth, they see a US Army truck coming towards them along a makeshift road – rescue is all the sweeter for being totally unexpected.

In *Friendly Fire* (1978), Gene Mullen (Ned Beatty) and his wife Peg (Carol Burnett) are the grieving parents of a Vietnam draftee inadvertently killed by his own side, one of those freak accidents which happen all too often in the confusion of battle. At first, the military PRs attempt a cover-up, both of the actual incident and of the alarming scale of its occurrence. When the anguished parents persist with their enquiries, they are summarily rebuffed and treated as trouble-makers, even by close friends who come to regard their criticisms of the behaviour of the Army as small-minded and unpatriotic at a time when the losses in Vietnam are depressingly high.

In the end, their persistence pays off, and the Mullens squeeze the admission they want from the military top brass, plus formal recognition of the fact that soldiers killed through ghastly miscalculations, that is, the 'friendly fire' of the title, are entitled to the same honours which military personnel killed in action automatically receive – a distinction all too easily overlooked in the grief which swamped families when their dead soldier sons were returned to them.

Friendly Fire was a modest, low-budget production with no star names other than those of the consistently under-rated Ned Beatty and Carol Burnett, but the thoughtful way it brought into the open a side issue of the War which deserved exactly this type of unsensational treatment makes it a notable, if little known, entry among the films which looked at the War and the conduct of those fighting it.

Two Robert Redfords for the price of one: Bill McKay (Redford) canvasses support above his election poster in *The Candidate* (1972).

CHAPTER THIRTEEN

GOODBYE, DEAR, AND AMEN

*W*atergate has been described as the biggest constitutional crisis to hit America since the Civil War. The arrest of the burglars who broke into the offices of the Democratic Party in the Watergate building during June 1972 was passed off, at first, as nothing significant, certainly nothing which could possibly rock the higher echelons of government. But one revelation led to another – the break-in was funded by the Committee to Re-elect the President (codename CREEP), which, in turn, was controlled and administered by President Nixon's personal staff.

The extent to which the Committee to Re-elect the President was prepared to go to destroy the opposition party's credibility is hard to believe even today. Tactics such as mugging squads to rough up political demonstrators, kidnapping radical leaders, sabotage, the use of prostitutes for political blackmail, break-ins to obtain and photograph documents, electronic surveillance and wire-tapping were all discussed under codenames. Even the Democratic Convention was not safe – a plot to sabotage the air-conditioning was dreamt up so that delegates would be seen on TV sweating unattractively in the 120-degree Miami heat.

Watergate confirmed the growing fear that too much power had accumulated in the White House. One criticism of the Kennedy years had been the degree of autonomy which close associates of the President enjoyed. They could wield power to suit themselves, and were rarely quizzed about the use it was put to, so that, in the end, no job was considered impossible, or too murky, if it solved a problem.

Watergate was another body-blow to American morale, which had still not recovered from the two Kennedy assassinations and the punishing South East Asian engagement. For over a decade, the nation had been shaken by successive shock-waves and there seemed no way out of the bitter political, social and racial divisions. The unthinkable had happened – the most powerful and influential nation in the world appeared ungovernable.

The painful years of readjustment after Watergate saw not just politics changing shape dramatically but also the attitudes and expectations of the electorate as a whole. The sense of betrayal was enormous and the determination to purge the recent past overwhelming. People sought reassurance that never again could the power of government either be misapplied or usurped for private gain. But how realistic was such an expectation? The mechanics for keeping the President in office had existed before Nixon. Wire-tapping, electronic surveillance, computerized lists for government use were already commonplace, so it was pointless to imagine that the clock could be turned back. What could be changed, however, was the kind of man who held the presidency. When the people were next offered a choice, it was to Jimmy Carter, a peanut farmer from White Plains, Georgia, that they turned, a man who could be trusted with the family silver.

Ronald Reagan, who deposed Carter in 1980, made shrewder use of the media, as one would expect of a former movie star, but he was careful not to appear too egalitarian. His image-men got it right and have kept it right, making consummate use of the stetson-topped off-duty rancher President to conjure up rock-solid frontier-style dependability, a true man of the people like Gary Cooper or James Stewart had been in their movies. Indeed, so great was the country's need to believe it, so badly did they want to repair the damage that, without question, they appointed as their new President a man whose grasp of the intricacies of, say technology, would hardly win him a university place.

Yet Watergate made politics watchable for the first time in screen history. For decades, films with political themes had done badly at the box office. Even the charismatic Kennedy years produced no outstanding box-office winner which could claim to be a breakthrough for politics as a film subject. Biopics about past presidents (or at least showing their run-up to power) had made money, but so too had biopics about well-known figures in the music and the criminal worlds. Films which offered insights, however distorted, into the personalities of public figures were popular, such as *Young Mr Lincoln* (1939) with Henry Fonda as the slow-talkin' Abe, and *The President's Lady* (1953) with a young Charlton Heston as Andrew Jackson, but these were not political films in the sense that they had relevance to twentieth-century politics.

Mr Smith Goes to Washington (1939) offered James Stewart as the homespun Wisconsin senator whose enterprising defence of libertarian attitudes helps weed out corruption in the high ranks but nearly destroys his own career in the process. It was both serious-minded and capricious, a typical 'thirties confection, breathless in its execution yet packed with enough substance to make you pause and think. The late 'forties had more politics going on outside the cinema than most people could stand, and because of the highly-charged climate, film-makers used a variety of allegorical disguises for their political statements. Nevertheless, a few biographical films with strong political overtones did emerge, most notably Robert Rossen's Oscar-winning *All the King's Men* (1949), a tough, outspoken drama about political string-pulling with Broderick Crawford as Willie Stark, the corrupt Huey Long-figure, assassinated at the end for the good of the people.

Frank Sinatra appeared as a political assassin in *Suddenly* (1954), in which the killers take over a house overlooking the President's route during a State visit. The storyline, which bears some resemblance to the Kennedy assassination nine years later, is tightly written and Sinatra's performance is excellent. He also co-starred with Laurence Harvey in *The Manchurian Candidate* (1962), another political assassination story, this time as the service buddy of a brainwashed Korean War veteran, Raymond Shaw (Harvey), who is turned into a mechanical killer by his politically ambitious mother and McCarthyite stepfather. At a major political rally where they are sharing a platform with their leading rival for the presentation nomination, Shaw has been programmed to kill the rival from a sniper's point high in the building. The effects of the brainwashing are starting to wear off, however, and as he conceals himself on the roof, Shaw's brain is in turmoil. His inner conflicts are resolved at the climax of the rally, which is also the climax of the film, when Shaw turns his telescopic rifle on his scheming mother and stepfather before killing himself.

Election in-fighting provided the interest in *Advise and Consent* (1962), Otto Preminger's jaundiced view of US politics, with Charles Laughton, as a hoary old Southern senator, spectacularly stealing the film. Co-starring with Laughton was Henry Fonda, who had a better role, politically speaking, in *The Best Man* (1964) as straight-backed William Russell, one of two candidates contesting one party's presidential nomination. His opponent is the unscrupulous, rabble-rousing Joe Cantwell (Cliff Robertson). The two politicians are polls apart, representing respectively old-style decency and new-style cynicism, cautious liberalism versus foul-play extremism. The party leader, a terminally-ill ex-president, Art Hockstader (Lee Tracy), assesses both before giving his endorsement to the one favoured to lead the party into battle.

Cantwell does his best to wrest the nomination from Russell, but when he tries to blackmail the dying leader, with documented proof of Russell's mental instability, he badly underestimates the old boy's indomitable spirit. Fighting off the intestinal pain, he refuses to be pushed around, and decency triumphs. Shot in black-and-white on a low budget, the film contains a curious nervous energy which captures the interest even though Fonda takes matters far too leisurely and Robertson's smarmy young buck has too much of the poolroom hustler about him to ever have made it that far.

In *The Candidate* (1972), an altogether better-composed parable about snatching a political nomination, Bill McKay (Robert Redford) has a crusty old senator for a father. McKay is a popular community lawyer who wears his causes on the liberal side and has no political ambitions other than voting for someone who takes civil rights seriously. He is spotted by a conniving agent, Lucas (Peter Boyle), who needs a bland, photogenic candidate to toss in against the incumbent Senator Jarman (Don Porter), someone who despite having a few pointers in his favour will decidedly lose. It is a ploy to keep the party machine oiled and project the illusion of democracy.

McKay at first demurs, but Lucas rounds on him as if he is turning down a chance to work miracles. O.k., so he has saved a few trees and managed to get a clinic opened. So what? He can pick up some useful publicity for his favourite causes, and there will be no necessity to compromise his beliefs because the machine will see to it that he loses. Once into the campaign, however, McKay's clean-cut charm begins to attract the voters. The semi-reluctant contender is forced to reappraise his entire philosophy. McKay's problem is, of course, that he is a political novice, and having won the senatorship, he is left muttering, 'What do we do now?' to the amazed Lucas. He was never anything more than a manufactured image, to be manipulated and sold like soapflakes, and that is how he ends up, the media's darling, but lacking any real conviction.

The Kennedy assassination in Dallas has been analysed in several movies and TV films. *Executive Action* (1973), which ponderously explores the conspiracy theory, is more fanciful than factual but is nevertheless intriguing enough to hold the interest. A bunch of influential right-wing businessmen, headed by the acerbic Foster (Robert Ryan), whose reach extends deep inside the White House, and Farrington (Burt Lancaster), a disillusioned CIA chief, decides it has had enough of Kennedy's soft-pedal approach to Communism. After Kennedy has declared his support for the USSR-proposed Test Ban Treaty, and vowed to get the troops out of Vietnam by 1964 irrespective of leaving the South Vietnamese in the lurch, the die is cast. 'The man is creating the climate for his own death,' comments Foster acidly.

Listen when Mummy's talking! Brain-washed Korean ex-prisoner Raymond Shaw (Laurence Harvey) fights his mother (Angela Lansbury), and his conscience, in *The Manchurian Candidate* (1962).

Everything is worked out carefully in advance. From the moment Kennedy's schedule is known to take in Dallas, the plans are finally laid. Kennedy's route is altered to make a sharp turn from Houston Street into Elm Street along Dealey Plaza which will bring him directly into the line of fire of the three marksmen, who are trained to hit a moving target.

Their fall guy is Lee Harvey Oswald, a Communist toady who supports Castro and has been photographed distributing leaflets. A lookalike for Oswald creates several rowdy scenes around Dallas shortly before Kennedy's arrival, exaggerating his prowess with rifles and expressing sympathy for Russia. Oswald's rifle is stolen and used by one of the assassins in the Texas School Book Depository, where Oswald works. The two other killers are allocated clear vantage points, and when Kennedy's car draws level, all three open fire. Senator John Connally, riding in the car just in front of Kennedy, is also hit and wounded, though not fatally.

After the three assassins go their separate ways, the focus shifts to the arrested Oswald, who is charged with the murder of a policeman, allegedly shot by Oswald as he left the bookstore. Dallas night-club boss Jack Ruby is arm-twisted into gunning down Oswald in the Dallas Police Headquarters underground car park during his transfer to the State penitentiary. Oswald was killed, according to the film, because he was charged with the Kennedy murder. Had he been, the evidence planted by Foster's associates would have convicted him, according to the original plan. When Oswald was charged with killing an unknown cop, the fall-guy option went out the window, and Oswald became superfluous to them.

To support its thesis, the film enlists at the end the support of a forgotten statistic, supplied by an unnamed actuary engaged by *The Sunday Times*, which states that in the three-and-a-quarter years immediately following Kennedy's assassination, eighteen material witnesses died, five from natural causes. The odds against this happening are quoted as being 100,000 trillion to one.

The acting of Lancaster and Ryan is faultless, even though Ryan was visibly dying from cancer during its making. Ironically, it is the Lancaster character who dies, from a heart attack, as the conspirators celebrate the success of the venture with a gentlemanly game of pool. Proponents of the conspiracy theory will vow that their case is proved, sceptics will wonder – despite the film's assertion that Secret Service agents assigned to protect the President were abysmally negligent – how the assassins managed to coolly pack their guns away and drive off from the scene of the crime. Even the killer holed up in the book depository calmly strolls from the building unchallenged.

Farrington's motives are never disclosed, nor does his disaffection with the system ever seem intense enough to require the President's head on a plate. The businessmen behind the plot seem unconcerned about the consequences of their actions, and no guarantees are either given or sought that their views will find a more sympathetic ear in Lyndon Johnson. And so it goes on, facts, half-truths, fantasies and wild guesses, all woven into a fascinating but scarcely convincing tale worthy of

Hitchcock. Despite the clever intercutting between newsfilm and studio material, our recollections of the real footage remain too vivid, too harrowing, for any reconstruction, even one doctored as cleverly as this, to engage us other than superficially.

The same thoughts apply to *Kennedy* (1983), a twentieth-anniversary compilation of JFK's presidency, beginning with his post-election euphoria and taking in the broad sweep of his achievements till Dallas. Despite doing his homework thoroughly, Martin Sheen, as the President, fails to capture the Kennedy magnetism. The brittle New England accent is faithfully reproduced, the hunched walk and the boyish grin are there, too, but it is not Kennedy, and no amount of imagining will bridge the gap.

The plot line is well-structured and the dialogue as crisp as it has to be, especially between the brothers John and Bobby. Kennedy emerges as a fundamentally decent man, alert, smooth when he wants to be and charming most of the time, coping solidly with the major crises of his day such as the Bay of Pigs episode, the Civil Rights marches, the blockade of Cuba and the Berlin visit.

Post-Watergate suspicion of the apparatus of government and the technology it uses were expressed in several 'seventies films. *The Conversation* (1976) gave an alarming view of the way in which the (then) latest surveillance devices could bug individual conversations in a crowd from several hundred yards away. The film makes the point that with all that sophisticated technology in the hands of professional snoopers like Harry Caul (Gene Hackman), privacy can only exist when Caul and his buddies decide to stop watching us.

Hired to record the conversations of two innocent-looking young people who appear to be illicit lovers in fear of their lives, Caul believes that he is being used by an unscrupulous client to set up a couple of victims. The theft of the tapes from his laboratory convinces him even more that the couple are in danger. Anxious to protect them, the conscience-stricken Caul books in at a hotel mentioned on the tapes on the day of the supposed attack and overhears through a powerful listening device attached to the wall the unmistakable sounds of a murder being committed. Too terrified to intervene, he waits until the violent noises in the adjoining room have subsided, and searching for clues afterwards, is horrified to discover blood in the waste disposal system.

Caul's suspicions are, in fact, correct. A murder has been planned and carried out in the hotel, but the twist in the story is that the young couple were the conspirators, and the victim – glimpsed briefly afterwards on a mortuary slab, the supposed victim of a car crash – is Caul's client, whose business empire the scheming couple are now certain to inherit.

Director Francis Coppola depicts surveillance in the way that Harry Caul does it as a deeply insulting, personal violation. He turns the tables on Caul by using the camera to observe him in the way Caul uses his electronic equipment, coldly, impersonally, snooping on him in his private moments, recording his intimate conversations with his girlfriend, and capturing his distress in the hotel room at the realization that he is involved in a brutal murder.

In Caul's apartment, Coppola points a static camera at one wall, which registers Caul's movements unblinkingly as he moves in and out of its fixed range, accentuating again the impersonal aspect of his profession. The final shot in the film is a splendidly ironic glimpse of Caul, sitting lonely and wretched in his apartment, viewed from a ceiling-level camera moving slowly from side to side, approximating the movement of a security video system. The emptiness and desolation of Caul's final moments are captured by the tools of his own trade.

Both *Three Days of the Condor* (1976) and *The Parallax View* (1974) depict a nightmare world dominated by devices and shady CIA types. In the former film, Joe Turner (Robert Redford), an amiable librarian employed by the information division of the Agency, narrowly escapes being murdered when an extermination squad wipes out the rest of his department while he is out to lunch. Panic-stricken and bewildered, he telephones his boss Higgins (Cliff Robertson) using his codename Condor, but another attempt on his life shortly afterwards convinces him that he has to solve the mystery before the hit squad finishes him off, too.

Turner goes into hiding, forcing his way into the apartment of lonely female photographer Kathie Hale (Faye Dunaway) and, after her initial alarm and antagonism subsides, enlists her help to force a meeting with Higgins, whom he believes authorized the killings. Turner's seven colleagues, it appears, perished because he had accidentally stumbled across an unauthorized plot by an unstable CIA official to 'destabilize' the Middle East in some perverted desire to safeguard future oil supplies.

Turner is appalled by the Agency's callous indifference to the murder of its own loyal staff, but Higgins has played the game by the rules. Individuals are always expendable; all that matters are results. The film's depiction of the CIA as a vast, bureaucratic animal prone to biting its own tail has some contemporary relevance, but we learn little about its ways or why it behaves in such a profoundly despicable way, and had this aspect been explored instead of Turner's preoccupation with saving his own skin, then a more thoughtful, timely film might have resulted.

In *The Parallax View* (1974) Joseph Frady (Warren Beatty) is Turner in a news reporter's role. Following the assassination of a presidential candidate in front of several witnesses, including Frady and TV newscaster Lee Carter (Paula Prentiss), a special investigation committee concludes that it was the work of a madman, working alone. The findings are arrived at rather quickly but nobody questions them, although Lee has a typical newshound's scepticism about all official explanations. When other witnesses meet their deaths 'accidentally', Lee's suspicions about a conspiracy increase. She confides her theories to Frady, who thinks they are too wild and unsubstantiated to have any relevance. He is forced to reconsider the possibility when Lee, too, dies suddenly.

From then on the film moves into top gear as Frady infiltrates the killer

Left to right: school buddies Terry (Charlie Martin Smith), Curt (Richard Dreyfuss), Milner (Paul Le Mat), Debbie (Candy Clark) and Steve (Ron Howard) get ready for a night's high rolling in *American Graffiti* (1974).

organization which masquerades behind a multi-million dollar enterprise known as Parallax and used brainwashed hit-men to eliminate political figures. Reminiscent in snatches of *The Manchurian Candidate*, but without the earlier film's more solid characterizations – neither Frady nor Lee are ever quite convincing as news reporters – the film nevertheless has sufficient tension and fluidity to sustain interest, and the harsh penalty which Frady pays at the end for his inquisitiveness comes as a nasty surprise.

Against this frightening backdrop of technology running amok, audiences longed for the simplicity of pre-electronic times, and since those days lay in the past, then the past had to be revisited, in order to make everything seem right again. Not by mischance was the long-running TV series about a group of 'fifties youngsters called *Happy Days*. Through the distorting mirror of time, those days really did appear happier, more secure and certainly less complicated.

The Last Picture Show (1971) recalled life in a small nowhere Texan town in the early 'fifties seen mainly through the eyes of two high-school friends, Sonny (Timothy Bottoms) and Duane (Jeff Bridges), who spend most of the film desperately trying to get laid. Nostalgia for his own youth is not enough for director Peter Bogdanovich. He delves deep into even simpler times through the character of Sam the Lion (Ben Johnson), a gnarled old cowpoke who runs the town's equivalent of a leisure centre, a fleapit movie-house and a rundown café-and-poolroom. This weathered relic from the days of the great cattle herds is the boys' – and one suspects, Bogdanovich's – hero, not the jukebox heroes of the period whose music endlessly blares from the soundtrack.

186

Most of the 'fifties nostalgia movies were about growing up and rock 'n' roll and jalopies. *Grease* (1979), *American Graffiti* (1974) and *Lords of the Flatbush* (1974) all showed groups of high-school kids raising hell before they finally split from school. Nothing much happens in any of the films, but the carefree, tomorrow-can-wait atmosphere is nicely sustained. In an unexpectedly solemn postscript to *American Graffiti*, we learn that Milner (Paul Le Mat), the film's closest approximation to a hero, was killed shortly afterwards by a drunken driver, and that the Toad (Charlie Martin Smith), a no-luck kid in glasses, was later lost in action in Vietnam, his luck rotten to the end.

Escape into the past fulfilled a deep yearning among audiences to be reminded of more comprehensible times, but it provided no solutions, offered no remedies and ultimately gave little heart to the troubled nation. Watergate had not suddenly happened; it had had a long build-up, through the accumulation of too much power and too little conscience among the top administrators.

Two films which dealt briskly and courageously with the events and the personalities behind the Watergate break-in were *Washington Behind Closed Doors*, a slickly-made television 'mini-series' based on John Ehrlichman's 'factional' novel *The Company*, and *All the President's Men* which was based on the best-seller by *Washington Post* reporters Bob Woodward and Carl Bernstein. *Washington Behind Closed Doors* depicted incidents which paralleled the Watergate affair, with an increasingly paranoic president (Jason Robards) and a corrupt, implacable chief-of-staff (Robert Vaughn) looking like the kind of men nobody in his right mind would let tarmac a driveway.

Washington is seen as a plush watering-hole for all sorts of unscrupulous wheeler-dealers in smart suits with expense-account lifestyles hatching their plots in an endless round of clandestine meetings. Keeping faith with the public, and almost alone in having a conscience, are an intelligence chief (Cliff Robertson) and the *Washington Post* newshounds.

All the President's Men (1976) was the only big-screen account of the Watergate affair, and delivers its blow-by-blow account of the investigations conducted by the two Washington newspapermen with style and conviction. Its starting point is the Watergate break-in and arrest, and the arraignment of the five intruders. Bob Woodward (Robert Redford), the reporter covering the story, wants to know how the burglars, all Miami-based with strong Cuban connections, can afford top-notch legal representation. The mystery deepens when address books in the possession of two of the arrested men name Howard Hunt, a former CIA chief well-connected with the White House, whom the reporters discover has been compiling a dossier on Edward Kennedy.

Woodward's discovery that the bank account of one of the burglars has recently been topped up by the Mid-West finance chairman of the Committee to Re-Elect the President establishes the first tangible connection between Watergate and the Committee. Dozens of doors are slammed in their faces before they tenuously tie in

Watergate with the notorious 'slush fund' used to sabotage opponents' campaigns, a discovery which forces former Committee treasurer Hugh Sloan to admit that 'the Committee is not an independent operation – everything is cleared by the White House!'

With a plausible but still uncorroborated link established between Watergate and the White House, and with the tacit approval of editor-in-chief Ben Bradlee (Jason Robards), the two reporters go after two of Nixon's top aides, campaign manager John Mitchell and chief-of-staff Bob Haldeman, both of whom they suspect of controlling the slush fund and rubber-stamping the whole operation. The *Post* names Haldeman, but Sloan, who gave the information, under pressure, retracts his comments, and with only a telephoned interview to back their story the two reporters come under heavy fire from Nixon supporters who bleat about 'shabby journalism' and 'hypocrisy'.

Bradlee's instincts tell him that 'the boys' are on the right track, and his faith is rewarded when Woodward's tame mole inside the Administration, mysteriously named Deep Throat, confirms that the fund was 'Haldeman's operation' and that the conspiracy is bigger than anyone could possibly imagine, involving the entire US Intelligence community, the FBI, the CIA and the Department of Justice. Bradlee's wry comment on hearing this is that nothing at all is riding on the allegations except 'the First Amendment of the Constitution, the freedom of the press and maybe the future of the country ... ' But proof exists and the truth must be told, and Woodward and Bernstein are instructed to pursue the story to the bitter end, with the abrasive warning that 'if any of you guys f--- up again, I'm gonna get mad!' And Bradlee getting mad is not a charming sight.

In the centre of the vast editorial room, a televised newscast shows the re-elected president triumphantly taking the Oath of Office while, oblivious to the speeches and the gun salutes, the two reporters pound out on their typewriters the story which will end an era. As a postscript, teleprinter headlines list the final agonies of the Nixon Administration, giving the exact dates when leading figures pleaded guilty to the various charges levelled against them, when Nixon finally resigned (9 August 1974) and when his top three aides, Mitchell, Haldeman and Ehrlichman, were found 'guilty on all counts' (7 January 1975).

Redford and Dustin Hoffman (who plays Bernstein) work well together as the newsmen, their initially brittle partnership maturing nicely as the scale of the cover-up becomes clear, but lesser-known actors would have been more believable. Famous faces make dirty jobs seem fun because we watch the faces, not the jobs. One learns nothing about them as people other than that Woodward's apartment is a rubbish tip and Bernstein owns a hi-fi system. Where are their wives? Do they prefer the movies to a ballgame? A little more insight into their characters would have benefited the film without losing either its pace or its excitement.

Long before the 'eighties, Hollywood's decline as a movie production centre was almost complete. The place itself had become a shell, like some grandiose studio set held together by adhesives. With the continuing decline in audience levels being counterpointed by a dramatic increase in the popularity of video-films, the range of subjects and the variety of treatments on offer have been badly hit. Nowadays, the prohibitive cost of making a film and the difficulty of raising the finance have forced studios to play safe, and one type of film which has come under the axe more noticeably than most has been the sociologically-orientated film.

Perceptive films dealing with contemporary issues do get made, but since 1980 they have been the exception rather than the rule. Two excellent Jack Lemmon films, in recent years, have examined politically explosive themes, much to the credit of both Lemmon and the producers. *The China Syndrome* (1982) is about a shoddily built nuclear plant which becomes a massive danger to the community; the cover-up involves murder and criminal conspiracy. Senior technician Jack Godell (Lemmon) becomes mentally unbalanced under the strain of keeping the facts from television reporter Kimberly Wells (Jane Fonda) and her colleague Richard Adams (Michael Douglas).

In *Missing* (1982), Lemmon played Ed Horman, the father of an American student (John Shea) who vanishes in the Chile of Pinochet. With his daughter-in-law (Sissy Spacek) he attempts to find reasons for his son's disappearance. It is an uphill struggle, and the quest, based on a real-life incident, is finally thwarted by what appears to be the combined resources of the Chilean authorities and the American government. Lemmon's performance as the worried but grittily determined justice-seeking father is one of the highspots of his unflaggingly engaging career.

Warren Beatty's *Reds* (1982), a lengthy, complex film which romanticizes revolution, co-stars Beatty with Jack Nicholson and Diane Keaton. The film's main point of interest turned out not to be the wonderful, perfection-chasing imagery or the controversial theme, but the fact that Beatty, the handsome stud, had finally shown proof of maturity, long expected and annoyingly overdue, but nevertheless worth the long wait.

The subject of divorce is more usually treated by Hollywood as comedy material, but the laughs came second to the raw emotions displayed by Dustin Hoffman and Meryl Streep as the battling couple in *Kramer vs Kramer* (1982), who end up in court fighting over the custody of their son Billy (Justin Henry). The film sensitively explores the jolting effects on an upwardly mobile couple of an irreconcilable split in their relationship, and how the harassed husband Ted Kramer (Hoffman), with a high-pressure job to preserve – the reason for the split, it appears – manages to glue together the fragments of his shattered life. He is helped by a sympathetic neighbour (Jane Alexander) who has been through the same experience herself. After thinking matters over, Ted's estranged wife Joanna (Meryl Streep) returns demanding custody of the boy, and the court's decision, predictably, goes in her favour.

The film contains a number of jarring images which crackle with honesty – an out-of-work Ted struggling to fix himself up with a new job at a humiliatingly low salary in order to stave off the certainty of losing custody of his child; the agonizing courtroom cross-examination of Joanna by Ted's brutally matter-of-fact attorney, Shaunessy (Howard Duff); the tense preparations before father and son are parted; the last-minute change of heart by Joanna, who cannot bear the thought of causing further suffering to Billy.

Another gritty, raw human drama which was helped enormously by the competent acting of the central players was *The Champ* (1981), a remake of the 'thirties Wallace Beery classic, with Jon Voight as Billy, the down-at-heel boxer-father, and Ricky Schroeder as TJ, the son deserted by his mother Annie (Faye Dunaway), who has subsequently married into money and returns to claim custody. Sensing that her impressive lifestyle will sway the decision her way, Billy makes one final attempt to earn sufficient money to keep the boy, by taking on a fight in which he is hopelessly outclassed. The melodramatic ending is as colourfully overdone as it was in the original, but Voight's simple-minded pug with a heart of gold is a joy to watch.

Curiously enough, the British film industry has given Hollywood a well-needed lesson in quality during the 'eighties, starting with David Puttnam's *Chariots of Fire* (1980) and Richard Attenborough's *Gandhi* (1981), both Best Film Oscar-winners; Puttnam's *The Killing Fields* (1984) came within a handful of Academy votes to winning him a second Oscar in 1985. People talk about a British renaissance but the reality is that Hollywood seems to have regressed into play-safe fantasy adventure films and empty comedies, which gives British films of the early- to mid-'eighties an illusion of superiority, well deserved in many cases.

It seems hard to believe that the days when Hollywood films contained the power and the imagery to shift attitudes and delineate moral standards are over. The artistry preserved on film since the early 'thirties, much of it revisited in this book, has at times been nothing short of amazing. Yet here is the cruel paradox. An industry apparently dying on its feet is crying out for the vision and perception which brought us *I Am a Fugitive from a Chain Gang*, *The Story of GI Joe*, *The Best Years of Our Lives*, *On the Waterfront*, *The Blackboard Jungle*, *The Defiant Ones* and *Days of Wine and Roses*.

Instead, what it gives us, in ever-depressing large doses, are brightly packaged movies with hollow insides, fantasy blockbusters, frighteners, escapist comedies and sex dramas. For every *A Soldier's Story* there are at least a dozen *Gremlins* and *Ghostbusters*; for every *Silkwood* there are ten times as many *Omen*s and *Cannonball Run*s.

Have films lost their appetite for making us question the real world around us, or for helping us to understand each other a little better? Perhaps not. In the cinema one can always turn up evidence to support or destroy any thesis one chooses. The evidence of the 'eighties, however, does suggest a marked decrease in the number and quality of films dealing with sociological subjects. All the more reason, therefore, for hanging on to the memories which we have, and which this book, in its own modest way, seeks to preserve.

INDEX OF FILM TITLES